*Language and the Distortion
of Meaning*

PSYCHOANALYTIC CROSSCURRENTS
General Editor: Leo Goldberger

THE DEATH OF DESIRE: A STUDY IN PSYCHOPATHOLOGY
  by M. Guy Thompson

THE TALKING CURE: LITERARY REPRESENTATIONS OF PSYCHOANALYSIS
  by Jeffrey Berman

NARCISSISM AND THE TEXT: STUDIES IN LITERATURE AND THE PSYCHOLOGY OF SELF
  by Lynne Layton and Barbara Ann Schapiro, Editors

THE LANGUAGE OF PSYCHOSIS
  by Bent Rosenbaum and Harly Sonne

SEXUALITY AND MIND: THE ROLE OF THE FATHER AND THE MOTHER IN THE PSYCHE
  by Janine Chasseguet-Smirgel

ART AND LIFE: ASPECTS OF MICHELANGELO
  by Nathan Leites

PATHOLOGIES OF THE MODERN SELF: POSTMODERN STUDIES ON NARCISSISM, SCHIZOPHRENIA, AND DEPRESSION
  by David Michael Levin, Editor

FREUD'S THEORY OF PSYCHOANALYSIS
  by Ole Andkjær Olsen and Simo Køppe

THE UNCONSCIOUS AND THE THEORY OF PSYCHONEUROSES
  by Zvi Giora

CHANGING MIND-SETS: THE POTENTIAL UNCONSCIOUS
  by Maria Carmen Gear, Ernesto César Liendo, and Lila Lee Scott

LANGUAGE AND THE DISTORTION OF MEANING
  by Patrick de Gramont

LANGUAGE AND THE DISTORTION OF MEANING

Patrick de Gramont

NEW YORK UNIVERSITY PRESS
New York and London

Copyright © 1990 by New York University
All rights reserved
Manufactured in the United States of America

Library of Congress Cataloging-in-Publication Data
De Gramont, Patrick, 1937–
Language and the distortion of meaning / Patrick de Gramont.
    p. cm. — (Psychoanalytic crosscurrents)
    Includes bibliographical references (p.).
    ISBN 0-8147-1829-9 (alk. paper)
    1. Psycholinguistics. 2. Meaning (Psychology)
3. Languages—Philosophy. 4. Children—Language.
    I. Title. II. Series.
    P37.D4 1990
      401'.43—dc20   89-14407
                                      CIP

New York University Press books are printed on acid-free paper, and their binding materials are chosen for strength and durability.

In memory of Mariette Negroponte de Thier

CONTENTS

Foreword by Leo Goldberger	ix
Introduction	1
1. What's Wrong with Our Notions of Preverbal Distortion?	15
2. The Problem of Representation	42
3. The Role of Language in Representing Our Reality	60
4. Language and the Objectification of Meaning	81
5. Language and Reflection	108
6. How Language Promotes the Distortion of Meaning	127
7. Language and the Creation of Meaning	146
8. The Literal/Metaphorical Dimension of the Self	177
9. Language and the Social Order	209
10. Psychoanalytic Failures in Integrity	225
Afterword	242
Appendix	257
Bibliography	273
Index	289

FOREWORD

The *Psychoanalytic Crosscurrents* series presents selected books and monographs that reveal the growing intellectual ferment within and across the boundaries of psychoanalysis.

Freud's theories and grand-scale speculative leaps have been found wanting, if not disturbing, from the very beginning and have led to a succession of derisive attacks, shifts in emphasis, revisions, modifications, and extensions. Despite the chronic and, at times, fierce debate that has characterized psychoanalysis, not only as a movement but also as a science, Freud's genius and transformational impact on the twentieth century have never been seriously questioned. Recent psychoanalytic thought has been subjected to dramatic reassessments under the sway of contemporary currents in the history of ideas, philosophy of science, epistemology, structuralism, critical theory, semantics, and semiology as well as in sociobiology, ethology, and neurocognitive science. Not only is Freud's place in intellectual history being meticulously scrutinized, his texts, too, are being carefully read, explicated, and debated within a variety of conceptual frameworks and sociopolitical contexts.

The legacy of Freud is perhaps most notably evident within the narrow confines of psychoanalysis itself, the "impossible profession" that has served as the central platform for the promulgation of official orthodoxy. But Freud's contributions—his original radical thrust—reach far beyond the parochial concerns of the clinician psychoanalyst as clinician. His writings touch on a wealth of issues, crossing traditional boundaries—be they situated in the biological, social, or humanistic spheres—that have profoundly altered our conception of the individual and society.

A rich and flowering literature, falling under the rubric of "applied psychoanalysis," came into being, reached its zenith many decades ago, and then almost vanished. Early contributors to this literature, in addition to Freud himself, came from a wide range of backgrounds both within and outside the medical/psychiatric field, many later became psychoanalysts themselves. These early efforts were characteristically reductionistic in their attempt to extrapolate from psychoanalytic theory (often the purely clinical theory) to explanations of phenomena lying at some distance from the clinical. Over the years, academic psychologists, educators, anthropologists, sociologists, political scientists, philosophers, jurists, literary critics, art historians, artists, and writers, among others (with or without formal psychoanalytic training) have joined in the proliferation of this literature.

The intent of the *Psychoanalytic Crosscurrents* series is to apply psychoanalytic ideas to topics that may lie beyond the narrowly clinical, but its essential conception and scope are quite different. The present series eschews the reductionistic tendency to be found in much traditional "applied psychoanalysis." It acknowledges not only the complexity of psychological phenomena but also the way in which they are embedded in social and scientific contexts that are constantly changing. It calls for a dialectical relationship to earlier theoretical views and conceptions rather than a mechanical repetition of Freud's dated thoughts. The series affirms the fact that contributions to and about psychoanalysis have come from many directions. It is designed as a forum for the multidisciplinary studies that intersect with psychoanalytic thought but without the requirement that psychoanalysis necessarily be the starting point or, indeed, the center focus. The criteria for inclusion in the series are that the work be significantly informed by psychoanalytic thought or that it be aimed at furthering our understanding of psychoanalysis in its broadest meaning as theory, practice, and sociocultural phenomenon; that it be of current topical interest and that it provide the critical reader with contemporary insights; and, above all, that it be high-quality scholarship, free of obsolete dogma, banalization, and empty jargon. The author's professional identity and particular theoretical orientation matters only to the extent that such facts may serve to frame the work for the reader, alerting him or her to inevitable biases of the author.

The *Psychoanalytic Crosscurrents* series presents an array of works from the multidisciplinary domain in an attempt to capture the ferment of scholarly activities at the core as well as at the boundaries of psychoanalysis. The books and monographs are from a variety of sources: authors will be psychoanalysts—traditional, neo- and post-Freudian, existential, object relational, Kohutian, Lacanian, etc.—social scientists with quantitative or qualitative orientations to psychoanalytic data, and scholars from the vast diversity of approaches and interests that make up the humanities. The series entertains works on critical comparisons of psychoanalytic theories and concepts as well as philosophical examinations of fundamental assumptions and epistemic claims that furnish the base for psychoanalytic hypotheses. It includes studies of psychoanalysis as literature (discourse and narrative theory) as well as the application of psychoanalytic concepts to literary criticism. It will serve as an outlet for psychoanalytic studies of creativity and the arts. Works in the cognitive and the neurosciences will be included to the extent that they address some fundamental psychoanalytic tenet, such as the role of dreaming and other forms of unconscious mental processes.

It should be obvious that an exhaustive enumeration of the types of works that might fit into the *Psychoanalytic Crosscurrents* series is pointless. The studies comprise a lively and growing literature as a unique domain; books of this sort are frequently difficult to classify or catalog. Suffice it to say that the overriding aim of the editor of this series is to serve as a conduit for the identification of the outstanding yield of that emergent literature and to foster its further unhampered growth.

Leo Goldberger
Professor of Psychology
New York University

INTRODUCTION

If you assume that reality reflects an independent world like a mirror, then meaning is what mirrors that reality, and distortion is what deviates from it. If I am standing in front of a cow, and I call it a horse; or if I persistently "forget" that I have failed to file my tax returns for the past ten years, the chances are that someone will tell me I am distorting reality. Like the photograph or the TV image you see on your screen, what we perceive is presumed to be a portrayal of an external reality that exists independently of how we perceive it.

If, however, you assume that reality is something we construct, then the standard of an external world cannot be used to determine its meaningfulness. Reality would be something that results from the interaction of what we bring, and the world we bring it to. A Cézanne painting of the scenery of southern France for example, is not a photographic image of what it depicts. You could not identify the Sainte Victoire mountain outside of Aix-en-Provence from his paintings. But once you have seen his paintings, you may never view the Sainte Victoire in quite the same way. His paintings give a new meaning to what we see. By the same token, if you believe we construct a reality, then meaning and distortion would not be measured according to the fidelity with which one reproduces a facsimile of an external world.

Today, given what we know about our physical world, and about how infants represent their reality, it has become very difficult to believe that we mirror an external reality. Philosophers and physicists have been making this point for some time, yet the kind of paradigm shift involved in adopting this view has only recently found its way to our models of meaning and of the mind. How are we to explain how we learn or alter what we know in a reality we construct? What is it we express with words, if our words do not refer us to an independent reality? What is the nature of meaning if meaning does not reflect a world "out there"? These are the questions one must consider in a contemporary theory of meaning and distortion. I would therefore like to start this introduction by wondering with the reader what such a theory would look like.

The first question we would ask is an obvious one, Where does meaning come from? The response one would have to work with today is one which has only recently emerged from what has been called a "revolution in infant observation" (Stern 1985). Infants, we are told, are biologically equipped with a system for representing a reality from the start of interaction. We don't have to explain where meaning comes from since it appears to be an inherent aspect of how we function. I will discuss the implications of such a view later. Suffice perhaps for the moment to point out that these findings support the idea that we construct our reality.

Our next question would be, How do you account for the role of language in an inherent meaning system? Once you assume that the meaning to be conveyed by language is inherent to our functioning, there aren't too many possible answers to this question. By most accounts (Saussure 1959; Peirce 1940; Mead 1934; Piaget 1951; Langer 1942; Eco 1976; among others), the sounds of language do not convey meaning directly, but must be interpreted as signs. That is, the sounds of language may be seen as signs which enable a listener to *infer* what we wish them to know, somewhat like the cloud that functions as a sign of rain, or the smoke that can be used as a sign of fire. Furthermore, if meaning is a biological given, then the success of language must depend upon the degree to which it permits us to communicate these meanings to others, and to infer the meanings others communicate to us. Distortion (from this perspective) would be understood as a deviation from what people are capable of inferring.

Unfortunately, this answer does not explain *why* meanings may be distorted. To do so, we would need to know how language enables us to infer meanings. Yet we still lack a consensually agreed upon theory as to how this works. Short of this knowledge, however, we may still use what knowledge we have to justify a *metaphor* of how it works, so long as the metaphor we pick may be challenged by observable events. This would be like the metaphor of the solar system that explained the atom before we had arrived at a more differentiated view.

One metaphor which seems appropriate to what we know about language is that language works like a filing system. Among the facts this metaphor accords with is that, like the file label, words refer to generalized episodes. A communicant will know what you mean by the word *cow*, even though the cows he has seen are very different from the ones you are acquainted with. A second point of accord is that once you have a file label, you can use it to point to a class of events, while your category remains independent of those events. In a similar way, words operate independently of the physical settings we find ourselves in; i.e., they can be used to refer to an "objective" world that exists independently of how we experience it. A third point is that, just as a filing system stores information for a particular purpose—the efficient retrieval of information—language organizes information for a particular purpose as well: to assure the predictable communication of information.

Further, the "language as a filing system" analogy permits one to understand the frequently noted distinction between the sense of a word, and its meaning. The sense of a word would pertain to the rules of language which regulate the communication of meaning. The meaning of a word would depend upon a file's content. If our words function like file labels, then the content of a file (the information it permits us to infer) is the nonverbal meaning we construct preverbally. In other words, the function of language is not to construct meaning, but to communicate meanings which already exist. This last point does not rule out the possibility that the organization imposed by language upon our preverbal meaning system alters preverbal meaning.

Clearly there are ways in which language may not be compared to a filing system, such as the fact that its structure is far more intricate than any filing system we are familiar with. The main point in presenting this metaphor will be to show how in adopting a language children initially confuse the file label with its content. It is this confusion of the medium with the message that will be taken here to be a principal source of distortion. For the moment, however, I would emphasize a frequently noted implication of this view of language. If language is an instrument for the communication of meaning, then the use of language is an intentional act. I could not use words in order to get you to infer what I mean, unless I wanted you to do so. The fact that one must intend to use language will also play an important part in explaining how verbal meanings get distorted.

Finally, since a language must be adopted, mature over time, and become a part of the language speaker's growth, we would need a way of showing how language participates in the development of the individual. Let us say that when a language is first adopted by a child, the signs of language refer to a limited range of meanings, and that this range gradually expands with the child's growth and development. The word *milk*, for example would at first be limited to the white liquid that comes out of a bottle, and would gradually include milk as the product of a cow, as well as the wealth of associations—milky way, milkweed, milking a situation—that contribute to its meaning. We could further assume (as noted above) that at first, when the signs of language are limited in what they refer to, the child confuses the word with the thing referred to. That is, the child "literalizes" meaning as being a property of the words used to communicate. The reason we would make this assumption is that the infant initially has no way of knowing how words permit us to infer meaning, since the emergence of meaning is not a conscious process. The word however, *is* conscious, and is used by the parent to indicate what he or she means. Under these circumstances, it seems quite natural to equate the word with what is inferred from that word. With development, the child comes to appreciate how words are "about" meaning (i.e., are used to *infer* meanings). This insight gives rise to a "metaphorical" dimension in which (it will be maintained) it becomes possible to generate new meanings.

We might compare the development I just described to the way some people view money. A coin for the child is at first literalized as *being* the value it represents. With growth and the accumulation of coins, money will come to be viewed as something one puts to work in order to generate more money. As with money, words are best viewed as a means to an end (i.e., the intentional communication and expansion of meaning), rather than an end in themselves. Areas will still exist however, where money resumes a literal significance, as when your partner in life wants to spend it.

At this point, my hypothetical account of how meaning is generated and distorted has vastly complicated a picture many of us might prefer to take for granted. One wonders if one wouldn't be better off with the

INTRODUCTION   5

naive realism of a mirrored reality! Not only have I ignored the conventional wisdom of our established theories (i.e., for a Piagetian, or a psychoanalyst) which attributes distortion to the way we initially construct meaning, I have introduced a notion that appears to violate common sense. If the range of what language refers to expands and grows, how could language refer us to an external reality? If words refer to things, then those things could not change in their meaning, else we would be unable to understand each other. If we require a language in order to establish both a literal and a metaphorical dimension, in what sense is our external world literal? Finally, if the metaphorical dimension introduced by language is necessary to the creation of new meaning, how do these creations pertain to a "real" (i.e., independent) world?

Intuitively, one may sense that an understanding of how we distort meaning would have to relate to our grasp of how meaning is realized. The problem is, if we construct our reality, that reality cannot be independent of the way in which we realize it. We cannot therefore (in our explanations) appeal to a world that is independent of how we perceive. We cannot, for example, say "This is a picture of a cow, because that's what *real* cows are like." We would have to say something like "I'm calling this a cow, because this looks like what I would infer for the word 'cow'." If I say this while looking at the picture of a horse, then the inference I make would have to be implicated in what went wrong.

Given the assumptions outlined above however, we have the following possible ways of accounting for how the adoption of a language causes us to distort the very inferential process it permits:

1. The development of meaning may be blocked at early, *literal* stages of development. For example, a child may have adopted the literal notion that bad acts make him a bad person. The child in question may then be stuck with what, for an adult living in an advanced industrial culture, is generally taken to be a distorted belief about the self; i.e., that his value inheres in an external standard of "badness" rather than in his ability to assume responsibility for what he does.
2. The metaphorical dimension of meaning may be literalized. For example, the conventional excuse of "I have a headache" has its place in warding off unwanted social obligations. For certain individuals however, this social excuse is adopted literally, as genuine pain. The location of this pain may not be where a

physiologist would tell us it is. Rather, it will be where the person thinks it should be. The social excuse has been literalized as a real headache. The metaphorical dimension of the social lie has been literalized as a physical event.

3. The metaphorical dimension necessary for the realization of new meaning may collapse. For example, in taking an exam, you will have mustered the courage to give your best effort. Suddenly you are faced with an exam question you are not prepared for. The sense you had of yourself as a generator of exam answers collapses. You find yourself floundering in a literalized world of failure and despondency. You have momentarily lost your ability to function in the metaphorical dimension of language as a creator of meaning.

These three examples must suffice for the moment to provide a sense of how the distortion of meaning is to be defined in this text. Meaning (it will be claimed) must be appreciated as an ongoing process of realization. In its preverbal guise, our meaning system is a built-in biological function which may be blocked or impeded by structural dysfunction or external deprivation, but not *distorted* (as that term is to be defined here). In its verbal guise, this inherent system must realize meaning within the constraints of the structure of language; i.e., meaning becomes an aspect of intentional communication. When this occurs, the potential for distortion arises in terms of whatever deflects this realization from its intentional function. By this view, the lie is not a distortion since it intentionally deceives a listener. The examples of literalized meaning described above, however, do stand as examples of distorted meaning because they show ways in which the intentional realization of verbal meaning may be aborted. The child who bases his sense of value on what he is told; the hysteric who turns the social excuse into a real headache; the student who becomes despondent over an exam; all testify to a specific vulnerability we share as the result of having adopted a language, i.e., the loss of its metaphorical function, and (as a result of that loss) the collapse of our capacity to *intend* the realization of meaning.

Having provided the reader with a preliminary view of the theory of meaning that I will attempt to justify in this book, I must mention a point which, if not addressed, calls into question the basis for all that follows. Namely, that when (as in this book, following Stern 1985) a theory of meaning is based upon the notion that the infant is born with an innate system for discovering and representing meaning, one must answer to the following question. How does an innate meaning system allow for freedom of choice? If the way we construct our reality is wired-in, how can it be said that we are responsible for what we learn, or that our knowledge has integrity, or that we act with purpose and intent? The reader who wishes to immediately consider these basic issues is invited to turn to the Appendix. Those who are willing to momentarily put off these questions, with the assurance that they will be addressed in the appendix, are invited to look over a description of what is to be found in the chapters which follow.

Chapter 1, "What's Wrong with Our Notion of Preverbal Distortion" examines the two prevailing theories on how we distort meaning—Piaget's cognitive psychology, and Freud's psychoanalysis. Both assume that distortion is inherent to the way in which infants are biologically designed to realize meaning. In this book, the kind of distortion described by Freud and Piaget is said to involve a faulty representation of reality, which in turn requires language. Freud and Piaget are therefore seen as attributing to preverbal meaning qualities that could only arise with language.

A founding assumption of Piaget's theory is that infants must learn to differentiate what is intrinsic to the organism from what is extrinsic. Piaget and his followers never questioned this assumption, since it is the kind of basic premise that only comes to be questioned once a theory has matured to the point of being ready for an overhaul. That is, it is the kind of premise the self-styled deconstructionist Jacques Derrida would single out revealing the limitations of the Piagetian system. For Piaget, our intelligence "organizes the world by organizing itself." The intrinsic and the extrinsic emerge in relation to each other, based on our knowledge of their interaction. Because this polarity of the inner and the outer is slow in being established, children have ample opportunity in their development to confuse what they think about an object with the object itself. This presumed "fault" in our meaning system (referred to as the child's egocentrism) has not been borne out by our most recent observation of infants. This should not surprise us, as the assumption that children do not initially differentiate the intrinsic from the extrinsic would be disastrous for our infants! They would all starve for want of not being able to tell what belongs to their body and what does not. Moreover, it can be shown that you need a language to make the kinds of mistakes Piaget attributes to the preverbal child. Yet it is but a short step from Piaget's thesis to the thesis of this text; i.e., to saying that the child confuses the idea with the object, *versus* saying that the child confuses the idea with the word. The difference is nonetheless critical, if you want a theory of distortion that respects the data of infant observation.

Freud's original premise was that infants hallucinate the desired breast when it is absent. This amounts to not being able to tell the difference between what you want, and what's really there. With the ego psychologist's systematization of Freud's theory, a hypothetical system of energy distributions was elaborated to explain how infants, in their development, transform primitive impulses into conscious, reflective, and goal-directed thought. Using Rapaport's presentation of this approach, it is possible to show that much of what he ascribes to the cathecting and countercathecting of energies is in fact the result of assimilating a language.

As some developments in psychoanalytic theory pertaining to the thesis of this book occurred too recently to be addressed in the main text, a word will be said here. In *Psychoanalysis: A Theory in Crises,* Marshall Edelson (1988) criticizes the energy metaphor of earlier psychoanalytic theorizers for not referring to observable events. Suitable observational practices should be applied to the work so as to make its explanations scientifically respectable. For Edelson the essence of what a psychoanalytic theory proposes is the "wish-fulfilling mental representation." It is because of the preverbal existence of these kinds of representations that infants distort their reality on the basis of their wishes and desires. The problem is, Edelson offers no theory of representation (which he claims is the job of general psychology). He therefore has no way of explaining how wish-fulfilling representations emerge to distort reality. In his scheme, he appears to have reified reality as a domain one validates through observation. That is, he appears not to have grasped the notion that what one validates is one's *theory* of reality (or of meaning, or of distortion), not reality per se.

In keeping with this last point, the theoretical scheme he does present may not be challenged, because the basic assumptions that should be open to question are taken for granted. That is, issues such as how infants represent their reality, or the role of language in that representation, are simply not raised, and so may not be challenged. Thus, while promoting a laudable emphasis on observation, Edelson is all dressed up, with no place to go! Without a theory of representation, there is nothing for one's observations (however observable) to prove. Having eliminated the energy metaphor (quite rightly, since it could not be observationally challenged) as theory, he had nothing to put in its place.

INTRODUCTION 9

Perhaps the most promising development to have occurred in recent years in this field, is the convergence of psychoanalytic thought with cognitive science and information theory. Horowitz (1988b) for example has edited a series of articles entitled *Psychodynamics and Cognition* (several of which are referred to in the appendix) which examine the tenets and the language of psychoanalysis in the light of what might be said from the perspective of cognitive psychology, neuroscience, and linguistics. While much clarity is brought to this domain, the approach to distortion is somewhat equivocal, insofar as the role of language is never considered. That is, the evidence used to support the existence of unconscious sources of distortion and defense invariably use a subject's verbal report. They may not therefore rule out the role of language in the distortion of meaning, as will be described in this text.

Horowitz's own approach to these issues (1987, 1988a, 1988b) introduces a theoretical dimension that was lacking in the original psychoanalytic metaphor, yet should be a crucial stage in the development of any theory. By elaborating a language for phenomenological states of mind *prior* to attempting to explain the inner workings of the mind, Horowitz establishes a working model that owes more to what patients say about what they think and feel than to what a metapsychology predicts about the mind. His explanation of distortion is concerned with a person's approach to the realization of meaning rather than to the fulfillment of biological needs alone. Thus for example, his use of the notion of *degrees of modulation,* whereby a person may be in an undermodulated state in which they are vulnerable to the intrusion of disruptive impulses, or an overmodulated state in which they are impermeable to the emotional significance of an event. Given these possibilities, states of mind may also be appreciated as enhancing each other, or as defending against each other in ways that emphasize the underlying contextual organization of the mind. Yet, however sophisticated and phenomenologically rich the detail of his account, Horowitz has no means of addressing the question of *how* a state of mind is modulated, or by what means the divergent aspects of a meaning context becomes integrated. An appreciation of the role of language would therefore be important to consider, since it may be claimed that the literalization of meaning with language (and its subsequent deliteralization with growth) play an important part in the modulation of our states of mind, as well as their degree of integration.

Chapter 2, "The Problem of Representation" discusses the role of language in representing our reality from the perspective of several philosophers of language and of the mind. While psychoanalysis and Piaget have ignored the role of language in how we represent reality, this has not been true of philosophers. A concern for the role of language is seen for example in the controversy that has emerged in response to the recent computation metaphor of the mind. Fodor (1987), who adopts a computation view, sees the mind as a "syntax driven machine." The mind by this view would have a built-in language with which to represent reality, referred to as "mentalese." A consequence of this assumption is that all meaning should be reducible to mentalese. Putnam (1988) has questioned this assumption by showing that one of the requirements of mentalese (that words have a fixed reference) is clearly not the case. Indeed, Quine's (1969) "relativistic thesis" goes so far as to claim that not only is it meaningless to seek an absolute reference for words, but that the meaning of words may only be understood *implicitly*.

Chapter 3, "The Role of Language in Representing Our Reality" examines the controversy between Putnam and Fodor in relation to infant observation studies (described in the appendix). How might one reconcile the way in which infants realize meaning preverbally, with the way language works? For Stern (1985) the verbal and nonverbal are described as discontinuous, on the grounds that language severely constricts the multidimensionality of nonverbal meaning. But if this is so, how does nonverbal meaning serve as a basis for verbal meaning as it surely must if it is built into our functioning? The solution offered in this text (borrowed from information theory) resolves the question raised by Stern's discontinuity thesis, as well as the points raised by Putnam in response to the computation metaphor. The shift from the preverbal to the verbal (it is claimed, borrowing a thesis from Watzlawick et al. 1967) involves a shift from an analog system of information to a digital system. This is where the language as filing system metaphor comes in, since digital information relates to analog information in the same way that a file label relates to the content of a file. While the file depends upon the nonverbal information of its content to have meaning, the meaning of the file label inheres, not in the information it contains, but in the file's ability to classify that information for the purpose of communication.

Since this last point supports a discontinuity thesis (i.e., the meaning of a file's label is determined differently from the file's content), a way must still be found to show how verbal meaning maintains contact with preverbal meaning. The answer suggested (in keeping with the file metaphor) is that while a content lends its meaning to a file label, it is not limited to that function. We are always free to "open a file" in order to reflect upon those aspects of its nonverbal content that are available to reflection; i.e., to reflect upon what Gendlin (1962) describes as our *felt* meanings. The idea that feelings operate like a language insofar as they represent nonverbal meaning has been adopted by computation theorists as well (Jackendoff 1987). In this text, Gendlin's seminal notion is used to bridge the discontinuity between the nonverbal and the verbal, and (later) to offer a (somewhat) novel account of the process of reflection. To do so, however, the holding function of language must be appreciated, since (following Mead 1934) reflection is made possible by language because it holds the nonverbal content of our thought. Language operates this way, it is claimed, because it is independent of the content it holds.

The importance of the independence of language as a system of rules is then examined in relation to Grice's (1957) theory of meaning; i.e., that language communication *intends* to affect a listener. This intentional use of language is made possible by the fact that the conventional signs of language are distinct from what they refer to, and reversible in the way they are used. The objectifying function of language is then discussed in terms of a variation of Grice's (1975, 1978) "cooperative principle"; i.e., it is because of the assumption that words *must* have meaning that we infer a commonly acceptable reference for the words we hear. Findings from the linguistic branch of "pragmatics" lend support to this idea, since it has been found that the reference of words is not due to language per se, but to the beliefs and assumptions we bring to communication.

Chapter 4, "Language and the Objectification of Meaning" starts with a metaphor comparing how language structures preverbal meaning to packing a set of suitcases. This is used to illustrate how language transforms preverbal meaning into a hierarchical set of classes, which in turn facilitates the objectification of meaning. An idea from Dretske's (1981) transformation of information theory into a theory of knowledge is used to describe the process of how this works. A research study by Gopnik and Meltzoff (1987) is then presented as evidence to the effect that the adoption of words does in fact alter the way in which infants classify events.

The transformation (with language) of the basic categories of nonverbal thought into hierarchical structures bears upon how recent infant observation studies invalidate the assumption made by Von Doramus (1944), Arieti (1955), and Piaget (1951), that the child is initially unable to grasp the difference between the salient part of an event and its significance as a whole. According to the data described by Stern (1985), children relate meaningfully to wholes from the start. But if this is so, and if we may no longer explain distortion the way Von Doramus, Arieti, and Piaget did, why do children's verbal reports reveal distortions? The answer proposed here is that children literalize meaning, by confusing the word with what the word refers to. This mistake may be shown to account for the kinds of thought disorder documented by Piaget and his followers.

However, when one maintains that distortion could not result from the preverbal misrepresentation of external reality, insofar as that reality is something we construct, then one must account for where our notion of an objective reality comes from. In keeping with the idea that it is with language that we establish an objective reality, this chapter then examines the reification theory of Alfred Schutz, and the deconstruction theory of Jacques Derrida as alternative explanations which fail to consider the role of language. The current debate among philosophers of science as to the nature of objectivity in scientific research is then related to the way in which language objectifies meaning.

Chapter 5, "Language and Reflection" starts with a brief history of this notion in Western philosophical thought. It then counters the positions of Ayer (1946) and Ryle (1949) who reduce reflection to a kind of behavioral disposition, and of Lyons (1986) who reduces it to a form of perception. Following Mead (1934) reflection is attributed to the way language permits us to hold a content so as to muse upon its meaning. In this text, this is said to involve a continuous process of refining the relationship of the word to its nonverbal content. That is, through the juxtaposition of disparate words, we learn to refine our grasp of the content of words via a deepening sense of their similarities and differences. This process, which is said in this text to be the basis for reflection, not only allows us to flesh out the generalized meanings of language. It enables us to deliteralize the content of words, and is the basis for the metaphorical dimension of meaning. That is, the act of reflection enables us to continuously integrate the verbal with the nonverbal by making the nonverbal contexts which support meaning more explicit.

Chapter 6, "How Language Promotes the Distortion of Meaning" notes that psychoanalysis is one of the principle approaches to meaning that has related the clinical findings of psychopathology to the way we are thought to represent our reality. Its principal failure however, is that it neglects the role of language in this process. Building upon a notion proposed by Bateson and Jackson (1964), the view of distortion offered

INTRODUCTION   13

here is that it results from a collapse of, or an inability to generate, the metaphorical dimension of meaning. If to communicate is to intend a communication, then communication is always about meaning. Any loss of this intentionality results in distortion. In *ideological capture,* our intent is waylaid by a borrowed notion of what we should be about, which bypasses the possibilities of reflective exploration. It occurs because with language, meaning need not be grounded in first-hand experience. In *affective capture,* meanings which have remained literal evoke anxiety, which in turn causes a collapse of our capacity for reflective awareness. Both forms of capture are said to be present in all distorted meaning.

Chapter 7, "Language and the Creation of Meaning" develops the notion that the deliteralization of words via our ability to reflect is a principle source of new meaning. Drawing on the writings of Mead, Ortega y Gasset, and Merleau-Ponty, the deliteralization of words is seen as a process of "decreating" the categories of language, so that they might be cast anew. An identical process is described for poetry by Vendler (1984). Winnicott's (1971) "transitional object," the "binary opposition" of Jacobson and Halle (1956), and the views of creativity proposed by Barron (1968), Getzels and Jackson (1962), and Hudson (1966), are seen as comparable, though these authors do not directly refer to the role of language. This view is then related to the interpretive process of psychotherapy, where a variety of psychotherapeutic schools all see the naming of previously unconscious contents as being essential to the process. When it comes to explaining *why* this works, these schools have remained in a Tower of Babel stage of understanding, as they all neglect the role of language. For this book, language plays a paramount role; i.e., it permits us to shift from a literal to a metaphorical mode; to explore the network of meaningful relations to other words; to better relate words to their contexts; and to promote transformations of meaning. The nature of psychoanalytic evidence is reviewed in relation to current shortcomings. An example of interpretation from the perspective of this essay shows how the analyst's various ways of promoting reflection in the analysand as well as the insights that come of deliteralizing meaning, are eminently observable.

Chapter 8, "The Literal/Metaphorical Dimension of the Self" presents three areas where the neglect of this dimension has limited the applicability of mainstream psychoanalysis to our lives. First, the mainstream view has misled us as to the basic nature of the human personality. A person's narcissistic core could not be a function of one's instinct, insofar as narcissism is a function of the self's awareness of being a self. This awareness, and the beliefs that support one's sense of entitlement, could only arise with language. The narcissistic core therefore corresponds to the literal beliefs we form as children that are basic to all that follow. This idea is compared to recent descriptions of the self's development by Mahler, Fairbairn, Winnicott, and Kohut. Second, there is no provision in mainstream theory for the effect of sociocultural patterns on individual development. The idea is developed that language is the medium for this effect; and that infants forsake a good deal of their natural inclinations because of the literal beliefs they form, with language, about the self. Third, the notion of a motive could not by this view be a direct translation of a biological need, as motives constitute a *belief* about the self and its possibilities. The effect of literal meaning on motives is also examined. Fourth, the notion of a conscience is mainstream psychoanalysis's most serious omission. Evil by this view may not be seen as a developmental failure, but must be appreciated as an essential component of our humanity, as it arises out of the very elements that constitute the self. The concept of morality is philosophical, not behavioral, and must be understood in terms of the symbolic elaborations of each culture.

Chapter 9, "Language and the Social Order" presents Jürgen Habermas's position on the role of language in "communal action" that shares a good deal with the perspective of this essay. The notion is developed that the integrity of knowledge depends upon our ability to question the premises that support our beliefs. The appropriation of Freud's drive theory by the Frankfurt school is presented as an example of a failure of integrity, as defined in this book.

Chapter 10, "Psychoanalytic Failures in Integrity" describes how a lack of integrity (as defined in this essay) may be discerned in the approach to treatment proposed by Robert Langs, which is then seen as an outgrowth of mainstream theory; and in the exegesis of the work of an interpersonal analyst by a mainstream analyst. Both examples are used to show how psychoanalysts have taken the assumptions which support their theory for granted. As a result, the principle theory we have as to how we distort meaning has been incapable of growth. An afterword examines the premises which support the thesis of this text from the standpoint of what is described as "pragmatic metaphysics." An appendix addresses the question of how, if you assume an innate ability to represent a meaningful world, you may also assume that the creation of meaning can be purposeful, responsible, and uniquely individual.

1.
WHAT'S WRONG WITH OUR NOTIONS OF PREVERBAL DISTORTION?

When the philosopher René Descartes (1596–1650) undertook his quest for a basic principle of certainty, he proceeded to push doubt to its ultimate conclusions, and arrived at the following familiar aphorism: the only certainty we have is the certainty of uncertainty! The reason for Descartes's scepticism is that we distort meaning. In a fever or a psychosis, or in our perceptual illusions, we may not always be sure of what we know. Since Descartes, the reasons for why we distort have become the province of the psychologist and the psychiatrist.

To the psychologist has fallen the task of explaining "normal" distortion. Children for example tend (in their verbal reports) toward animistic and magical thinking. A child will describe a string as feeling twisted, or insist that his or her movements influence the movement of the moon. Considerable ingenuity has gone into explaining how these (and other) examples of distortion are normal, insofar as they are a function of how we normally realize meaning.

The situation is different for the psychiatrist and the clinical psychologist who specializes in abnormal behavior. The hysteric who turns a headache into a real one, or the schizophrenic who hears voices that exist only in his or her head, are not appreciated as examples of how we normally realize meaning. Rather, they are seen as disturbed and in need of being cured. Why the contradiction? How is it that those who study distortion from the perspective of normal behavior see it as a normal phenomenon, whereas those who study it from the perspective of abnormal behavior see it as an abnormal one?

The answer I would propose is that we have (for the longest time!) subscribed to a theory of meaning whereby we duplicate a facsimile of a world "out there." One consequence of this assumption is that we must be endowed with abilities which enable us to learn how to construct such a facsimile. Such in fact is the role of the British empiricist's laws of association, and of Piaget's process of assimilation-accommodation. It then follows that distortion must be a function of this learning, either as a result of what normally occurs, or of some interference with this normal function. And since (until very recently) we have had no real evidence as to how children duplicate an external reality, the interpretation one makes of distortion has depended upon the frame of reference one adopts. If like Piaget, your frame of reference is normal behavior, then you will see the distorted thought of the child as a function of how the normal mind functions. If, like Freud and his followers, your frame of reference is abnormal behavior, then you will see the repressions and dissociations of your neurotic patients in terms of what can go wrong with normal functioning.

Today, we have evidence (reported in the Appendix) which is clear on this score. Distortion could not be due to what occurs when the child learns to duplicate a reality for the simple reason that children do not have to learn this ability. It is there from the start. Furthermore, children don't duplicate something "out there"; they bring a reality into being. Meaning, we may now say with some confidence, is a built-in biological function. Given this evidence, we may also say that Piaget and Freud were wrong in the assumptions they made regarding the distortion of meaning. In this chapter, I will discuss Piaget's theory of egocentrism, and the systematization of Freud's theory by David Rapaport (1951) in order to demonstrate two related points. First, that in Piaget's case meaning could not become distorted in the manner he prescribed. Second, that both Piaget and Freud attributed qualities to preverbal meaning that could only exist with language; and that these qualities are necessary if one is to ascribe distortion (as defined by Piaget and Freud) to the child. My goal in this analysis will be to show that if these two influential schools have failed in their explanations of distortion, it is because both neglected the role language plays in the distortion of meaning.

A CRITIQUE OF JEAN PIAGET'S THEORY OF EGOCENTRISM

Though initially trained as a zoologist, Jean Piaget (1897–1980) went on to do postdoctoral work in two psychological laboratories, as well as Bleuler's psychiatric clinic in Zurich. Later, while working at standardizing tests with Parisian children, Piaget characteristically took greater interest in the kind of mistakes the children made than in the answers themselves. Pursuing an interest in child development, he proceeded to question many of the conventions he found in this field. The child, he argued, does not merely reflect a reality as is presumed by the associationism of British empiricism; rather, the child actively constructs a reality, so that we need to account for far more in terms of how this occurs, than had previous investigators. Piaget did not push this notion to its ultimate conclusions, but continued to adhere to the idea of an independent reality as objective standard. He nonetheless transformed our understanding of the child in ways which many today take for granted.

In the course of his investigations, Piaget noted that when you go by what children say, much of their development consists in learning to correct distortions in thinking which appear to be inherent to how the child's mind works. To account for this data, Piaget assumed that infants start off in a totally egocentric or undifferentiated state, and ascribed the thought disorders of the child (e.g., the magical, animistic, and realistic thinking to be described shortly) to this initial egocentrism of the child. The term *egocentric* is somewhat misleading in that it normally connotes an exaggerated concern with the self, whereas what Piaget intends by this term is quite the opposite. That is, it refers to a state in which the notion of the self does not yet exist! So that there is as yet little sense of the difference between self and other. How did Piaget arrive at such an assumption?

Piaget's theory is built upon a metaphor of organismic functioning which pictures the mind in terms of what may be presumed about any living organism. Organisms take in nutrients, in the course of which the nutrient must be assimilated to the organism's needs; and organisms accommodate their structure to what has been assimilated, once it is taken in. In this manner, a dialectic is established between the organism and its milieu, whereby every interaction serves to further define and differentiate each in relation to the other. Since the mind is seen as emerging from this dialectic, Piaget assumes that the organism and its milieu initially exist in a state of undifferentiation. Development is therefore seen as proceeding from this initial state of undifferentiation (which is what Piaget refers to as egocentrism), toward an ever expanding capacity to differentiate the inner from the outer. Piaget writes: "Intelligence thus begins neither with knowledge for the self nor of things as such but with knowledge of their interaction, and it is by orienting itself simultaneously toward the two poles of that interaction that intelligence organizes the world by organizing itself" (1951, 400).

The neonate, in other words, is presumed not to be able to tell the difference between his or her actions upon a thing and the thing itself. Only gradually do infants come to a sense of the independent existence of the objects upon which they act. Sensations and perceptions are presumed to be fused with the objects which are not at first accorded any separate permanence outside of the infant's sensation. It is upon this presumption —that the child's subjectivity interpenetrates with his universe—that Piaget has built his entire view of congitive development.

When Piaget writes that intelligence begins with a knowledge of interaction, one must assume that he includes a knowledge of what pertains to the organism and what does not. Were the infant not equipped to make this differentiation, he or she would starve; there would be no means of separating what is integral to the body from what (such as food) is to be assimilated by that body. The functional process of assimilation-accommodation presumed by Piaget presupposes such a differentiation. His assumption that we initially lack a knowledge of self or of things could not therefore mean that the child cannot tell that the object is extrinsic to its own functioning. And yet this is precisely what Piaget does mean, since the distortion that egocentrism brings to the child's reality is in the child's not being able to differentiate the intrinsic (pertaining to the body) from the extrinsic (pertaining to physical reality).

There is another question raised by the assumption that the child could confuse its experience with the object of that experience. Assuming that I must always experience the object (i.e., I may not apprehend it extrasensorily), then I could only confuse my experience with some other experience. But if this is so, in what sense might I be said to be confused? In one sense, confusion would relate to an inability to identify one's experience in relation to a discernible setting. For example, if I enter my living room in the dark, and am alarmed to see a stranger there, I will experience a moment of confusion before realizing that I had glimpsed my own reflection in a mirror. But this is not the kind of confusion Piaget is referring to, as it merely results from not making sense of a particular experience.

For Piaget, the child confuses its experience with the object—a feat which, short of extrasensory perception, must entail the ability to attribute what pertains to the object, to one's experience, or to attribute what one experiences *to* that object. In terms of the latter possibility, I would have to be able to falsely assume that the meaning of my perception is in fact attributable to the object and not to my body that has it. For this to be possible, the object must be understood as existing independently of my experience, or I could not ascribe my experience to it. To attribute my own thoughts to someone else, for example, I must first have identified that other person as being independent of myself. Far be it from me to deny that we are in fact capable of just such a distortion, and that the process Piaget places at the center of cognitive development represents an all-too-familiar aspect of relating. The question is, could such a distortion arise without language? Herein lies my principal criticism of Piaget's notion of egocentrism; that to confuse my experience with the object evoking that experience, I must conceive of my experience and of the object as existing independently of each other. But if, as is described in the Appendix, the child *constructs* a reality, that reality could not be conceived of as existing independently of the child. If the child participates in the emergence of his or her reality, some features of that reality must be experienced as *extrinsic* to the child's functioning. But what emerges could not be experienced as *independent* of the child, any more than the experience of touching the surface of a table could be conceived of as independent of the person who is touching the table. To conceive of this experience as independent of the person who has it, one needs a system of representation that can operate independently of the setting in which the experience occurs.

What this amounts to is that the notion of our existing independently of our reality is itself in need of an explanation. Not only is language (as is spelled out in chapter 4) *not* a medium for expressing the objectivity of an independent reality (as was presumed by Piaget), language is responsible for our ability to perceive reality as independent of our experience. Thus, to conceive of my experience as existing independently of the object, I must (by the position adopted in this book) have language.

How does the question I have just raised apply to the kinds of evidence

Piaget used to support his assumptions? Before turning to some examples, I must refer to a point that is elaborated in the Appendix (p. 258). Infants, we may today assume, are born with expectations about their world. These expectations are not (and cannot become) conscious. One might therefore say something like "little Johnny did 'so and so' because of the way he constructs meaning." But one could not say "little Johnny did 'so and so' because of what he thought *about* his own behavior, or *about* the object of his behavior." The second statement is questionable because it attributes to little Johnny a reflective ability that he could only acquire with language. Until then, he cannot make conscious assumptions about the effects of what he does. As we shall see, Piaget has the preverbal child making these kinds of reflective judgments long before they could occur with language.

Turning now to some examples of the evidence, one of Piaget's best-known observations is the so-called A not B error. Babies between about eight and twelve months manage to retrieve a toy hidden in place (A), but then when they see it hidden somewhere else (B), often wrongly look for it in its original hiding place. Piaget's explanation is that this shows how the child is not able to separate the object's existence from his or her own actions; i.e., the child thinks (according to Piaget), that his or her original action of reaching out somehow creates the object, and should therefore recreate it. As described by Piaget: "The elaboration of the universe by sensorimotor intelligence constitutes the transition from a state in which objects are centered about a self which *believes* it directs them although completely unaware of itself as subject, to a state in which the self is placed, at least practically, in a stable world conceived as independent of personal activity" (1951, 395, my emphasis).

The question is, could the self believe it directs the object without being self-consciously aware of itself as subject? To expect that the object will be there because one has created it implies a self-conscious awareness of one's act. Furthermore, for the child to assume that his or her act creates the object, is to presume the object's independence as well, since it is something that must exist independently if the child is to take responsibility for it. Yet if the child may not at this stage separate the object's independent existence from his or her own actions (as Piaget correctly states), it could not be because the child fails to differentiate what it does from the object. As noted above, such a differentiation must exist from the start or we would all starve. Rather, it must be because the self and the object may not yet be *conceived of* as independent of each other. In short, one may endow the self with implicit beliefs which guide its behavior. But one may not present the self as having beliefs about itself or its object, without presuming the very thing one would want to explain; i.e., the conceived independence of the self and the object. Having smuggled in a characteristic of thinking that could only occur with language, Piaget is virtually fated to ignore the actual effects of language when they do appear, and to attribute those effects to egocentric thought.

A further example. Piaget states that "the infant may consider the picture which he contemplates as the extension, if not the product, of his *effort to see*" (ibid., 8, my emphasis). In this statement, Piaget is assuming a reflective capacity in the infant, insofar as the infant is said to consider its own behavior in terms of that behavior's effect. To consider one's act of seeing in terms of its effect requires a reflective sense of self as agent. Granted, Piaget describes the infant as trying to prolong or recapture the pleasing image by continuing to look, to listen, or to grasp, which would not of itself imply a self-conscious effect. But perceiving the picture to be an extension of his or her effort to see does require the self-consciously reflective thought of language.

A further example, taken from Piaget's account of his son Laurent at the age of two months: "I look at him through the hood of his bassinet and from time to time I appear at a more or less constant point; Laurent then watches that point when I am out of his sight and *obviously expects* to see me reappear" (ibid., 9, my emphasis).

What is obvious from Piaget's description is that he has succeeded in drawing Laurent's attention. But there is no reason to assume that this entails an expectation (as he later states) which "assimilates" the sight of Piaget to Laurent's own act of looking. To form such an expectation, the infant would have to be capable of reflecting upon its act of looking as something that can produce an effect; i.e., that Laurent be capable of musing reflectively to himself (had he language), "If I look at this particular spot, I will cause whatever that strange thing was to reappear." Yet prior to adopting a language, Laurent cannot be conscious of having expectations. He cannot therefore be said to be assuming that his father will reappear because of the assumption that he causes father's appearance. With experience, Laurent will come to anticipate events such as his father's face peering into his bassinet. But this cannot be said to indicate that he reflectively draws the conclusion that his act causes this event to occur.

A similar point may be made in relation to Piaget's description of how children achieve a sense of object permanence prior to the assimilation of language. For example, with his daughter Jacqueline, Piaget effects a series of displacements with a coin: "I put the coin in my hand and move my closed hand sequentially from A to B and from B to C; Jacqueline sets my hand aside, and searches in A, and in B and finally in C" (ibid., 79). Flavell, in commenting upon this example concludes:

> Quite independent of his own actions with regard to it, the child now imagines a series of possible loci for an object conceived as substantial and permanently existing in the common sense. The object is now definitively seen as a thing apart, subject to its own laws of displacement just as the child himself—and the object—is subject to them. (1963, 134)

However, the child's discovery that objects can be hidden and found could not of itself indicate that the child conceives of the object as existing independently of the setting in which the act occurs. The fact that Jacqueline has learned the notion of "covering and uncovering things" does not mean that she can conceive of the coin as being a separate entity which exists by itself, apart from the very setting which is essential to its meaning. From the perspective of this text, this independence would require that the object be named, so as to be abstracted out of its setting. The example does indicate that the object is experienced as extrinsic to the self, but this is not (from the perspective of this essay) a discovery, as a sense of the extrinsic must exist in the child from the start, if the child is to survive.

Questions may also be raised with regard to Piaget's assumptions about the origins of representation, insofar as they are challenged by current observational evidence. Piaget assumes that a representation is the internalization of an imitative act. As noted in the Appendix, since Piaget wrote the text from which these examples are drawn, we have learned (Meltzoff and Borton 1979) that three-week-old infants can recognize objects visually that had only been perceived by touch—a feat which not only rules out the egocentrism presumed by Piaget, but also indicates that the ability to encode a representation of events is there from the start, and therefore need not be learned.

The main point of this critique of Piaget's notion of egocentrism, however, is his failure to perceive language as our principal source of distorted thinking. To borrow Derrida's term, Piaget logocentrized cognition. That is, he made it the starting point and inevitable cause of all that follows, ignoring the role of language. In *The Language and Thought of the Child* (1926) for example, language is seen as necessary to the expression of underlying intellectual operations, but not as contributing to the way we realize meaning. Here and elsewhere, Piaget summarizes a good deal of data as pointing to the fact that the child is the unwitting center of his or her universe. By this he means that only the child's point of view can figure since he or she is unaware that others see things differently. That is, the child is seen as assimilating reality to his or her own perspective, and as thereby endowing that reality with his or her own motives and needs. The question posed by this assumption (once again) is this: is this egocentrism of the child due to the nature of early cognitive functioning, or to the reification of the child's experience with language?

Later in chapter 3, I describe how language literalizes the child's reality —the word for the child *is* the thing it refers to (in the sense of being fixed in its reference)—so that the child's perspective is transformed from the participatory mode inherent to preverbal thought, to the linear-sequential, objective reality created by language. In adopting language, the child establishes a representational system that *reifies* preverbal meanings in the form of discrete *things*. An example of this effect is seen in Piaget's demonstration that in certain relations such as the child's understanding of right and left, young children lack a sense of the relativity of these terms. Children of about five to eight years old may correctly identify their hands, but not the right and left hands of a person facing them. At this stage, right and left correspond to fixed positions. Complete relativity is not achieved until about eleven or twelve years of age, when the child may appreciate the problem as involving a set of relations, rather than fixed positions in space.

From the perspective of this essay, the child takes time to integrate its innate ability to discover relations within the structure of language. Language must be deliteralized to allow the child to express these relations verbally. The child's innate understanding of relational and reciprocal meanings is sacrificed to the literal meanings of language; an outcome that will not be countered until the maturation of the ability to reflect. That is, it is the reflective ability introduced by language which permits the self-conscious reversibility demonstrated by the twelve-year-old in correctly naming the hands of a person facing them. For Piaget however, "it is because (the child) fails to grasp the *reciprocity* existing between different points of view that the child is unable to handle relations properly" (ibid., 134). And yet the preverbal ability to engage in reciprocal interactions such as reciprocal smiling, patty cake, and so on, shows that children can adopt an alternating role and reciprocal to that role long before this capacity is ascribed to the child by Piaget.

A further question concerns the kinds of thought disorder uncovered by Piaget. Piaget and his coworkers offer a wealth of examples to the apparent effect that preoperational children fail to discriminate between psychological and physical events. Thoughts, feelings, wishes constantly interpenetrate and become confused with the objective reality upon which these experiences bear. The following is an example of realism; i.e., the child's tendency to substantiate psychological events such as a dream, as physical things:

> Barb (5½): Are dreams true?—*No, they are pictures we see.*—Where do they come from?—*From God.*—Could I see your dreams?—*No, you would be too far away.*—And your mother?—*Yes, but she light the light.*—Is the dream inside the room or inside you?—*It isn't in me or I shouldn't see it.*—And could your mother see it?—*No, she isn't in the bed. Only my little sister sleeps with me.* (1929, 94)

Do these responses truly indicate a confusion of the psychological with the physical? Or may we view Barb's responses as a valiant attempt to struggle with a communication mode that reifies relational meanings? Barb appears to justify Piaget's thesis in that she clearly objectifies her dream as a thing; anyone close enough could perceive it. Yet a careful reading of her answers shows that she has good reason for describing dreams in this fashion: *"It isn't in me or I shouldn't see it."* One could not wish for a clearer statement of how the child's reality becomes reified with words. With the objectification of our reality introduced by language, the world becomes something that is "outside," and separate from the knower. It is then but a short step to assume that anything I perceive (such as a dream) is outside, else "I shouldn't see it."

Barb nonetheless distinguishes between physical reality and dreams (in blatant disregard for Piaget's claim!), by referring to the latter as a *picture*. From the perspective of this essay, Barb only *appears* to offer a good example for Piaget's thesis, because she has come (with language) to attribute what she experiences to a world that is "out there," and not to the body that has it.

A similar analysis may be made of Piaget's examples of animistic thought.

In the following sample, a child appears to demonstrate egocentric thinking by ascribing thoughts and feelings to an inanimate object:

> We hung a metal box from a double string and placed it in from of Vel, in such a way that, on letting go of the box, the string unwound, making the box turn round and round. Why does it turn?—*Because the string is twisted.* —Why does the string turn too?—*Because it wants to unwind itself*—Why? —*Because it wants to be unwound*—Does the string know it is twisted?— *Yes.*—Why?—*Because it wants to untwist itself, it knows it's twisted!*—Does it really know it is twisted?—*Yes. I'm not sure.*—How do you think it knows?—*Because it feels it is all twisted.* (ibid., 175–76)

Here, clearly (it would seem), Vel is attributing thoughts and feelings to the twisted string. Hence the assumption that Vel *assimilates* the string to his own nature. Does this mean that Vel can't tell the difference between a person and a twisted string? Or might his mode of expression be due to the limitations of language as a communication mode; limitations which require that the child express his understanding in the form of an analogy, as poets have done for centuries! The difference between the poet's metaphor and Vel's analogy, however, is that whereas the metaphor is understood to be like what it has reference to, Vel's analogy is taken quite literally; a literalness made possible (it is claimed here), not by the egocentric nature of his thought, but by language. If anything, Vel demonstrates a very unegocentric capacity for projecting his feelings! Thus, while Vel correctly surmises that some property of the string "seeks" to regain its original shape, he as yet lacks the notion of the string's elasticity, and so expresses this idea in terms of what he is familiar with—his own feelings.

Were Vel not already quite advanced in his mastery of language, he would not be able to speculate metaphorically on what a string *is like* (though he does so in a literal way). To discourse upon the sensed nature of things requires the reflective capacity of language. Given Vel's demonstration of this capacity, and its effect upon what he says, it would seem quite inconceivable to assume that Vel's responses merely reflect his thought, without regard to the role language plays in the elaboration of that thought. In short, realistic and animistic thought cannot be explained in terms of preverbal cognition, since they presuppose a conceptual level of functioning that could only occur with language; or rather, they presuppose a potential confusion that arises in the course of establishing the verbal identity of objects and therefore the independence of objects from one's experience. I could not substantiate my dreams and animate physical objects unless—as is true of Barb and Vel—I were in the course of developing a verbal notion of things that obscures my sense of their functional constancy.

The point is critical, not only because it uncovers a confusion at the heart of Piaget's theory; but because it highlights the fact that we need a different kind of explanation for the child's "thought disorder." To round out this analysis, I will raise a final point which, given the complexity of some of Piaget's theory, is itself a bit complex. Piaget is perhaps best known for his description of how the child acquires a sense of the objective independence of things, which he referred to as object constancy. As has been noted, from the perspective of this essay the object constancy described by Piaget requires language. The child must have access to a mode of thought that is itself independent of the settings in which it is used. What I will be claiming is that Piaget's notion of object constancy invokes a contradiction within his own system. As noted by Flavell (1963):

> A mature conception of the object most of all demands that an object be seen as an entity in is own right which exists and moves in a space common both to it and to the subject who observes it. Moreover, and very important, the continued existence of the object must be construed as separate from and independent of the activity which the subject intermittently applies to it.... A necessary consequence of an independence and permanence imputed to the external world, is the recognition that the self is also one object among others, which, like the others, has its own space-filling properties and its own movement in the common spatial field. (129–30, my emphasis)

Further on, Flavell states: "Piaget feels that behavior of this kind [demonstrated during the preverbal mastery of invisible displacements] strongly presumes an object concept which is developmentally mature in terms of the criteria stated earlier" (ibid., 134).

While accurately reflecting Piaget's view, Flavell's object concept points to a contradiction in Piaget's position on how object constancy is attained. That is, Flavell's description attributes to the sensorimotor stage a capacity which according to Piaget could only appear in the later stage of operational thinking; namely, that for the self to exist as an object among other objects, it would have to exist for the child as both a subject *and* an object. To experience the self as both subject and object, the child would have to have achieved what Paiget refers to as the reversability of formal operational thinking.

The reversibility of cognitive structures is shown, for example, in what happens to red, white, and blue beads strung on a wire, if the wire is rotated by 180 degrees. In this rotation, the original order of the beads has been reversed. Only when the child has mastered operational thinking, (which means that he or she can imagine this rotation without having to witness it) however, will the thought system involved be reversible. Stated differently (and in terms not used by Paiget), only when the child's assimilation of language has matured to the point of permitting the child to reflect upon his or her experience, might the child self-consciously imagine what a rotation would be like, as this kind of imagination requires an act of conscious reflection.

In a similar vein, for the conservation of the self and the object to occur for the child so that the self becomes "an object among others" (as described by Flavell), the observing self and the observed other would have to have achieved reversibility. That is, the ability to imagine the self as object entails the ability to imagine the self as seen by another, as one might perceive that other. As each is defined in relation to the other, the child would have to be capable of self-consciously holding a notion of the self so as to imagine (as in the rotation of the beads) what being the reciprocal-other to that self would be like. As described by Mead (1934): "I know of no other form of behavior than the linguistic in which the individual is an object of himself, and so far as I can see, the individual is not a self in the reflexive sense unless he is an object to himself" (142).

Only with language do we develop the consciously reflective capacity necessary to grasp the self and other as consciously reversible. The same must be said of the independence of objects. To develop the notion that the object I perceive has an existence which is independent of my act of perception, I would have to have the capacity to think about myself as a person who perceives; and I'd have to be able to think about the object as something that exists in its own right.

In this analysis, I have maintained that what Piaget took to be a deficit in human cognition is not in fact a feature of preverbal thought at all. Rather, egocentric thought and the variety of distorted thought it gives rise to may all be understood as the result of the incursion of language in our development. I should at this time make a point that extends to psychoanalysis as well: it is not the accuracy of Piaget's observations that is at issue. Indeed, he and his coworkers were so accurate in their perceptions, that they documented virtually all of the effects language has on the thought of the child. They may therefore be said to have anticipated the thesis of this text, were it not that they attributed these effects to egocentrism, rather than to language. I do not, therefore, wish to impugn the justly deserved reputation of one of our most prolific and discerning psychologists. Indeed, this book builds upon the understanding gleaned from Piaget concerning the dialectical growth of knowledge; a growth whose very existence depends upon a willingness to err, so that one's error might (in being corrected) add to our knowledge. Far from wishing to discredit the importance of Piaget's oeuvre, I have in fact modeled the basic idea of this book upon his studies in genetic epistemology on the historical genesis of knowledge. In so doing, I have simply factored in the role of language, which had not yet come to the forefront in Piaget's time.

A CRITIQUE OF DAVID RAPAPORT'S *TOWARD A THEORY OF THINKING*

When Freud and his followers invented a structure that evolves out of sexual energy as metaphor of the mind, it was for lack of a better alternative. A metaphor had to be invented because no one had as yet hit upon a medium for these developments that could be observed, or that could be inferred from what could be observed. After all, the discoveries that emerge from a practitioner's consultation room could always be used to alter the metaphor where needed. Nonetheless, these pioneers of psychoanalysis were in the position of the proverbial blind men, each holding a part of an unseen elephant. A team of blind men willing to challenge and learn from each others' discoveries might at some point have come up with a fairly accurate account of what an elephant is like. In the early history of psychoanalysis, however, this was not to be the course followed. Freud attached such importance to the role he attributed to sexual energy that a failure to subscribe to this belief became grounds for being drummed out of the corps. Adler and then Jung were but the first of a list of revisionists who were forced to sever their ties with a group they had themselves helped to establish. Even analysts whose writings are now enthusiastically embraced by today's mainstream adherents were met with a similar rejection. D. W. Winnicott for example suffered a heart attack after presenting to the New York Psychoanalytic Association, presumably in response to the abuse he suffered from his psychoanalytic colleagues for not hewing to the exact word of Freud.

Why couldn't these people agree to disagree? How could the members of this elite group of mental health practitioners behave in such a rigid, autocratic fashion? There is a story that when Michelangelo was painting the Sistine Chapel, he became so absorbed in his work that when he finally descended from the scaffolding to change his clothes, the boots he was wearing had to be cut off and removed with parts of his flesh adhering to the leather. Such is the absorption that comes of dwelling among the gods!

Today we are witnessing a new and heartening era of ecumenism—at least among some members of the American Psychoanalytic Association as will be described toward the end of this section. Yet there are grounds for claiming that the growing ability among psychoanalysts to challenge earlier assumptions is missing a critical piece of the puzzle. From the perspective of this book, Freud's metaphor (as systematized by Rapaport) was a highly prescient formulation of the effects of language upon the mind. The time may now have come to complete what a loosening of the earlier reified beliefs has begun; i.e., a deliteralization of the metaphor so as to uncover the premises that support its beliefs. To see if this is so, I will start by presenting Rapaport's systematization of Freud's theory and then examine a sample of views from today's mainstream followers of Freud.

While there is no denying the impact of an innovator on the development of a school of thought, the thought itself cannot be ascribed to one individual. A school of thought includes the work of a collection of like-minded individuals, each drawing upon earlier sources, who share a number of common basic assumptions. Such a school can be identified as long as these assumptions are preserved. David Rapaport's systematization of Freudian psychology may be seen as one of the last great flowerings of the Freudian metaphor. Since that time, the innovations represented by the self psychologists and the object relations analysts have so altered the basic framework, that one commentator (Horowitz 1988a) has suggested a different term—psychodynamic—for the most current developments in the field.

The development of psychoanalysis from Freud to Rapaport maintained a feature not to be found in today's self and object relations theory; i.e., a theory of how we *represent* our reality. Granted, the theory was cast in the form of a metaphor, and the metaphor chosen is one that cannot be challenged by observation. Nonetheless, the care given by its adherents to the observations which served as a basis for its metapsychology (its theory of the mind) and the explicitness of their formations, did much to bring us to the point where we may challenge what they had to say. Had they not been as steadfast in adhering to the basic principles of their metapsychology, we would not today have reached the point of seeing beyond those principles.

Born in Hungary, David Rapaport came to the United States soon after completing his doctorate in psychology at the University of Budapest. He eventually became director of the research department at the Menninger Foundation, and is considered today, along with Heinz Hartmann, as one of his generation's most important interpreters of Freud's text. Rapaport's *Toward a Theory of Thinking* appears as a conclusion to his *Organization and Pathology of Thought, Selected Sources* (1951). In this book, he draws upon the literatures of psychology, psychiatry, and psychoanalysis, that were published in foreign languages, in order to present a variety of methods of investigating how we think. His *Theory* is described as an attempt to extract a conception of thought processes that he feels is implicitly sketched in these papers. It is in fact a work very much in keeping with the aim of the Hartmann article included in his text *(Ego Psychology and the Problem of Adaptation)*. Namely, to offer a systematic examination of the basic tenets of psychoanalytic theory, so as to clarify its premises, and to address some of the contradictions and anomalies that arise as a result of adopting these premises.

Rapaport starts by adopting Freud's basic premise that humans have *drives* (instinctual urges), and drive-objects (such as the maternal breast) toward which the drives are directed. Instinctual urges introduce tension or energy disequilibrium, and drive objects are means of tension reduction or drive satisfaction. Since the purpose of the mind is to maintain equilibrium, whatever reduces tension becomes an important feature of the mind. Given these basic assumptions, thoughts are said to originate in the following manner. When need-tension mounts and the need-satisfying object is absent, a hallucinatorily vivid image of the object and the gratification experience comes to mind as a thought. That is, a memory trace of the object is charged with energy by the drive, and thereby becomes conscious. Rapaport's primary model of thought is therefore: Mounting drive tension—absence of drive-object—hallucinatory image of it as a thought.

Notice that the question as to how infants orient themselves toward reality is taken completely for granted. Not only is the ability to feed at the breast assumed as a given; the ability to perceive meaningful events, to store them in memory, and to recall them as needed are all assumed as innate capacities that the infant brings to its environment. Rapaport's main concern is with how the infant comes to *represent* its reality, as it is this process that presumably goes astray in neuroses and in other pathological conditions. At the heart of this model is the notion (adopted from Freud) that it is the body's system of energy distribution which allows the individual to represent his or her reality in a way that manages tension, and permits the development of inner controls.

Rapaport accounts for how this occurs in the following way. When a need such as hunger is gratified, the memory of this pleasant experience is thereafter capable of being charged with energy or cathected. The energy in question is taken to be a sexual energy, which Freud and his followers took to be a basic sort of life force. While this energy is understood by Rapaport and others in a literal sense, it may also be understood metaphorically, as for example the organism's way of marking or flagging important events. When not in use, this energy remains as a kind of reserve to be called upon, much as you might call upon a cup of coffee to lift your spirits. It is this energy that summons our representations, since it enables the memory to be recalled when the infant is frustrated. One might assume that this becomes something the infant can then use to maintain equilibrium. This assumption however would be wrong, since the explanation being proposed is one in which these processes occur automatically. That is, because of the energy derived from earlier gratifications, cathected memories are automatically summoned under conditions of need, much as the metal object is summoned in the presence of a magnet. This could create a problem for the organism since, in the absence of a gratifying object, the delay of discharge would further energize the memory trace and create serious discomfort for the infant. Since it is assumed that the raison d'être of the mind is to maintain a state of equilibrium, a way had to be found to account for how excessive stimulation is dealt with by the infant.

As noted earlier, structures such as perception and memory are in place from the start, or the infant could not seek its objects, and store gratifying memories. Since memory traces are energized by delay of discharge, they come to be organized around the drives whose delayed gratification they represent. Thus the primary organization of memories occurs around drives. Since at this early stage, there do not yet exist discrete and well-delineated objects or ideas (which are said to be diffuse), these cathected energies can freely move and center on any representation. When drive tension exceeds the limit of the organism's tolerance, it may change to a bound form, or it may be repressed so as to prevent the discharge of the energy. In other words, given enough energy, the idea becomes conscious; given too much energy, the idea has to be repressed so that it cannot become conscious.

Repression occurs in a way that is analogous with the organism's *stimulus-barrier* (which protects it from too much stimulation). The stimulus-barrier works by using the organism's own energy to scale down intense stimulation to manageable proportions. In repression, an energy-charge is pitted against the drive-cathexis, becoming a *countercathexis*. A countercathexis must borrow energy from the memory trace it represses. Rapaport likens the process to a river, which, where it is slowed down, builds up sand bars to slow it further. A countercathexis (like the working of a pump), becomes more probable once it has been primed. Thereafter, if thoughts become even remotely connected to repressed drives, they may themselves be repressed. These countercathecting operations operate, not on the basis of a particular memory, but of the energy charge they contain. Rapaport compares the situation to having a unified front in a war. Instead of a series of fully manned posts, the countercathexes dispose of energies as a kind of reserve to reinforce the posts of a garrison as needed.

Once a generalized system of countercathecting energy distribution has been established, it controls all drive discharges. Drives which are not repressed are nonetheless altered in their rhythm and discharge conditions. These altered drives (drive derivatives) are more amenable to delay, and are more attuned to reality, as well as to the greater variety of objects and activities that will serve as gratifiers. Drive derivatives therefore give rise to new forces, some of which have an autonomy and energy of their own. The transition from one idea to another is no longer determined by a relationship to the same drive, but by a "connectedness among the pathways in reality toward the need-satisfying object" (1951, 697). This new form of thought-process is said to be ordered and goal-directed.

Through the establishment of countercathecting energy distributions, delay becomes a potent factor in the development of the overall organization of controls. This is conceptualized as the ego, which when fully developed, corresponds to those structures which regulate attention, consciousness, and secondary process thought. Secondary process thought— which is reality oriented—is imbued with all the qualities brought by language (i.e., is conscious and reflective). The ego can cathect all memories except those that are repressed. Secondary process has the all-important capacity to accept or reject, not on the basis of immediate pain or pleasure but by detours, or by reality testing. The reflective awareness of conscious thought results from what Rapaport describes as a "pattern of hierarchic progression of cathected organizations."

Primary process thought is unconscious, and cathects only drive representations. It therefore represents the part of the self that has escaped the psychic structures of the ego. In primary process thought, reasoning "does not move inductively from the parts to the whole, or deductively from the whole of its parts, but from part to part with the assumption that the step will hold for the whole (conceptualized as 'transduction')" (708–9). The assumption is that our natural inclination is to distort our reality; and that only with the emergence of the inner structure that arises out of the constraints of countercathecting energy distributions, does our thought become reality oriented.

At this point I will pause to consider how Rapaport's metaphor compares with what might be said today of the infant's mind. In one sense, the metaphor compares well. Given the infant's innate ability to discover meaning (described in the Appendix), he or she has the abilities presumed by psychoanalytic theory. The attempt to explain pain in terms of tension, and pleasure in terms of tension release seem less likely today. The discovery of pleasure and pain centers in the brain's limbic system, and of the body's ability to secrete natural morphines for example, suggest that physical pleasure and pain are more direct responses to environmental events (i.e., are not mediated by states of tension). For this and other reasons, the role of tension release as the mind's raison d'être has given way (in today's prevailing metaphors of the mind) to a view of the mind as information processor.

What of the relationship of the body's innate meaning system to language? At the time Rapaport elaborated his systematization of Freud's theory, our zeitgeist had only begun to consider the importance of language in the way we think. Having ignored the role played by language in the structuring of the mind, Rapaport's metatheory may nonetheless be seen as a way of accurately describing the effects of language, even though these effects are ascribed to energy distributions. For example, he held that it is the conceptual organization of memory out of its drive organization which accounts for the dual organization of the mind, since memory comes to play a double role. Starting as an inborn, autonomous apparatus, memory is organized around drive organization on the one hand, and the registration of reality sequences on the other. The conceptual organization itself becomes progressively autonomous via the cathecting dynamics; i.e., these establish a hierarchic layering of organizations in which the laws or drive organization and the laws of realistic (logical) organizations are balanced against each other.

In other words—and this is a critical point if psychoanalytic theory is to account for a reality that is independent of our knowledge of drive-objects—the rise of the ego-organization of memories from their drive-organization frees us from the limited world of drives. That is, thinking and action still serve drive-gratification, but at the same time have an independence which guarantees that valid knowledge of reality can be acquired by thought. One view of this description is that Rapaport intuited (as did Freud) the split introduced into the mind by language. The differences he describes between the conceptual and drive organizations anticipate the differences described in this book between verbal and nonverbal meaning. Indeed, one need only substitute "inherent meaning" for "drive organization," and "language" for "hierarchic layering" to have the thesis of this book.

Today it is clear that the ego, as the self-conscious, purposeful agency of the mind, is inconceivable without language. To be goal-directed, to tolerate frustration, to consciously and deliberately reflect upon one's behavior, all of these so-called ego functions presuppose the objective sense of self and the capacity for self reflection that require language. A similar point may be made regarding the defenses that are said to emerge in response to our need to contain and repress impulses. The ability to deny, to dissociate, or to displace meaning, for example, all presuppose a capacity to refuse to acknowledge contents that pertain to the self. To permit such a refusal, one must have a point of reference that is independent of the settings in which meaning is realized, which is to say, one must have a language.

But what of Rapaport's notion of primary process? Surely here, we are faced with a form of preverbal thought that distorts our reality, and yet is unrelated to the use of language. Rapaport's notion of primary process thought constitutes a critical point of difference between his theory and the thesis of this text. The transduction Rapaport attributes to primary process thought—taking the part for the whole—is a thought disorder. Yet our current evidence presents the infant as relating to wholes from

NOTIONS OF PREVERBAL DISTORTION   35

the start. From the perspective of this book, language is necessary to distort the inherent integrity of the child's perception, giving rise to processes like Rapaport's transduction that could not arise preverbally. The primary process thought described by Rapaport would therefore correspond to meanings which have been captured during an early stage of language assimilation, and which have remained literal and primitive in content.

One of the important effects of ignoring the role of language in representation is that Rapaport has no means of accounting for how "objective" reality enters into his system. We may not today merely assume that our objective reality corresponds to what is "out there." To say that countercathecting energy distributions enable us to become more reality oriented, is to assume that objective reality inheres in the reality we become oriented to, once these constraints are in place. But why should this process render our reality more objective? His explanation merely presumes what it would explain.

When we come to the problem of accounting for change, however, Rapaport does so in a very ingenious manner. As we saw earlier, cathected energies account for the structural changes that form the mind. Once this system is in place however, the model Rapaport adopts for change is one of creative discovery:

> First, when an unconscious idea rises to consciousness, the ego suspends its "censoring" function momentarily, only to resume it again. This formal characteristic of creative activity has been stressed by Kris. In terms of energy-dynamics: the countercathectic energy-distributions become momentarily ineffective, and part of their energy is probably used to hypercathect the arising repressed idea. This is the "inventive" phase of creative thinking, which abides by the rules of the primary-process. The idea so arising in consciousness may take various forms—a vague general "feel," a sense of relationship, a schematic pattern, a verbal or visual fragment, and so on. In any case, it is characterized by a paucity of relationships to other contents of consciousness: repression and other defenses deprive drive-representations of these relationships, the presence of which gives full consciousness to a thought. The "elaborative" phase of creative thinking establishes these relationships, and turns the idiosyncratic "inventive" product of the individual into the social communication of art or science. (720)

The emergence of a novel idea is understood as a violation of existing rules. That is, the mind must suspend its normal censoring function in response to some kind of intuition or hunch. The hunch is hypercathected because the normally repressed energy of an unconscious idea has somehow broken through, promising to reveal a meaning that has yet to be integrated within the individual's thought processes. Hence the need for an elaborative phase in which the newly discovered meaning is aligned with (and in turn reorganizes) our habitual modes of thought.

One of the consequences of adopting the thesis of this book is a view of meaning as undergoing a continuous process of dereification. Individually as well as collectively, our insights into the nature of things start as literal metaphors and only gradually shed their concrete imagery for a more differentiated view. An obvious example of this process is the fact that the early Greeks, in spite of their political sophistication, saw numbers as referring to real entities, and divided nature into sacred and profane spaces (Kuhn 1959). Rapaport's description of the emergence of new ideas is an example of this process. Today we would not consider the role of an impulse without questioning the meaning it has for the person who has it. That is, to have a conscious meaning for the individual, the body's biological functioning must be interpreted from the perspective of a system of representation such as language. The significance of a biological impulse would therefore be seen in terms of the difficulties that arise in integrating one's experience within the self's representational system, not in terms of the impulse qua impulse.

Yet we could not today appreciate this fact, had it not grown out of earlier formulations. The early psychoanalysts were pioneers in the exploration of our motivational states. They had the courage to stretch their metaphor to its ultimate implications. Only because of their steadfastness might we today be clear that their metaphor is due for an overhaul.

What of the current state of Freud's theory in the United States? A recent supplement to the *Journal of the American Psychoanalytic Association* (1988) on the concept of structure in psychoanalysis presents a sample of the state-of-the-art among today's mainstream followers of Freud. In his discussion of these articles, Roy Schafer (1988) states:

> My reading of the panel papers on psychic structure, as originally presented, shows that current usage often departs significantly from Freud's structural-energetic propositions and that these propositions no longer strictly control psychoanalytic theorizing and research. In what seems to be a shift toward minimalism in theoretical formulation, modern structural theory is increasingly situated in a different conception of explanation; for example, there is less or no concern with how basic human tendencies are possible in the first place. Emphasis now tends to fall on the development, organization, and function of stable psychic organizations. (295)

Referring to "a quiet revolution in psychoanalytic theorizing" that is "a basic but mostly unacknowledged shift away from Freud's dual instinct theory" (ibid., 301), Schafer goers on to ascribe these developments to "a change in the idea of explanation itself." The notion of drives has shifted from being an explanation of how the mind works, to a manifestation of a "state of affairs." An explanation of "how is it possible" is no longer called for. Rather, there is a new kind of demand on theory which he characterizes as a shift toward minimalism in which "one proposes that we develop or retain no more theory than is essential for clinical analytic work" (ibid., 304). He offers as an example the work of Brenner (1982) who has "pretty much reduced the idea of explanation to dynamic explanation" (ibid., 304). Schafer sees Brenner's shift as comparable to his own attempt (1976a, 1978, 1983) to dispense with "presuppositions about propulsive forces, expenditures of energy, restraining and regulating structures, and other such mechanistic and substantialist terms or metaphors and their many entailments . . ." (ibid., 304).

For Schafer, this new kind of explanation is one that is currently favored by our cultural era. Today, we no longer give much credence to explanations in terms of instincts or structures in our psychoanalyzing. We want our theories to be cast in the language of process, of subjective experience, and of human relationships. Thus, while the concept of psychic structure is "bound to lose its appeal [it has become 'an empty shell of its former self' (ibid., 309)], the concepts of conflict, organization, and change remain undisturbed, although we do use them in revised, personalized, and more experiential contexts" (ibid., 310).

A point not made by Schafer in this article is that the change he describes corresponds in large measure to an assault led by Schafer (1976a, 1976b) Gill (1976) Klein (1976a, 1976b) Holt (1976) and Holtzman (1976) among others against the reifications of psychoanalytic theory. When a metaphor is used to explain psychic events, reifications tend to set in from taking the metaphor literally. For example, affects and identifications come to be viewed as "things" residing "in" an id, or "in" a superego. An unfortunate by-product of this literalization is that the notion of psychic structure comes to be used to depict people as passive victims of inner forces. Thanks to the challenges waged by these authors, we are today better able to question this misuse of our theoretical concepts.

However, having been alerted to the dangers of reifying one's metaphor, should one's next step be the elimination of all metaphors as explanatory devices for psychoanalysis? An alternative would be to view the metaphor as but a first step in the process of elaborating explanations. Once established, metaphors by this view must be dereified via an examination of the premises that support their meaning. As described by Zucker (1989)

> A field takes its directions as much from the premises embedded in its concepts as from the concepts themselves. Whether sex or security is the more fundamental motivation also involves a methodological debate over the relative significance of constitutional vs. social influences. Whether more or less permanent characteristics are formed primarily in response to early universal traumas implies a methodological position on the significance of general experience in psychological development. Premises are thus bound to infuse a concept with meanings that are not necessarily expressed in the content and can in this sense remain unexamined and inadequately assessed. (1)

In other words, the process of explanation must eventually lead to our uncovering the assumptions and beliefs that support what one has to say. Only then might one challenge those beliefs so as to deepen one's grasp of their meaning. The fact that we are today placing more emphasis upon what a person experiences may well be a function of the natural dereification of our concepts that comes of challenging a point of view. To neglect this aspect of theory building is to suggest that in expressing one's view of reality, one is simply describing what is there, rather than presenting a point of view based upon a set of beliefs. The question I would therefore raise is, does Schafer's minimalism correspond to a genuinely new approach to theorizing? Or is it merely a kind of lower-level theorizing that is being pursued for want of a deeper grasp of the premises that support one's position?

From this vantage point, the mainstream Freudians who today eschew the mechanistic tenets of drive theory and no longer ask "how is it possible," have not in fact eliminated a concern for the nature of their premises; they are simply not telling us that they are! The situation is similar to what Edelson (1988) proposes when he states, "Psychoanalysis, indeed, might be said, in its concern with mental contents and their interrelations, to take psychological capacities for granted" (150). Edelson also maintains that the only way to verify a particular point of view is to submit it to the challenge of alternative explanations. But if the capacities one assumes are taken for granted, how is this to be done?

In this book for example, I claim that we need a language in order to represent and distort reality, as those terms have been defined by psychoanalysis. If Edelson takes the fact that we represent reality for granted, how is he to challenge what I say?

An example of this point will be presented in relation to an article from the supplementary issue of the *Journal of the American Psychoanalytic Association* (1988) described above. In his paper, Pulver (1988) shows how the terms *psychic content, process, function,* and *structure* are frequently confused in the literature, owing to unclear definitions. If psychic content is defined as the items of our experience, then a process may be defined as a sequence of psychic acts that have some impact on psychic content. A psychic function is then the goal-oriented outcome of the action of organized psychic processes. Psychic processes are not something we can be aware of. We infer them from their effect upon our experience. A defense mechanism is an example of a psychic process in that it structures our experienced meaning in a particular way. The emphasis upon goal-directedness in Pulver's definition of function is necessary for viewing organized psychic activity in terms of a purpose. For example, the defense of reaction formation is a *process* in which unacceptable motives are repressed; but it also has a *function* which is to maintain a certain peace of mind.

The pay-off to this clarification is that it permits one to form a dynamic definition of psychic structure. A structure is any organized group of mutually related psychic contents and/or processes which carries out a specific function. For Pulver, this definition is in keeping with Freud's structural-functional analysis of the mind, whereby a structure is any organization of mental contents and processes which carries out the various tasks of the psyche in a systematic way. Given this view, a reaction formation for example is a defense *structure* in that it carries out the ego function of defense. According to a minimalist perspective, we should all rest content with this important clarification of our terms, and leave it at that! Yet there is a question some might still wish to raise. Pulver does not question the basis for drafting these definitions. Why should Pulver's ability to describe how processes impact on contents, how functions are goal-oriented, and how structures are processes with a function, strike us as so clear?

The explanation I will offer (though I won't pursue it in detail, since that is the function of the rest of this book) is that Pulver owes the clarity of his definitions to the fact that he is tapping into some of the basic assumptions we must make in using modern (Western industrial) languages. Language does two things which are reflected by Pulver's definitions. Language literalizes events (as will be described in chapter 3) so as to dichotomize our experience in terms of subjects and objects; it then becomes possible to express what subjects do to objects, or processes do to contents. And it becomes necessary to refine these descriptions in terms of actual meaning contexts, as Pulver does in his paper, though the examples he gives have not been presented here. Language also allows us to *deliteralize* the content of words (as will be described in chapter 5) when we broaden the frame of reference our terms refer to. An example of this process is when Pulver questions the static view of structure as organized and enduring patterns, and proposes that structures must have a function. In raising this question, Pulver is doing two things as well. He is following the evolution of the idea of organic structure in natural history as described by Foucault (1973); i.e., from the taxonomists who classified on the basis of visible static structures, to a taxonomy based on a structural-functional analysis. And from the perspective of this book, he is also deliteralizing the notion of structure itself toward a broader, more comprehensive understanding of the assumptions underlying its use.

In short, we could not describe Pulver's clarifying definitions as minimalist without ignoring the premises that support what he has to say. To do so is to assume that his clarity stems from the fact that his definitions conform to what reality is "really like." That is, to ignore the premises of what we claim (as in minimalist theories) is to reify one's discourse and to objectify one's reality. To understand why Pulver's definitions work, one must (by this view) uncover the premises which support them—in this case one would include the assumptions built into language itself—and the way in which these assumptions structure our beliefs.

In keeping with a theme which will be elaborated in subsequent chapters, one may not hold any point of view without having first adopted premises (including assumptions about ultimate concerns and values), regardless of whether or not these premises have been made explicit. Thus, rather than take the fact that we represent reality for granted (as in minimalist theorizing), I will pursue this inquiry into the role of language in distortion by looking at how our current philosophers of the mind are addressing these issues. One issue in question (how language enables us to represent and to distort our reality) should not surprise the mainstream followers of Freud, as it is nowadays frequently alluded to by mainstream analysts. For example, in the supplement issue of the *Journal of the American Psychoanalytic Association* described above, Greenspan (1988) explores the hypothesis "that thought disorders emerge from auditory-*verbal* pro-

cessing difficulties coupled with caregivers providing confused meanings
..." (20, my emphasis). In the same group of articles, Shapiro (1988) not only points to how the notion of structure must include conscious and unconscious aspects of linguistic organization (356); he also claims the linguistic sciences as a part of psychoanalysis (and psychoanalysis as a part of linguistics): "Because of its structural regularities, language can be construed and speech events interpreted. If to construe means to interpret, then psychoanalysis itself is of necessity a part of the linguistic sciences, and if language structures are psychologically mapped, the linguistic sciences are part of psychoanalysis" (357).

Could it be that the structure alluded to (and intuited) by Freud is in fact the structure of language? The question must appear as outlandish to some. It is worth asking, not only because it will enable us to clarify the meaning of our terms, but because it may be an answer to the question ("how is it possible") we no longer dare to ask.

2.
THE PROBLEM OF REPRESENTATION

THE PROMISE OF LANGUAGE

The "problem" noted in the chapter heading refers to the fact that until recently, we have not had observable indications of the way in which the mind represents its reality. This is a problem because without these indications, a theory of the mind may not be challenged. The "promise" as subheading refers to the possibility (developed here and in the next chapter) that language offers our best hope of such a measure. I will start by discussing these issues in relation to psychoanalysis.

Starting with Freud, the goal of psychoanalytic metapsychology (its theory of the mind) has been to forge a model of how the individual structures an inner reality. As described in the last chapter, this was done in terms of a metaphor of energy distributions, also known as drive theory. The problem with the drive theory is that, given what we now know about how infants relate to their reality, it is a very unlikely explanation. Thus, while a term such as *neutralized drive* will continue to have currency for as long as a particular group finds it useful, it will not be because it could lead to discoveries in the areas it was intended to address.

But why should this matter? Psychoanalysis isn't a theory of cognition or perception, it's a theory of meaning. As long as agreement exists among its practitioners to view development in a certain way, based upon the assistance this provides in doing clinical work, why rock the boat? One reason is that the nature of these terms points to the *inescapable circularity* of this approach. While all theoretical terms are circular, some escape their circularity by being presented in a way that may be challenged. Challenging a theoretical term enables one to clarify its meaning. This, clearly, is not the case for the terms of psychoanalytic drive theory. When for example, I say "Johnny must have neutralized his anger because he now embraces his sister instead of biting her," I have presumed the very state I wish to explain. That is, since neutralized anger assumes a transformation of hostile impulses, I can apply this notion to the fact that Johnny no longer bites his sister as an explanation of why Johnny is behaving as he does. But I will not have discovered anything new about Johnny, since the explanation is built into the assumptions I bring to observing him. What I very much need, then, is some way of checking the validity of this statement that is independent of the assumptions made.

Because of recent developments in the philosophy of science, a good deal of confusion exists today in our approach to these issues. No less a philosopher than Hilary Putnam (1988) observes that most of twentieth-century philosophy of science has consisted of the gradual overthrow of the view "that the meaning of a sentence should be given by (or capable of being given by) a rule which determines in exactly which situations the sentence is assertable" (8). What we came to realize, according to Putnam, is that "theories cannot be tested sentence by sentence. . . . As Quine puts it, sentences meet the test of experience 'as a corporate body,' and not one by one" (ibid., 8, 9). Notice however, that Putnam's claim refers to the meaning of a sentence, not to whether or not it is accepted as true. And Putnam himself spends a good deal of effort arguing (in *Representation and Reality*, 1988) for a "pragmatic realism" whereby we have clear-cut communal (normative) procedures for deciding upon the different kinds of "truth" in our world.

In other words, the truth of a neutralized drive cannot be the same as, say, the truth of a proton. As long as I cannot point to an index of neutralized drives in a way that is independent of the assumptions I make in defining neutralized drives (as I may with protons), my theory will be incapable of growth. That is, it will be immune to revision in response to the events it purportedly explains. Freud himself found an ingenious way around this difficulty, which bears a marked resemblance to the solution proposed by the philosopher psychologist, Jerry Fodor (1987). The answer is to assume that one's terms will one day be shown to be true (in the same way that a proton is accepted as true), and proceed accordingly. One day, for example, a certain biochemical state of the brain will be independently shown to result in desire; i.e., we will have a measure that shows that psychological desire depends upon the biochemical state of the brain. Given the recent advances made in mood-altering medications, these assumptions do not, in our day, seem farfetched. Yet the equally plausible objection is raised that to assume as much, is to assume you could alter the scenario of a televised program by altering the tubes that transmit it. Be that as it may, the point is that for the present, we lack such a measure; and acting as if one day we will have one, does not alter that fact.

A possible counter is that I am pursuing a misguided notion of what a theory of meaning should be. Comparing neutralized drive to proton is like comparing apples and oranges. A proton among other things is an inference based upon observation; whereas a neutralized drive is a metaphor that refers to events that cannot be observed. The notion of neutralized drive is immune to challenge for a reason far more critical than the circularity of the way it is defined. There is no viable alternative to take its place! General psychology has failed to provide a view of how the mind represents its reality that inspires unanimous agreement from its practitioners. That is, psychologists as well lack a way of describing these processes independently of the assumptions used to define them. So that even if the point about theoretical growth is valid, it simply can't be applied to a theory of meaning. As far as we can tell, the workings of the mind do not (and may never) have observable correlates.

The problem with assuming that you can't have a verifiable theory of meaning, is that this tends to discourage people from looking for one. At the heart of all scientific investigation is the belief that whatever assumptions you make, you must have good reasons for making them; i.e., reasons that other knowledgeable people would agree to. These reasons must meet acceptable standards of proof, and be capable of withstanding the challenge of opposing views. Any system which fails to live up to this expectation will be justly suspect in the eyes of the scientific community. Must we accept the notion that psychoanalysis will never be scientific? I would hope not!

Yet the situation is not helped by the fact that today, having lost faith in the suitability of drive theory as a theory of representation, psychoanalysts have failed to search for an alternative. The situation is akin to one in which a job applicant says to a prospective employer, "I've forgotten where I obtained my degrees, so you'll just have to assume that I have them." A profession in which basic beliefs may not be questioned is suffering from a fundamental lack of integrity. As long as the beliefs which support the system may not be questioned or challenged, the system will (by default) be grounded in dogma. The pursuit of a verifiable theory of representation is therefore seen in this text as critical to theories of representation such as psychoanalysis.

The point of writing this book may now be stated. It is to present the view that an independent measure of how the mind represents its reality does exist! The reason it has taken us so long to discover this measure, is that we have (till recently) failed to appreciate how language participates in the representation of our reality. The theories we have constructed to explain how we establish representations—Freud's psychoanalysis and Piaget's cognitive psychology for example—must today be seen as metaphors of the mind that left out a critical ingredient in failing to consider the role of language.

When language is considered as an actual structure of the mind, one has an index of the workings of the mind that is observable to one and all. That is, one has a basis for the agreement which had eluded those who concern themselves with the operations of the mind. There are a number of recent developments which, taken singly, are impressive enough. Taken together, they amount to an understanding of how language structures our thoughts. In child development, the discovery that infants have an innate ability to represent their reality has revolutionized our assumptions about infant perception. In the philosophy of language, Grice's theory of meaning, and the important questions about language functioning introduced by W. V. Quine, and more recently by Hilary Putnam, are complemented by the past twenty years of discovery in the linguistic branch of pragmatics. Add to this already impressive list the influential ideas that have come to us from information theory via the ingenious work of Bateson and Jackson, and more recently, of Fred I. Dretske, and you have what amounts to a prescription for understanding how language represents reality.

If the thesis of this book is correct, our understanding of how we represent our reality need no longer depend upon theories that are limited to being metaphors of the mind which presume what they should explain. In the text which follows, the basis of what is maintained is observable— in the ear and on the page—so that all might question what is claimed. I will present a theory of representation that is capable of growth, and that could become a basis for transforming psychology and psychoanalysis into what Thomas J. Kuhn has described as "normal science"; i.e., a science in which the practitioners agree to a basic view of reality, because a way has been found to relate that view to independent observations all might agree to. Given this agreement, these practitioners might then work upon clarifying the premises and implications of their paradigm, until it yields to a more encompassing discovery.

For this to be possible, however, one must account for how the preverbal meaning that is wired-in is transformed into verbal meaning. To attempt such an explanation, I will start with a description of preverbal meaning as a preliminary to discussing the relationship of the verbal to the nonverbal.

THE VERBAL AND THE NONVERBAL

As described in the Appendix, the recent revolution in infant observation is based largely upon the finding that infants represent their reality from the start, and therefore need not learn how to do so. That is, infants have an innate ability to tune into the invariant features of what they perceive, and then to use these features to recognize past events. Most startling of all, they accomplish this feat *across modalities!* That is, infants by the first week have the capacity to experience an object in one modality (such as touch), and then later recognize that object visually. As described in Stern (1985): "Infants are predesigned to be able to perform cross-modal transfer of information that permits them to recognize a correspondence across touch and vision [as well as other modalities]. . . . No learning is needed initially, and subsequent learning about relations across modalities can be built upon this innate base" (48).

What this amounts to, states Stern, is that infants have an innate capacity to encode information "into a still mysterious amodal representation, which can then be recognized in any of the sensory modes" (51). Given this ability, what might one infer about the quality of how infants perceive their world? First, (following Stern, 51, 52), the infant experiences a world of perceptual unity which is not of sights, sounds, touches or nameable objects, but of shapes, intensities and temporal patterns. That is, infants experience the more global qualities of experience insofar as they form and act upon abstract representations. Furthermore, these amodally derived integrations would constitute distinct, characteristic experiences. Borrowing an example from Stern (ibid., 176), in perceiving a patch of yellow sunlight on a wall, the infant would experience the "intensity, warmth, shape, brightness, pleasure, and other amodal aspects of the patch." The child (for Stern) maintains a "highly flexible and omnidimensional perspective on the patch," which is very different from the quality of the experience one assumes when it is communicated with words.

This new understanding of how infants perceive has brought to life a problem which, though a perennial one for philosophers of the mind, has not (till recently) been the concern of many psychologists. How does the preverbal meaning system of the infant—this innate ability to tune into the invariant properties of events—undergo the kind of transformation which must occur with the adoption of a language? Verbal meaning differs from perverbal meaning on virtually each of the points mentioned above. Rather than being global in the multidimensional sense described by Stern, verbal meaning is linear-sequential. That is, meanings are abstracted out of their settings, and are arrayed in a sequence. This sequence severely constrains the dimensions referred to by words. At the same time, the concrete specificity of the particular setting is lost to the generalized statements of words. Words operate effectively in communication because they refer to events that are removed from their nonverbal context. In this manner, words may conform to standard meanings that a community of speakers will understand, but they do so at the expense of the lived specificity of nonverbal understanding.

The differences between verbal and nonverbal meaning generate a host of questions. Is the verbal system a transformation of the nonverbal system? What are the effects of this transformation (if that's what it is)? In the more modern terminology of today's philosopher of the mind, how does language supervene upon our preverbal system (i.e., how is it functionally related to that system)? How do the categories of language individuate the preverbal system (i.e., how do they slice it up into verbal categories)? Finally, the infant observation studies reported by Stern indicate that infants do not in fact represent their reality, in the sense of reflecting what's "out there." Rather, they appear to construct a reality out of a synthesis of what they bring in the way of amodal perception, with what they find. If this is indeed the case, does language participate in this construction? That is, if language does not operate on the basis of reflecting a reality "out there" (and it's hard to imagine that it would, if nonverbal meaning doesn't), how do verbal meanings evolve and change? And how are these changes related to the preverbal system that precedes language?

In order to convey the importance of this issue, I will borrow Mead's metaphor in which each individual consists of a "biological self" and a "social self conscious self." With the assimiliation of language (by Mead's view), a split or "bifurcation" is introduced between the individual's nonverbal biological meaning system, and his or her verbal self-conscious system. To borrow another analogy from the pragmatists, the biological self might be viewed as money in the bank which the verbal system draws on in order to communicate (which is one reason why one is enjoined to "put your money where you mouth is!"). In drawing upon this fund, many problems may arise; i.e., the funds may be in short supply, or they may be blocked, or the computer that controls the system may break down, and so on. Translated into clinical terms, the bifurcation of the self introduced by language may generate problems in integrating the biological part of the self with its verbal and socially self-conscious counterpart; a failure which may result in serious misconceptions as to the nature and limits of our being. This analogy compares in some ways to Freud's metaphor of the self in terms of a topographical bifurcation between an unconscious id, and a conscious ego. In Mead's metaphor however, the emphasis is upon the transformation that one system effects upon the other, in the course of forging a medium for interpersonal communication.

Having alerted the reader to the importance of how the biological self relates to the verbal self, I will now turn to the questions which arise when one speaks of representations. These questions will orient us toward those problems which a theory purporting to address the inner world of the individual must address.

REPRESENTATION AND THE PUTNAM-FODOR DEBATE

When Rapaport, Hartmann and other ego psychologists undertook the systemization of psychoanalytic theory, they had two separate agendas, one explicit, the other implicit. The explicit agenda had to do with the fact that the infants' abilities to perceive and remember had been assumed to arise as a result of the frustration of biological needs. As it became clear that the very enactment of these needs requires a modicum of perception and memory, these abilities were designated as "conflict free" areas of functioning. That is, it was assumed that perception and memory may be attributed to the infant from the start, and that this conflict free area of functioning enables the infant to establish representations. The role of instinctual need would then be to shape these representations in a way that protects the organism from too much stimulation.

The implicit agenda had to do with the growing recognition that one must envisage some area of the self where the competing demands of the id and the superego might give rise to the integration of synthetic solutions. That is, in addition to the mechanistic transformation of energy into psychic representations or constraints (which is not under the individual's conscious control), one would want a sense of how we arrive at solutions as a result of the conscious pursuit of discoveries and goals. This agenda is described as implicit, for the area in question is necessarily symbolic. The solutions it addresses require the reflective capacity of a language. As psychoanalysis had yet to appreciate the important role language plays in the creation of meaning, the agenda was translated into giving greater importance than had been done previously to the ego in the child's development.

Given these developments, one would think that psychoanalytic theorizers would have proceeded to question the assumptions being made about representations, and to work at resolving the problems that arise from these assumptions. This has not, for the most part, been the case. The innovations of the past thirty years have focused upon the preoedipal period of the infant's development, and upon speculations as to the kind of parenting necessary for the self's emergence. Of the authors who have contributed genuinely new ideas to mainstream psychoanalysis (such as as Melanie Klein, Margaret Mahler, Fairbairn, Winnicott, and Kohut for example) only one has questioned the role of biological drive in our development of representations. (Kohut and his followers describe how they believe the self arises in a way that eschews drive theory, but they presume the representation process, rather than explain it.) Indeed, the notion of representation has scarcely changed since the revisions of the ego psychologists of the 1950s. This is not for want of having been challenged. Questions raised as to drive theory's inability to account for the symbolic or hermeneutic aspects of the mind (e.g., G. S. Klein 1976a; Gill 1976; Schafer 1976b) have until very recently had little impact. In spite of the contradictions these authors point to, and Roy Schafer's (1976a) valiant attempt to bring psychoanalysis up to date with his "action language" these challenges have not yielded an alternative to drive theory's explanation of how we build an inner world.

As a result, while metapsychological speculations about energy and neutralized drives have virtually ceased in most psychoanalytic publications, there has been no effort to find something to take its place. It is as if psychoanalysts have collectively decided that they no longer have to account for what representations are, or where they come from. The problem however, is that the premises that ground the theory continue to be based upon Freud's original biological model, so that even if one no longer refers to neutralized drives in mainstream psychoanalytic circles, the notion continues to pertain to other psychoanalytic assumptions still in circulation, such as "instinct," "need," and "repression." Furthermore, if you fail to make your premises clear, then your beliefs may not be challenged, and you risk adopting the immutable presumptions of the autocrat. The point being that while the psychoanalytic perspective still assumes that we represent our reality, one may not look to psychoanalytic metapsychology for a well thought-out theory of *how* we do so. Yet such a theory (as the earlier Freudians well understood) is critical if you wish to question the premises that support what you have to say.

In order to proceed with my presentation of the problems of assuming that the mind represents its reality, I must turn to those who have taken the trouble to formulate thoughtful theories. That is, I will present a debate over representation currently being waged, not by psychoanalysts, but by philosophers. The debate is over whether the mind can be seen as having an innate language with which to represent reality, as has been proposed by Jerry Fodor (1987) for example. This position is countered by Hilary Putnam (1988), who believes that you cannot reduce notions of representation and reference to what goes on in the mind alone. As trained philosophers, these authors share an interest not always evident among psychoanalysts. They keep a keen and constant eye upon the premises that support what they say! For our purposes, the usefulness of what they say will therefore be to the degree that they alert us to some of the problems that arise with regard to the notion of representation.

Before presenting the Putnam-Fodor debate on representation, I will offer a very brief historical context for this issue. Following Putnam's discussion (1988, Chap. 2), since Aristotle philosophers have for the most part assumed that the way in which we have meaning is by establishing some sort of inner representation of our environment. By this view, our natural languages (such as English and French) have meaning because they refer us to this inner system of representations. Thus for example, the word *table* is said to have meaning, because it refers to an inner representation of a table. And if the synonyms we have for the word *table* and the translation of this word into another language are in turn meaningful, it is because they refer us to the same inner representation.

Departing now from Putnam's exposition, the questions which have mostly preoccupied philosophers and psychologists about these internal representations have had to do with how they emerge, and what laws regulate them. From the British empiricists to the behaviorists for example, it was assumed that these representations were literal copies of an external reality. Our environment as reality (it was thought) imposes itself upon the virgin substance of the mind as an idea (for the empiricist) or a stimulus (for the behaviorist). The mind in turn has certain inherent laws (associations, conditioning operations) for combining these events in a way that duplicates the reality "out there."

Other theoretical views such as those of Jean Piaget and psychoanalysis have assumed that our representations are fated to somehow distort our reality. Thus, these theoreticians view development as a process of learning how to correct the distortions of egocentrism (for Piaget) or of the defenses we institute in order to moderate our libidinal impulses (for the psychoanalyst). But these positions continue to share an assumption with the associationism of the empiricists and behaviorists; i.e., that what one needs to discover are the underlying laws which govern our ability to represent reality.

All of this by way of introducing a recent metaphor for the mind that has seized the collective imagination of a new breed of investigators, the cognitive scientists who have taken over many of our academic centers in the field of psychology, and appear to be well-represented among philosophers as well (Hunt 1982). This "computation" metaphor will be briefly described here, as it answers some of the questions posed above regarding representations; and because it is a starting point for the Putnam-Fodor debate, insofar as Fodor embraces it, whereas Putnam (who initially championed it) now repudiates it.

According to a computation metaphor, the mind (in keeping with the associationistic, psychoanalytic and Piagetian views mentioned above) operates on the basis of internal representations; but these representations are more akin to a computer program than to associations, cathected images, or reversible structures. For example, the symbol *2* operates on the basis of constraints as to what can be referred to in the nonpsychological world, as well as how it might combine with other symbols, such as *3* and *4*. Which is to say that computational symbols not only reflect real states, but have the power to *effect* the events they reflect, as well as *each other*.

To imagine how this would work, envisage the mind (following Fodor 1987) as a "syntax driven machine." Borrowing again from Fodor, the syntactic structure of a symbolic system is like the geometry of a key. Just as a key's structure tells you what locks it will fit, a language's syntax determines "what goes with what." In a symbolic system of representation, the syntax is what connects the causal properties of the system (its ability to affect real events) with its semantic properties (its relationship to real events). Having a computational model is therefore like having a model of the real world, but with a quasi magical property. The operations one effects upon the parts of this model (as when we think through a problem, or plan for the future) are the same as the operations we effect on the real world! It is as if you have a television screen that depicts the events of your life in such a way that whatever changes you bring about on the screen are the same as would occur in relation to real events (assuming that you can tell the difference between a rehearsal and the real thing!).

One advantage of a computational model is that it alerts us to a number of properties a representational system would have to have, that we hadn't thought of before. The mind by this view, would have to be structured like a language system, since this is the kind of structure that, by our current standards, best answers to what a representational system would have to be able to do. Borrowing a term from Fodor, if we describe this language as "mentalese," then representations in mentalese would have to bear two kinds of functional relations. They would have to be functionally related to physiological states of the organism (if one assumes with Fodor that brain states must participate in this process). And they would have to relate to states in the nonpsychological world. That is, if a change x occurs in one's representational system, then a change y would have to have occurred in one's brain state, and a change z would have to be manifested in one's milieu. Without for the moment inquiring too closely into how these covariations arise, the potential interest of this metaphor of the mind should be obvious. If all meaning is ultimately reducible to the innately determined, universal representations of mentalese then all one need do to unlock the secrets of the mind is to decipher the inner workings of mentalese! And lest the fainthearted doubt the feasibility of such a venture, one need only look to the promising developments in artificial intelligence where computer models of the brain are tantalizingly close (some would claim) to duplicating the mind's ability to generate its own assumptions and beliefs.

A critical question posed by the computational model of the mind to be examined here, has to do with the role of language in meaning. Namely, are natural languages merely vehicles for the communication of mentalese? Or does language itself play a role in the formation of our thought? The question is called critical, since a positive response to the latter (language *does* play a role) would call into question the assumption that all meaning is reducible to mentalese. From the perspective of Mead's metaphor of a biological and a social self, Fodor's notion of mentalese is like saying that the social self may be reduced to the biological self; it therefore counters Mead's view that language brings to the social self a dimension that does not exist in the biological self. The relevance of these questions to the psychoanalyst would not simply bear, therefore, upon the hope of unlocking the secrets of the mind. In proposing an innate meaning system based upon biological drives, Freud might as well have been talking mentalese! If he didn't refer to some version of mentalese in his theory, it was only (one might say with hindsight) because he had not as yet familiarized himself with the requirements of a system of representations.

As brought out most recently by Putnam (1988) the notion that the mind is structured in mentalese is vulnerable to the following objection. If you look at how language is used, you find that it does not in fact conform to what a proponent of mentalese would predict. If (as in mentalese) you relate meaning to a pre-existing, nonverbal mode of comprehending our nonpsychological world, then it would follow that the meaning of our words must refer to mentalese, since it stands in for the world it refers to. That is, our words would be synonymous with the mentalese representation they refer to, and would therefore have a fixed meaning. This last point refers to the fact that if mentalese is inherently in the mind, then the meaning of mentalese would be universal and not subject to the variations that arise in particular contexts.

And yet words do not have fixed references. Rather, their meaning evolves. To borrow an example from Putnam, were you to encounter the word *plant* in a novel written two hundred years ago, you would bring to this word a knowledge about chlorophyll and about the plant's dioxyde-oxygen cycle that did not exist when the novel was written. And yet our concept of *plant* has maintained an identity through time which must have as much to do with a community's norms for justifying a particular belief, as with purported mental representations. In short, meaning is (at least in part) a normative process, which depends upon a particular community's procedures for using words.

Borrowing another example from Putnam, words are often associated with meaning which not every speaker who uses the word has access to. The whole meaning of a word like *gold* for example, is known only to a group of experts—scientists who know about atomic numbers, or jewelers who know how to test for gold—and may not therefore be reduced to an individual's grasp of what *gold* would be in mentalese. From these and other considerations, Putnam concludes that the reference of a word —what it refers to for the people who use it—cannot be reduced to a mental representation that is inherent to the brain's functioning. Our natural languages are a form of cooperative activity that is socially determined, not just a function of what is stored in the brain. Mental representations do not suffice to fix the reference of a term.

And yet, in describing the revolution in infant observation presented by Stern in the Appendix, the point is made that today, infants are understood as having an *amodal* or abstract way of relating to their nonpsychological world that exists from the start of its social existence. Wouldn't this inherent ability to tune into patterns and shapes constitute a kind of mentalese? That is, if this ability doesn't have to be learned, it must be that the amodal features of the infant's nonpsychological milieu already have a meaning in terms of an 'inner syntax' that is applied to this information. And 'inner syntax' sounds like a pretty good synonym for 'mentalese'. However, the existence of amodal perception is by no means a validation of Fodor's mentalese, insofar as it supports a notion of meaning which Putnam and Quine refer to as "meaning holism."

The basic idea of meaning holism is that to understand an event, one must *interpret* that event. That is, one understands the event based upon the knowledge one already has as to what things mean. Any meaning will therefore depend upon the assumptions of one's meaning system as a whole. For the infant, if he or she is capable of recognizing patterns from the start, one must assume a meaning system that operates in terms of meaning holism.

As described by Fodor (1987), meaning holism has become the "received doctrine in current philosophy of language" (57), and he spends a good deal of time refuting this doctrine. Were meaning holism true to how we have meaning, meaning could not depend upon brain states but would relate to the totality of interrelations of an individual's meaning system. Since it is unlikely that two persons (let alone the same person at different times!) could share the same state of mind under these circumstances, it becomes impossible to believe in a psychology of mental representations such as Fodor's, that is grounded in brain states.

For the purposes of this book, it will not be necessary to describe the debate over meaning holism further. My purpose in referring to this debate is to enable us to appreciate some of the issues that arise when one considers what it means to believe that the mind represents its realty. To return to how all of this is relevant to psychoanalysis, I believe it is possible to draw an analogy between Fodor's position, and the one originally staked out by Freud. Fodor's concern is for what he calls a "commonsense" psychology. He wants a way of showing that our commonsense view of people as having attitudes, beliefs, and desires, and as having an impact on the world, can be made to correspond to a more refined analysis in terms of mental representations. This is not far removed from Freud's attempt to ground the whole of human knowledge in terms of primitive biological needs. Both approaches presuppose an inherent capacity of the mind upon which the individual's socialization is built.

Fodor and Freud part company, however, when it comes to specifying the nature of this primitive aspect of the mind. But the basic intuition as to how meaning emerges in development is the same. And both are concerned with the importance of the individual as agent or center of action (though Freud's *ego* had to be rescued by ego psychology from an overly mechanistic view).

For Putnam, Fodor's mentalese is a way of presenting the mind as a cryptographer. "The mind thinks its thoughts in mentalese, codes them in the local natural language, and then transmits them (say, by speaking them out loud) to the hearer" (1988, 6). What's wrong with this metaphor of the mind as cryptographer? First, it suggests that the language we adopt, far from being essential to thought, "is merely a vehicle for the communication of thought" (7). Second, it is but the latest form (for Putnam) of a tendency in the history of our thought to think of concepts as "psychologically real" entities in the mind or brain. Only for this reason, states Putnam, do we need to postulate desires and beliefs as "functional states" of the brain, that can be defined in terms of computational parameters and biological imputs.

Mentalese reflects (for Putnam) our age-old desire for a "God's eye view"; i.e., for a special kind of knowledge that comes of reducing events to something prior which can be discovered and controlled. Looking for a God's eye view, states Putnam, denies the "open texture" (ibid., 120) of our notions of objects, reference, meaning, and reason itself, which are all interconnected. We reduce the meaning of events to prior events at the risk of denying what is really there. Truth, for Putnam as for the pragmatists, does not transcend use. And yet Putnam also says that we must distinguish between fact and convention. But if normative convention determines what we take to be true, in what way is a fact different from a convention? Furthermore, if one objects to putting too much into the mind, one still has to account for the mind's role as agent, or relinquish (as per Fodor) a good deal of what we take for granted about human beings; i.e., the fact that we have desires and intentions. In a similar vein, one needs to establish a sense of continuity between preverbal and verbal meaning, else how are we to account for the meaning of language?

Fodor's counter to Putnam appeals to a principle that has been around for some time, and which may offer a way of reconciling these differences. The principle in question is that systems which supervene upon each other (which are functionally related) may be *isomorphic* to one another. That is, a system may preserve or reflect certain relations of another system, without existing in a point for point similarity. The usefulness of this assumption would be to enable us to see how one meaning system such as natural language could supervene upon another system such as nonverbal meaning, in such a way that the meaning of language is *a function* of nonverbal meaning, yet does not directly *reflect* nonverbal meaning.

To illustrate this possibility, one might take the example of the map as isomorphic system. A map works, *not* because it duplicates the topography of the area it represents point for point, but because it preserves certain critical relationships. In this manner, the map and its referent may be said to covary (much as the proton and the indices manifested by the scientist's instruments covary) in such a way that the one is mapped onto the other, without being a direct reflection of the other. In this manner, enough of the content of nonverbal meaning could be preserved in language to allow for continuity, without ruling out other sources of reference, as are described in Putnam.

Alas, the potential hope for this solution has been dampened by the observations of W. V. Quine (1969). Let us assume for the moment that we may show how nonverbal and verbal meaning relate to each other as isomorphic systems; i.e., that the first meaning system can be mapped onto the second in such a way that the meaning of language is captured from nonverbal meaning. This possibility would still not tell us how words come to refer to things. A language *appears* to refer to things "out there" by defining and describing these things. But the definitions of language depend entirely upon how the words are used in a sentence, not on the thing per se. For example, the word *green* may be used as a general term that refers to specific things such as "a green lawn," and as a singular term that refers to a general notion such as "the color green." Short of the way the word *green* is used in a sentence, there is no objective criteria to tell us how to detect the difference between these two uses of the word *green*. Pointing to a lawn for example, will not communicate which of these meaning you have in mind.

What this means (following Quine) is that in referring to things, we are completely dependent upon a coordinate system of terms and predicates that can only tell us how things are defined within a language system. When we use language to refer to things, we don't really say what they are, since it is only relative to this system of coordinates that we may communicate about things. Two points follow from this observation. First, it is as meaningless to question the absolute reference of a word, as it is to question absolute position or velocity in physics. In both instances, what exists is relative to a system of coordinates which tell you how the event is located, not in reality but within that system. Second, just as questions as to the position of a spatial coordinate system can only be answered relative to some further coordinate system (until the regress halts with something like pointing), so too will the theories we establish to explain reality. Ultimately, the theories and mathematical languages we elaborate as explanations can make sense only because they refer to some "background language," that is itself taken at face value.

Perhaps the most troubling aspect of Quine's observations (for those seeking to ground meaning in terms of a theory of representation), is the question it raises as to the basis upon which we take the words of ordinary language at face value. Quine has pointed out that the meaning of words may not be directly expressed in terms of formal rules and definitions (as was thought possible by Carnap for example), but may be understood only *implicitly,* by attending to their actual use in everyday life. What this means, according to Quine's "relativistic thesis," is that not only do we lack a means for formally specifying these assumptions, but there is nothing to specify, other than the interpretation itself! That is, we never (for

Quine) reach a background theory based on assumptions that are more fixed or determinate than the language into which it has been translated. Linguistic meaning itself derives from the possibility of such translations, rather than being a basis for it.

Stated differently, understanding what thing a word refers to requires that we be able to ask "is this thing the same as that one?" Yet the assumptions that moor our language, and permit us to define things are not themselves grounded. As observed by Quine (1969, 50) "What makes sense is not to say what the objects of a theory are, absolutely speaking, but how one theory of objects is interpretable or reinterpretable in another." The same point may be made about the objects of language; i.e., that it is the comparison we establish between two systems that determine what these systems mean, and not what a particular system is able to determine in isolation.

Yet how would Quine respond to the data presented by Stern? In describing how infants have amodal perception, is Stern not describing a background language that *can* be taken at face value? That is, wouldn't a built-in system for comparing patterns qualify as determining meaning in a way that doesn't require a translation? Not necessarily. The fact that infants make sense of their world from the start does not mean that they do so by referring to things. If we go by Stern's description, infants don't have to slice up their reality the way we do with language, because they relate to their environment in a global, omnidimensional way. That is, they use the information of their sense receptors to respond to what is invariant in a particular pattern. This kind of perception need not be in the form of discrete objects. One may therefore conclude from this brief foray into Quineian philosophy of language, that any theory that purports to address the problem of how words come to refer to things will have to account for the problem of how language translates the background of amodal meaning into the definitions of language.

To recapitulate what has been said so far in this chapter, I have discussed the notion of representation, and the role it plays in psychoanalytic theory. One way of constructing a belief-desire psychology (such as is presupposed by psychoanalysis), is to assume that the innately given meanings we start off with are basic to our mental representations; and that any meaning system which follows is built upon this preverbal meaning system. The problem however, is that these assumptions do not concur with the way language works. The reference of our words is in many instances determined by social norms, not mentalese. To maintain a belief-desire psychology, one must address the possibility (raised by Quine) that the way words refer to things is in fact indeterminate. And find a way of showing how language is nonetheless a function of nonverbal meaning.

3.
THE ROLE OF LANGUAGE IN REPRESENTING OUR REALITY

Is the infant a human being prior to the adoption of a language? Psychoanalytic authors have long claimed that an ability to empathize with another person is instilled in the infant before, or independently of, the appearance of language. Among the more philosophically minded however, language is seen as essential to the development of this distinctly human quality. The eminent Alfred North Whitehead, for example, has gone so far as to claim that "the souls of men are the gift from language to mankind" (1938, 41).

In order to address the ways in which the preverbal mind is altered by language, I will consider two related questions concerning the impact of language upon man and womankind. First, what are the areas of continuity or discontinuity between preverbal and verbal meaning? Second, in what ways does language *transform* meaning and communication? In keeping with the title of this chapter, these questions will bring us to an understanding of how language comes to represent a reality that could not in turn exist without language.

IS VERBAL MEANING DISCONTINUOUS WITH PREVERBAL MEANING?

We know from recent studies that infants are born with an ability to represent their reality. It would seem unlikely that language would bypass this innate meaning system. Adopting a language must therefore be a function of language's fitting in with the system that is already known to the child. This, briefly stated, is a principal argument for the continuity between nonverbal and verbal meaning. Not all authors who write about language agree with this position. Daniel Stern (1985) is among those authors who claim that language is discontinuous with preverbal meaning. For Stern, prior to the assimilation of language, the child's perception is unsuited to being adapted to language. He describes the child's act of perception as

> engaged in a global experience resonant with a mix of all the amodal properties, the primary perceptual qualities, of (for example a) patch of light—its intensity, warmth, and so on. To maintain this highly flexible and omnidimensional perspective on the patch, the infant must remain blind to those particular properties (secondary and tertiary perceptual qualities such as color) that specify the sensory channel through which the patch is being experienced. (176)

Stern assumes that if words are to have meaning, the child must single out those properties which specify the sensory channel through which something is experienced. That is, a word would have to refer us to a particular sensory mode such as vision or hearing, so as to be a clear and predictable referent. To prepare the child for language, he or she must therefore be weaned from the omnidimensional mode of nonverbal meaning, and this occurs (for Stern) when a caretaker says something like: "Oh, *look* at the *yellow* sun*light*" (ibid., 176). By emphasizing the qualities that specify the sensory channel being used (e.g., vision), this statement orients the child toward a unidimensional reference. The infant's perception must therefore be anchored to a single modality if it is to be yoked to language as a communication mode. Were intensity and warmth included as experiences referred to by the word *light,* this would presumably generate ambiguity, and make it difficult to anchor the word to a specific meaning. But the infant pays a high price for this kind of clarity: "By binding (a single modality of sensation) to words, they (the words) isolate experience from the amodal flux in which it was originally experienced. Language can thus fracture amodal global experience. A *discontinuity* in experience is introduced" (ibid., 176, my emphasis).

Stern's description of this process raises a critical question. If the child's experience is rendered discontinuous with preverbal meaning, how is the continuity of meaning maintained? To draw an analogy, if I cut a patch out of a fish net, the strands that maintained the patch's connection to the net would be severed, and the patch would unravel. Similarly, if (as per Stern) the anchoring process whereby our words come to refer to our perceptual understanding severs the child from its amodal perception, how is meaning maintained? One must assume that if language is so readily adopted by the child, then a language system must somehow fit in with the information processing of the central nervous system. If this is so, then language could not divorce the child from the omnidimensionality of amodal perception; it would have to operate in a way that accords with how we perceive our reality to begin with.

And yet, one could hardly argue with what Stern is saying. To be intelligible and communicable, words would have to refer to denotable experiences that are relatively free of ambiguity. Granted, a caretaker's statement "Oh, *look* at the *yellow* sun*light*" could not of itself bring this about, as the infant must first know what these words mean in order to respond to this directive. But Stern is articulating a commonly held view; i.e., that words operate by referring us to an experience. It is undeniable, for example, that words represent or stand in for the physical reality of our settings, since they in fact free us to refer to those settings in their absence. Words also appear to refer to *things* as existing independently of our expectations or contexts, as when the milk that is an inseparable part of the feeding context in which it exists becomes something that exists by itself because it can be named. Finally, words permit us to establish an identifiable self who has a name and can be referred to as an independent being.

The problem as to whether or not words actually denote things poses a dilemma which ever way you look! If words don't refer directly to things, then how is it that we use words as if they were in fact capable of denoting the things and events we talk about? On the other hand, if words *do* denote things, how do they do so, given Quine's observations described earlier? And if words must capture preverbal meaning (as is claimed in this essay) to *have* meaning, how does the global, omnidimensional character of preverbal thought come to slice up the world in terms of objective things, as in language?

The semiologist-novelist Umberto Eco (1976) has devised a solution this problem that appears to indicate a way out. Eco has proposed that the thing should itself be viewed as part of a meaning system. If this is in fact true, then all you need to know is how to make one system such as language, coincide with another system such as "physical properties of the world." To support his position, Eco observes that when one points to a cat, it is difficult to explain the word *is* in the statement "This *is* a cat." If the cat is an empirical thing, *is* could not be a sign, since a sign (for the semiologist at least) could only connect with other signs. Furthermore, *is* could not be a pointer, since a pointer (as when I point with my finger) points to the thing that *is to be* connected to the sign. The word *is* performs this connection itself. The only solution envisaged by Eco is to treat *the cat* as being itself a sign. In this manner states Eco, when we say "This is a cat," we are "comparing two sets of semantic properties and /is/ can be read as /satisfactorily coincides/ (That is, the elements of the content plane of a code coincide with the elements of the content plane of another code; it is a simple process of translation)" (165).

Eco's solution (to consider all realms of meaning as semiotic systems, and to relate these systems on the basis of a "simple process of translation") would appear to be what we're looking for. If the preverbal, amodal language of mentalese constitutes one semiotic system, and the language of socially and historically determined words another, and you know how to get from one system to the other, then you don't really *have* a problem! Yet a problem clearly remains. Eco doesn't really explain how the "content planes" of two semiotic systems come to coincide. In order to follow Eco in his leap toward a "simple process of translation," we need to know how this translation takes place. How, for example, could statements that are true based upon an amodal system of perception (as in the preverbal infant), also be true in a system where the truth is determined by social norms, as with language?

Eco approvingly quotes Strawson to the effect that "to give the meaning of an expression . . . is to give general directions for its use to refer to or mention particular objects or persons; to give the meaning of a sentence is to give general directions for its use in making true or false statements" (Eco 1976, 163). But how do you translate these directions from the nonverbal to the verbal? To illustrate this point, one may say "This is gold" because it is a hard, shiny, yellow metal, which refers to gold's nonverbal qualities. And "This is gold" because it has the correct atomic weight, which corresponds to a definition imposed by language. How do you translate from one to the other? Is there some way to map a verbal system onto a nonverbal system? It seems unlikely that the directive about what gold looks and feels like could be mapped onto the statement about gold's atomic weight. The scientists' measure of gold is a reference to the characteristics of gold that are meaningful only in relation to his or her measurements.

When a scientist looks at an instrument, he (or she) is not really experiencing the qualities of gold per se. He is noting that the instruments indicate a certain category of belief; i.e., the basis for agreement (among scientists) that a certain reading is an indication that the substance under consideration is gold. Yet one may also say that the reason instruments work, is that they take for granted the intermediate states that contribute to our understanding of a reading of gold's atomic weight. Mead makes a similar comment about the bear track; i.e., that it serves to summarize a great deal of information as the hunter stalks his prey. Our ability to perceive things this way—to pass from a detailed observation, to featuring one aspect as representative of a context—is a familiar aspect of how we function. These two modes of perceiving are referred to respectively as "analog" and "digital" forms of processing information (Watzlawick et al. 1967). Dretske (1981) describes the difference between the two modes as follows:

> In passing from the sensory to the cognitive representation (from seeing the apple to realizing that it is an apple), there is a systematic stripping away of components of information (relating to size, color, orientation, surroundings), which makes the experience of the apple the phenomenally rich thing we know it to be, in order to feature *one* component of this information—the information that it is an apple. Digitalization (of, for example, the information that s is an apple) is a process whereby a piece of information is taken from a richer matrix of information in the sensory representation (where it is held in what I call "analog" form) and featured to the exclusion of all else. (61)

How would this distinction pertain to translating one system of representation into another? If a translation occurs between two analog systems, the actual relations are preserved, as in a map and its terrain, or a picture and its subject. If the translation is between an analog system and a digital system however, an event in the analog system corresponds to a *category* in the digital system. That is, when certain qualities of gold are picked up by the scientist's instruments, these are read as indicating a category of meaning referred to as gold.

For these reasons, language may be viewed as a digital system of communication (Watzlawick et al. 1967). That is, the categories of language are seen as referring us to generalized events that are in turn related to nonverbal meaning in the same way that a scientist's measures are related to gold. One may therefore imagine Eco's translation as one in which the nonverbal meaning system of the child is related to the categories of language in the same way that language is related to the binary operations of the computer. Both systems operate on the basis of summarizing a great deal of information that is implied, but not directly referred to.

Given this way of understanding how we translate the nonverbal into the verbal, we still have to address the problem of individuation (how language slices up the world into defineable objects), and of supervenience (how language establishes a functional relationship to preverbal meaning). As this aspect of language functioning can be extremely complex, I will propose a metaphor for this phenomenon. The metaphor which I believe best fits the data to be addressed, is to compare language to a filing system.

THE "LANGUAGE AS FILING SYSTEM" METAPHOR

Filing systems have two distinguishing characteristics which enable one to compare them to the way language works. First, they operate on the basis of the fact that the information to be filed has meaning before it is filed. Second, the system under which the information is filed is geared, not to the information per se, but to an ulterior purpose. For example, if I file my correspondence alphabetically, the classification I use has nothing to do with the correspondence in itself; rather, it is a function of wanting to retrieve letters easily and efficiently. In the analogy being drawn, language corresponds to the system I use to file my information, while the information itself corresponds to what I know based upon my preverbal meaning system. Another example will seek to bring out the role of these two kinds of information.

I may know what a cat is (i.e., recognize a cat I've seen before) in terms of my nonverbal perception of its amodal properties, along with whatever feelings I experience in response to this cat, without knowing that it also belongs to the general category *cat*. This second kind of information would arise as a result of learning how to file my preverbal knowledge under the filing system of language; i.e., according to the criteria specified as to how the word *cat* is to be used in communication. In this manner, I will have two ways of knowing what a cat is; a nonverbal way, and a verbal way. These two systems are related digitally (in my file metaphor) insofar as the first (nonverbal) system is a basis for the second (verbal) system. That is, I could not establish a generalized category for *cat* in communication, unless I were in a position to identify specific cats in the first place.

But why bother with a filing system if you already have a way of identifying specific cats? One reason is to reorganize the information it stores from the perspective of a single, prevailing purpose: to assure *predictable interpersonal communication*. An actual filing system is useful because it enables you to retrieve information in a far more efficient way than if you have to go through piles of paper each time you need to find a letter. In addition, the categories we use to file things are extremely useful for the purposes of communication because they are more predictable. Communicating the labels of a filing system rather than its content gives you a better chance of being understood. When I say "I saw Bill at the supermarket," I have a better chance of being understood, than if I attempt to draw a picture, or seek some other facsimile of Bill. There is little ambiguity in the understanding mathematicians have of their notation systems, insofar as these are geared solely to the uses (and communication) of computation. Language differs from mathematical symbolic systems in that the underlying purpose of language is not computation, but communication itself. That is, while the meaning of the file depends upon the nonverbal information it contains to have meaning, the meaning of the file as label inheres, not in the information it contains, but in the file's ability to classify that information.

But how could a file depend on its content to have meaning, and yet be meaningful in terms of the file's label? The nonverbal content of a file is information that we take for granted, since it is built into the organism's way of processing information. Nonverbal meaning corresponds to Quine's "background language." It operates beyond our conscious control, in the background, yet it is the basis for what we find meaningful. As background, the nonverbal is the meaning we accept implicitly, so as to then forge the categories of language, based upon the requirements of communication. To draw an analogy, the biochemical makeup of the heart's tissues constitute an important aspect of how the heart works. When a physiologist explains the workings of the heart, however, it is in terms of its blood-pumping function. Similarly, the basic contribution of nonverbal meaning is taken for granted in explaining how language works, since the function of language is not to generate meaning, but to communicate it.

It would appear, however, that we are still left with a discontinuity

THE ROLE OF LANGUAGE IN REPRESENTING OUR REALITY   67

between the verbal mode and the nonverbal mode. If the meaning of the label has little to do with the content of the file, then Stern was quite correct in describing how language "fractures" the amodal organization of preverbal meaning. Herein, I would reply, lies the real advantage of the language as file metaphor. In taking this metaphor quite literally, it enables us to imagine how preverbal meaning continues to operate in relation to verbal meaning without being fractured. That is, (given this analogy), even though the preverbal system has been taken over digitally for the purposes of communication, the preverbal system continues to operate alongside the verbal system, as the file's content.

To appreciate how nonverbal meaning could operate in this fashion, one must grasp a thesis proposed by Eugene Gendlin (1962). Gendlin describes how, when we reflect upon the meaning of a word, we focus upon a *felt* meaning, which is to say that we summon the nonverbal meaning that the word (as file label) captures as its content. Gendlin spends a good deal of time describing situations in which what we have access to when we reflect, is something felt, as opposed to something thought with words. For example, when we forget a word, there is a stage (when one fails to recall a normally familiar word) in which one senses a searching geared to a feeling. Upon recovering the word, one senses that this as well is preceded by a feeling of recognition. Both instances (the *felt* search, and the felt recognition) are for Gendlin, signs of the role of felt meaning in the way we use language.

Gendlin's thesis anticipated by over twenty years a conclusion drawn by an author who has provided us with a computation view of consciousness. For Jackendoff (1987), since we cannot be conscious of how the mind computes our reality, we have to assume that our affects have the job of conveying to our awareness the results of these computations. Following up on Gendlin and Jackendoff's observations, we may assume that when we communicate, the words we use to convey meanings are like file labels. That is, they depend upon felt meanings to have meaning, much as a file depends upon the information it stores to have meaning. But while a file label tells a communicant what file to look up (i.e., what general area to focus upon, if one is to summon a felt meaning), it doesn't require that you summon that content. When I say "two" for example, this alerts my communicant to the fact that I'm referring to a file which contains specific events having to do with two of a kind. My communicant need not reflect upon this content each time it occurs. He or she already have a sense of its implicit meaning. But one may always open the file to examine its contents whenever a closer sense of meaning is called for. In this manner, the events each of us refer to may differ in their specificity, while not interfering with our sense of what our communicant means.

It should by now be obvious that the language as file metaphor is a way of responding to Quine's observations about language; i.e., that the meaning of a reference is always implicit, and that the reference itself may not be objectively determined. The metaphor is also a way of responding to Putnam's observations about the historical nature of words. A world like *plant* evolves over the centuries, given the discoveries we've made about how plants grow. A way must therefore be found to account for how the meaning of a word would grow while remaining constant in its meaning. It would be tempting here to claim that the filing label remains constant (since it is what we may explicitly refer to, in terms of verbal meaning) whereas the file's content changes. Yet the content (as defined here) refers to the background, amodal understanding that exists independently on the file's label. What changes then, is the degree to which the file's content has been put into words. That is, we generally discover new ways of expressing ourselves with words, as in the discoveries that come of reflecting upon our felt meanings so as to be more aware of how we experience our world; or in discovering how things work, as in the oxygen-carbon dioxide cycle of the plant. These discoveries broaden the field in which our words operate, since more and more of the nonverbal content of a file may become subject to conscious reflection by being articulated with words. Hence the importance of Putnam's point, that a language is a dynamic system insofar as the meaning of a word may expand in relation to the social and cultural events of the individual's zeitgeist. What will be stressed in the following text is that this expansion of the meaning of words is a necessary feature (in health) of each individual's development as well.

A further aspect of the language as file metaphor, is that initially, there is a loose fit between the file label and its contents. The generalized episodes referred to by words (the file label) are related to specific episodes only in the broadest sense, as in the child who uses the word *big* to refer to anything that goes with adults. Gradually, over the course of development, the file labels (i.e., what we communicate with words) become more finely attuned to specific events, in that we learn to use language (as a system of coordinates) to differentiate among the various possible references of a single word for example, or to pinpoint finer shades of meaning. In this manner, as we become familiar with the intricate workings of this complex filing system, we also become more adept at communicating what we mean, by learning how to translate our more subtle and personal feelings into words. While the overall designation of the file does not change, its contents are susceptible to ever-finer differentiations of meaning, within the broad constraints of the filing system itself.

Another aspect of the language as file analogy is that once you have assimilated the rules and conventions that a particular language system requires for including certain kinds of information in its files, you will find that the system enables you to impose categories of your own. You might for example establish a take-action file for matters that must be attended to quickly; or a suppressed contents file for the events you'd rather forget about; or even an X-rated file for those events you aren't supposed to let other people know that you know. What this suggests is that (borrowing Strawson's [1960] description), a language as filing system will tell you the "general directions for its use" as filing system, but it won't tell you about the information you are filing beyond the assumptions of the filing system itself. What this amounts to, (and here I believe, is a point that is most difficult to grasp), is the idea that the meaning of a particular file (e.g., the category *cats*) is not determined by its content (e.g., "real cats I have known"), any more than the tax bracket a person is in tells you how they make their money. The reason this point is difficult to grasp, is that once you have a language meaning (e.g., rules for defining the category *cats*), you can use it to refer to its content as actual event ("In his tax bracket, he doesn't have to worry!"). For this reason, we naturally assume that our knowledge of *cats* comes from knowing specific cats.

Stated differently, the language as file metaphor provides an understanding of what was wrong with the logical positivist's belief in verification. Logical positivists thought that for a sentence to have meaning, it had to refer to a situation that you and I could both experience. The problem with this notion however, is not the idea that observation is a basis for agreement (which it surely is!). Rather, it is that the positivists thought that the meaning of a sentence must depend upon the observations it refers to. This is like saying (in terms of the language as filing system metaphor) that the meaning of a language category depends upon the information or content *in* its file. From the perspective of this essay, this is a mistake, since the meaning of a file category depends upon how language works as a system of definitions for the purpose of communication. By this view, the contents of a file can be used to check the appropriateness of your definitions only by being placed in another file. That is, only another file could challenge the file in question. For example, a filing system that tells you to feel shame in response to sexual feelings because "they're bad," has to be challenged by an alternative system that defines shame in a different way.

This last point is similar to one made by Putnam (1988) who uses the following, familiar analogy. If you ask a group of people in a room to tell you how many objects are in the room, you will get a wide range of responses depending upon how each person defines *object*. These might range from the person who insists that every molecule is an object, to the person who sees the room itself (and its contents) as a single object. What you "see" in your verbal report, will depend upon the purpose you bring to your definition, and the interpretive strategies of the system that are applied to the definition. The question might then be asked, why bother with observational evidence, if the meaning of your data depends upon how you use it? Why not just accept whatever frame of reference seems most useful?

The answer proposed here is that the relevance of observational evidence arises *after* you have a theory, not before. A theory is not something you deduce from your experience (though your experience may trigger an insight by challenging what you take for granted). Our theories enable us to arrive at new ways of defining our world. Once you have a theory, *then* you may apply it to observation, and see if it pans out. Unless one's theory can be applied to observations, it won't be capable of growth. Observational evidence enables one to clarify the details of what a theory says, by pointing out its anomalies and contradictions. But a definition of reality (a file label) must exist if these observations are to make sense.

The language as filing system metaphor obviously leaves many vital question unanswered. How, for example, does the preverbal content lend its meaning to words? Is it altered in the process? Does it remain as content in the filing system in its amodal mode, or does its integration with language change its character? And most puzzling of all, how does language manage to convey meaning, when it is not, in itself, responsible for the meanings we have? Some of these points will be addressed in the sections which follow.

HOW LANGUAGE TRANSFORMS MEANING AND COMMUNICATION

In the previous section, I offered a metaphor with which to appreciate the transformation of meaning that occurs with language. In this section I describe some of the characteristics of language which are responsible for this transformation of meaning. These must be touched upon as they will enable us to address (in the next chapter) how language is responsible for our having an objective reality.

The American pragmatist George Herbert Mead had a highly developed sense of the role language plays in the realization of thought. For Mead, you have to have a language in order to have a mind. This is how Mead puts it: "Mind arises in the social process only when that process *as a whole* enters into, or is present in, the experience of any one of the given individuals involved in that process" (1934, 135, my emphasis). The words seem startling even today! How could the *whole social process* (whatever that might mean!) enter into the mind of a single individual? The answer of course is through language. That is, through Mead's notion of language, which is different from Fodor's or Chomsky's, though quite close to Putnam's.

For Mead, the importance of language is that it is predictable. You can understand what your conversation partner says, because you would mean the same thing by what he or she says, if you were to say it. Thanks to this characteristic of language, we may reflect upon our thoughts as a way of predicting how someone else might respond. And yet (as described earlier, p. 46) preverbal meaning is tied to its contexts; it is always a function of a particular time and place. Given the contextual basis for preverbal meaning, I would have little reason to understand the meaning conveyed by another, unless we happen to be sharing the same contexts. How then, do we manage (with language) to communicate as well as we do?

The answer proposed by Mead is that language does not convey meaning by referring to specific episodes. It does so by evoking generalized events. Stern has provided a graphic description of how this is true of words:

> Words apply to classes of things ("Dog," "tree," "run," and so on). That is where they are most powerful as tools. The generalized episode is some

kind of average of similar events. It is a prototype of a class of events-as-lived [...] going to bed, eating dinner, bath time, dressing, walk with Mommy, play with Daddy, peek-a-boo. And words get assembled with experience as life-as-lived at this general level of the prototypic episode. Specific episodes fall through the linguistic sieve and cannot be referenced verbally until the child is very advanced in language, and sometimes never. We see evidence of this all the time in children's frustrations at this failure to communicate what seems obvious to them. (1985, 177)

In other words, language permits us to communicate ready-made generalizations about what we do. Does this imply that the generalized episodes are *in* language? For example, we all know what the expression "He's gone to pot" or "Heavens to Betsy!" mean (if we learned English in the United States), without having been on a farm, or knowing who Betsy was. We glean the meaning of these expressions from the way they are used, rather than from what they specifically refer to. And their use makes sense because they evoke human experiences (our states of dissolution, or excitement) we've all had as people. Has language therefore evolved over the centuries as a structure for the expression of prototypical experiences? If such a view implies that the content would have to be *in* language, it would be counter to the metaphor of language proposed by this text. From the perspective of this essay, it is the assumptions one must make in order to make sense of a sentence that are basic to the way language works. That is, it is the *communicative intent* of language, and the *interpretive strategies* applied to the words used, that are responsible for the generalized nature of language, as will be elaborated shortly.

Mead's notion of the generalized meaning of words has many important implications. It accounts, for example, for the fact that each individual has access to the "social process as a whole," since language provides a tool for sharing in the assumptions of a group. Mead's thesis also explains why our notion of what is objective in our reality is not a function of what's "out there." Rather, the generalized reality we convey with language, exists *because of language*.

In the following sections, I consider two aspects of language functioning which have come to light since Mead stated his thesis, yet which build upon points he made, and which enable us to appreciate how language applies to classes of things. The first has to do with the independence of language (as a structure) from the meanings it expresses. The second, with the fact that much of what language communicates makes use of the beliefs and desires of those who use language, without actually referring

THE ROLE OF LANGUAGE IN REPRESENTING OUR REALITY   73

to those beliefs and desires. I shall emphasize the role of the conventional sign in several ways. Not only is the conventional sign of a language system essential to the intentional communication of meaning. It also plays a critical role in establishing the generalized meanings of our reality. To arrive at a sense of how this works, we will be using Grice's theories of meaning and implicature, along with the most recent view of how we attribute reference to words, as seen from the linguistic branch of pragmatics. This frame of reference will then permit us to see how, using an idea borrowed from Dretske (1981) and some research evidence from Gopnik and Meltzoff (1987), the conventional sign becomes a basis for forging general meaning.

ON THE IMPORTANCE OF THE CONVENTIONAL SIGN

From the perspective of this discussion, language works because it yokes our innate meaning system to the requirements of interpersonal communication. In this vein, a language system may be compared to the harness that is imposed upon a beast of burden. The animal lends its functioning to the harness, which exists independently of the beast it is attached to. As applied to language, the term *independent* means that the rules that regulate the conventions of language—its syntax, its semantics, and its lexicon—are independent of the meanings expressed by language. Like the file that exists independently of the information it files, a language system communicates meaning based upon the requirements of a set of rules; rules which pertain to the operations of the system, not to the meaning per se. For this reason, a language system may be compared to the laws of a community which prescribe the kinds of behavior which that community deems acceptable. The procedures to be followed are specified in advance. As with the law, a language applies to specific circumstances, but is specifiable in the absence of those circumstances. What may be specified are a series of rules having to do with how to combine the expressions of its lexicon into well-formed constructions; and how to derive the meaning of each construction from the meaning of its parts. These rules, which pertain to the use of language as a medium, are independent of its message. Why should this matter?

If you say "Pass the sugar," I must realize that your words are a request. That is, I must understand that what you say depends (for its meaning) upon my ability to appreciate your wish to have me do something as a result of what you say. This, in essence, is the basic idea of H. P. Grice's (1957) theory of communication. For Grice (as for Mead), communication works because those who communicate realize its *intentional* nature. With language, a sender causes a receiver to think or do something, by getting the receiver to recognize that the sender is trying to cause that thought or action. But what does this have to do with the independence of language as a medium?

In the argument which follows, I will draw upon the treatment of the importance of conventional signs by Kenneth Kaye (1982), who in turn brings together the ideas of Saussure (1959), Peirce (1940), Mead (1934), Piaget (1951) and Langer (1942).

If I wish to communicate to you the fact that I am in pain in order to arouse your sympathy and concern, I might moan, and hope that you catch on. The problem with moaning, however, is that it may not enable you to distinguish between my moan as a sign, and the pain it represents. You may respond to my moan, *not* because it refers to an intent, but because it permits you to experience my pain empathically. Only if we *both* realize that my moan is an appeal for sympathy, will it assume this characteristic of a conventional sign. You could say that responding empathically does just as well. Yet it misses a critical feature that can only be conveyed with conventional signs; i.e., it fails to communicate my *wish* to arouse your sympathy. Only when the sign can be treated as being separate from what it designates, as when we both agree to treat some part of a setting as a sign, might a listener become aware of a speaker's intention. The importance of the independence of language as a system is therefore that the conventional sign (which is a function of this independence), is necessary for intentional communication.

There is a further feature of the conventional sign that is important for communication (as defined by Mead and Grice). When my cat Rover meows to go out, she clearly intends to have an effect upon me. But the effect of Rover's meow is not reversible. That is, meowing does not call out a comparable response in her. If I meow to Rover, she gives me a puzzled look, but she does not appear to think to ask what my meow means; and she never attempts to open the door for me. Rover does not use signs with the understanding that they intend a meaning, so as to call out a response in the other. She cannot use signs this way because she does not have access to a system of conventional signs that are distinct from what they stand for. She is therefore limited to signs such as meowing and rubbing my leg, that stand in a fixed relation to what they signify. Rover cannot use the sign to adopt the perspective of the other, as Mead would say. If the sign is to mean the same for you as for me (as it must in intentional communication), it must be capable of calling forth the same response in me that it does in you.

GRICE'S PRINCIPLE OF COOPERATION, AND THE ROLE OF IMPLICATION IN LANGUAGE

A second notion that permits us to elaborate on Mead's thesis is the idea that the objectivity of language has to do, not with the content of what we say, but with the assumptions that support our way of saying it. The objectivity of our reality is normally ascribed to what a language says, not to how it is said. If I insist that the earth is flat, it is the content of my sentence that is objected to, not its form. Yet the premises we rely upon when we use words to explain our reality may be seen as more basic to what we take to be objective than the content of the words used. To bring out this point, I will start by borrowing Wittgenstein's analogy of language to a set of tools.

To use a hoe, you must have learned how it works. But you also must know what kind of hoe is appropriate to the task at hand. Like a set of tools, language also depends upon the uses we put it too. You would not attribute beliefs and intentions to the hoe you use, any more than you would to language (unless you wish to reify its role). And since a principal use of language is the intentional communication of our beliefs and desires, then much of what language does cannot be ascribed to the structure of language per se. This is the idea conveyed by the language as file metaphor, insofar as the file aspect of language communicates meaning, but does not generate it.

There is a view of language which would attribute beliefs and desires to language. Were this position correct, it would discredit the metaphor of language as a filing system used in this essay. Fortunately, this position is itself largely discredited. The position I refer to is one which claims that language suffices in communicating to a listener that which a speaker intends. As described in Green (1989), up until the 1960s it was widely assumed that because language has a conventional syntax, semantics, and lexicon, any utterance constructed in accordance with those conventions would automatically be understood by a listener as was intended by a speaker. A syntax tells you how to combine the expressions of your lexicon into well-formed constructions. A compositional semantics provides rules for deriving the meaning of each construction from the meaning of its parts. The meaning of a sentence (by this view) is therefore to be explained in terms of the conditions which must be fulfilled by these rules, if the sentence is to truthfully describe a situation. If you can account for the conditions under which a sentence is true, you can account for the relation between that sentence and the proposition it expresses; and between what the sentence expresses and its referent.

Twenty years later, it is clear that none of the above (i.e., the sentence's reference, truth conditions, or propositions) can be derived from language alone. Borrowing an example from Green (ibid., 8), the sentence "He fell down," according to a truth conditional semantics, tells you that a sentient male came abruptly to a point lower than his previous position, at a time prior to the asserting of this sentence. In order to determine the propositional content of this statement, however, it must make reference to an agent who is uttering the sentence, and to the time of its utterance. Even then, the sentence does not determine a proposition because *he* does not determine a referent. What we have come to appreciate, is that the genius of language is precisely in the fact that it does not fix a reference, or a propositional content. Rather, it leaves those slots open so that they may be filled by those who are communicating, based upon the setting their communication pertains to, and the assumptions they make about what they say. An analogy to this aspect of language is the inkblot of the Rorschach test. In this test, abstract forms are presented on cards to a subject so as to invite an interpretation of whatever he or she happens to see. With the Rorschach, the adequacy of your response depends upon how well you articulate what you see, in relation to the actual properties of the blot; and upon your ability to see what most others see in response to the cards. With language however, a speaker must be capable of investing his or her words with meaning in a way that anticipates what the listener will hear.

The language as file metaphor therefore agrees with the recent findings of a relatively new branch of linguistics known as pragmatics. Described by Green as the study of "the factors that influence a speaker's choice to say something the way she does, and a hearer's interpretation of what has been said, and what was meant by it" (ibid., 159), pragmatics takes the following fact of our symbolic lives into account: in order to communicate, we must infer what our respondent knows, in relation to what we would like her (or him) to know.

In terms of the language as file metaphor, the truth conditional semantics described above (as attributing beliefs and desires to language) amounts to saying that the file component of meaning can tell you exactly which content to look up so that a communication will be understood as intended. It ignores the fact that a communication may only be meaningful in relation to the frame of reference a listener brings to a particular context. As noted by Nunberg (1978), to figure out what he means by *jazz* when he says, *Do you like jazz?*: "My theory of jazz is relevant only insofar as it happens to coincide with the beliefs that somebody else might reasonably attribute to me."

Today it is clear that what we communicate depends upon a good deal more than the language we use to express what we mean; it depends, not only upon what a speaker believes, or believes the addressee believes, but "on what the speaker believes the addressee believes (the speaker believes) others believe" (Green 1989, 159). This kind of inference could not inhere in the truth conditions of a language file. Bar-Hillel noted as early as 1954, that even the interpretation of expressions like *here* and *you* require an estimate of the speaker's beliefs and intentions. More recently, Green summed up the past twenty years of research in this area with the statement that "ultimately, it is guesses about what the speaker intended the addressee to assume or infer that determine what a form or expression will be taken to refer to" (ibid., 35).

How does a speaker infer what a listener will hear? One way identified by Grice (1975, 1978) is based upon the following observation. If you listen for what is being taken for granted in a communication, you will get a sense of the assumptions that underlie that communication. Grice found that the assumptions one discovers in this way have to do with the basic integrity of communication; i.e., that it be truthful and appropriate. We use language, it would seem, with the understanding that it is for the cooperative exchange of ideas. According to Grice (1975), human beings follow what he calls the cooperative principle in communicating: "Make your conventional contributions as is required, at the stage at which it occurs, by the accepted purpose or direction of the talk exchange in which you are engaged" (45).

To paraphrase the four applications of this principal to particular requirements, to communicate with another, one must: a) fit with the accepted purpose and direction of the exchange one is engaged in; b) be relevant to the context of the discussion; c) be brief and orderly, and d) avoid obscurity and ambiguity. While these are said to be implicit assumptions we make about what communications are supposed to be like, Grice is not saying that we invariably adhere to these standards in communicating. Rather, his point is that these principles are assumed by those who communicate (though not necessarily consciously), so that when they are *not* followed by a sender, the receiver will nonetheless believe (contrary to appearances) that they have been adhered to. To borrow an example from Levinson (1983, 102), if person A says, "Where's Bill?" and person B answers, "There's a yellow volkswagon outside Sue's house," then A (following Grice's principles) will assume that this must be a truthful and pertinent statement, and that therefore if Bill has a yellow VW, he may be in Sue's house.

A further use of this notion is that a principle may be overtly and blatantly *not* followed in order to exploit it for communicative purposes. Taking an example from Grice, if A says, "I do think Mrs. Jenkins is an old wind bag, don't you?" B's response, "Huh, lovely weather for March, isn't it?" would be understood as indicating, "Watch out! Her nephew is standing right behind you!"

A principle question raised by Grice's principle, is why, if cooperation is basic to our use of language, do we not always cooperate? Why would we only assume cooperation when the communication becomes cryptic? When I lie, I do not appeal to a basic principle of cooperation. My communication is a function of my ability to distort the meaning of what I say, and my communicant (by the age of seven), is aware of the possibility of such a distortion. From the perspective of this essay, lying is as important a function of language as is cooperation, insofar as both pertain to the uses one may put language to. The underlying assumption one might call upon which encompasses both possibilities, is the principle of communication, which states: At the heart of any use of language, lies the assumption that words *must* communicate meaning. Therefore, if you get a cryptic message, you have to figure out what it means. Language makes cryptographers of us all!

There is a further reason for substituting *communication* for *cooperation*, as a basic assumption of language use. Grice's theory is derived from the fact that we exploit the cooperative premises basic to communication when we cannot, or do not wish to state a meaning more directly. Hence the use of implication when (in terms of the examples) we wish to avoid a complicated description, or alert a friend to a embarrassing situation.

But in view of the arguments and examples cited from Green, and in the second chapter of this text from Putnam and Quine, one would have to say that all language statements operate in this fashion; i.e., by implicating the reference that constitutes their meaning. For example, the sentence "He fell down," discussed earlier works only because it implies an agent who is uttering the sentence at a particular time and place as well as a referent for *he*. Otherwise, the sentence would make no sense. Herein lies a principal reason for the notion of language as a filing system. The principle of communication does not work because it refers us to contents. It works because it enables words to *imply* the meaning they refer to, based upon the settings in which they are used. Most of what language expresses can only make sense if you know who is saying it; for whom, where, and when it is said; and what the communicants presume about each other. In addition, you have to assume that words *must* make sense, else why would you fill in what's missing?

But why the *generalized* nature of what language conveys? The fact that we adopt the assumptions identified by Grice does not explain why words express generalized episodes, or how these episodes constitute our objective reality. To grasp why language works this way, one must appreciate the deconstructive strategy at the heart of Grice's theory. Normally, one would assume, we must first discover whether a word refers us to a particular object or event. Only then might we say that a word has meaning. Grice has turned this assumption on its head (in true deconstructive fashion) by saying the reverse: It is because of our assumption that words *must have* meaning, that we surmise the meaning of the event they refer us to. I have merely added the proviso that while there must be meaning, the meaning need not be true. Meaning is therefore more basic than cooperation. For example, because (according to the communication principle) the sentence "He fell" must have meaning, we infer that there must be someone who observed this event at a particular time and place, and a person who corresponds to "he." "He fell," conveys a general event because it can be filled in. The specific content needed to flesh out its meaning is provided by the listener.

So far (in this view of how language represents reality) I have started by showing how preverbal and verbal meaning can be seen as continuous. Language, as a digital system, may be said to organize the analog information of preverbal meaning the same way a filing system organizes the contents of its files. To appreciate how language performs this holding function, one must grasp the radical way words transform our preverbal meaning system. First, words as conventional signs are independent of the content they hold, and are reversible. Words therefore enable those who use them to engage in intentional communication. That is, in using words, communicants engage in an activity that presupposes their ability to infer what each wants the other to understand. Second, given this basic assumption about language, when we use words, we do so with the idea that they *must* have meaning. That is, we take it for granted that we ourselves must fill in the slots provided by language so as to render them meaningful. Thus, Mead's notion that language introduces the "generalized other" to the individual's mind may today be understood in terms of this aspect of how language works. Language provides us with slots which we fill based upon the assumptions we make in communicating. One might then intuitively sense that the objective nature of language is a function of how these empty slots permit our categories of meaning to exist in a way that has consensual validity for those who use them. How this works will be addressed in the next chapter on language and objectivity.

4.
LANGUAGE AND THE OBJECTIFICATION OF MEANING

Imagine that you are about to take an extensive trip, and that you have a closet full of clothes to pack into an assortment of suitcases of varying sizes and shapes. These suitcases in turn will all have to fit into the cargo space allotted to you in the plane that will transport them. Assume now that you make many of these trips, and that gradually you become more systematic about what you put into each suitcase. The suitcases and the cargo space in this analogy stand for language; the clothes for the nonverbal meaning that must be called upon to fill the slots. On your metaphorical trip, you won't get to pack all your clothes, but you will include what's essential. Gradually, the clothes you pack will become better suited to the suitcases they are allotted to, and will assume characteristics of the particular case they belong to. You would have your trunk clothes, and your duffle bag clothes, just as you have *subject* words and *verb* words. Granted, once you've made your trip (i.e., had a conversation) the clothes needn't stay in their containers. For relaxation, you might indulge in very different ways of using them, as in the nonverbal activities of music and the plastic arts.

This analogy, like the file metaphor, is an attempt to convey how the omnidimensional, global nature of preverbal meaning is transformed into the linear sequential form of verbal meaning; or how language slices up preverbal meaning into denotable objects. I will propose that (along with the conventional sign and the independence of language as a system of rules) there are two further characteristics of language which help to understand how this transformation occurs. A first aspect (to be developed in the next section) refers to the conclusion drawn in the last chapter concerning Grice's principle; i.e., that from the moment we adopt a language as children, we assume that because the words presented by our parents are used by them to refer to meaning, then they must have meaning. Thereafter, it remains our assumption that some way must exist to, for example, "fill the suitcase with clothes." That is, because language is a tool for the cooperative communication of meaning, then a way must exist for stuffing our preverbal understanding into the slots of language. The second aspect of how language slices up preverbal meaning to be addressed here pertains to how, if the same kinds of clothes are repeatedly placed in a particular suitcase, that suitcase will function as a category; i.e., as a container or slot for an indentifiable set of meanings. This analogy falls short however, of explaining why the sets of meanings should be general. Why for example, wouldn't we establish a category for every individual item? And on what basis do we establish a hierarchy of classes, which includes superordinate and subordinate classes?

To imagine how this could work, picture a child who is told that the person who just left the room is named Bill. The child is also told that Bill is his brother-in-law, and that he works in insurance. The child also notes that Bill is a grown man, and has curly hair. At first, these properties of Bill will not all make sense or be seen as distinct. Only gradually will statements like "Bill is my brother-in-law" refer to the specific fact that "he married my sister"; or that "Bill's in insurance" come to refer to the more specific fact that he works as an insurance salesman. In other words, when a child assimilates a language, the identities he or she establishes with words undergo a gradual change in the direction of specificity. The semantic content of "Bill is my brother-in-law" gradually excludes all information that is not specifically related to the content which fits that slot; i.e., which is specified by the community in which it is used.

What would induce our children to go through this selection process prior to knowing that words have specific contents? How can you look for it if you don't know it's there? One could call upon Grice's principle (amended here as a principle of communication) and assume that from the way words are used, we glean the fact that their communication potential lies in their ability to select as semantic content the most specific meaning for any given sign. Ergo, in communicating, look for the most specific semantic content as a way of inferring what your communicant means. As described in Dretske (1981), the most specific bit of a set of information in information theory is the one that implies all of the other bits in the set, without itself being implied. A square for example is also a rectangle, a parallelogram, and a quadrilateral. These other bits of information are all nested in (implied by) the fact that a particular shape is a square. Nested information my be imagined as a series of concentrically arranged rings, which become progressively more specific as you move from the peripheral ring to the central ring. In this manner one may begin to imagine how we establish the semantic content of our words, as well as how we arrive at hierarchical systems of classes.

To recall an example used before, in being told a name such as *milk* the child will initially ascribe the semantic content of this word to the perceptual features of the setting in which it occurs. Only gradually will milk come to refer to the white liquid in the bottle. Once this occurs, the other features (the bottle, the nipple, and so on) become subsidiary features of the semantic content of *milk*. The word is necessary to establish a semantic content, as it anchors that content to something that is independent of the setting. But the child must still work its way through a series of meanings—like the series of concentric circles used to depict nested information—which go from the peripheral to the most central meaning for that particular set of information. Like the proverbial blind men who each have a piece of the elephant, the child initially attributes a peripheral part as the word's semantic content. Unlike the blind men however, he or she must at some point break through to the specific content of each word as category. In discerning what is essential to the beast, the child also retains the more peripheral contents as parts of a whole. Once this occurs, it allows one to set up hierarchies such as *animal, cat, rover* based upon an item's location in the information nest. On the outermost ring for the semantic content *animal* is the item *(Rover)* that is particular to a fixed reference. The most specific item however *(animal)* is the one that (from the perspective of information theory) includes all the others. The progression from peripheral to central contents is referred to in this book as a process of *dereification*. It is when a content is at the outermost, peripheral information ring that the child is said to confuse the word with its content or to *literalize* meaning.

The point is, words are essential to this process because they serve to anchor the semantic content to a conventional sign that is independent of the settings to which it refers. The reader might at this point question the role being attributed to language. Aside from briefly describing a semantic content in terms of "specific" information, I have provided hardly any evidence for this view. To do so, however, I will have to refer to a discussion in the Appendix on the nature of our reality. In the Appendix, the claim is made that we have evidence to the effect that infants do not reflect a reality, they bring one into being. Why should this matter with regard to language?

If you adopt a Piagetian point of view, language is a medium for the expression of ideas. Before a child is ready to assimilate a language, a certain level of cognitive development must therefore be attained. A critical assumption relating to this view is that for Piaget, the basis for objective meaning exists extrinsically, "in" the world, independently of the child who perceives it. The critical word here is *independent;* it is the child's growing ability to differentiate *inner* from *outer* that prepares the child for the symbolic functions of language. But if the child constructs a reality (as described in the Appendix), that reality could not be independent of the child. A constructed reality emerges out of a synthesis of what the child brings, with whatever in the environment impinges upon that child. The independence of our world may not therefore be used to explain how we come to discover an objective reality. Rather, this presumed independence becomes something we need to explain, insofar as the child (by this view) may not in fact be said to exist independently of a reality he or she constructs. How, then, do we come to the notion that we exist independently of our reality?

Herein lies a major change in our understanding relating to the paradigm shift described in the Appendix. Piaget's notion about language must be turned on its head! Not only is language *not* a medium for expressing the objectivity of an independent reality. Language is itself *responsible* for what we take to be objective in our world. That is, language provides the child with a means of categorizing events in a way that generates the generalized, communicable episodes described by Mead and Stern. Fortunately, we need not limit ourselves to what may be inferred from earlier infant observation studies to support this point. Thanks to the work of researchers who have adopted the paradigm shift described in the Appendix, and are therefore working at the cutting edge of discovery (including Andrew Meltzoff yet again!), we now have evidence which permits us to say with some certainty that language plays a formative role in the child's ability to categorize objectively.

At issue is Piaget's claim that children must have achieved a level of cognitive development in order to adopt a language, versus the thesis that language is partly responsible for this cognitive achievement. For Piaget, you couldn't use language unless you had arrived at the stage six problem-solving level, and had achieved object permanence, and the ability to produce symbolic play and deferred imitation. Yet the evidence shows (e.g., Gopnik and Meltzoff 1985) that children can use words before they show signs of stage six cognitive abilities. That is, there are relationships between language and cognition, but these are very different from what Piaget predicted. Gopnik (1984) and Gopnik and Meltzoff (1984) have shown that children acquire words relating to very specific types of meaning, such as disappearance words like "gone," or success and failure words like "There!" and "Uh-oh."

Most interestingly, children start to try actively to categorize objects at a time which coincides with what has been called the "naming explosion" when they suddenly develop an intense interest in naming objects, and sharply increase the number of names they use. Gopnik and Meltzoff (1987) found a clear relationship between the development of the highest level of categorization (the ability to spatially displace eight objects from their original location, into two clear groups) and the development of the naming explosion. That is, there was a significant correlation between the age at which children first sorted all the objects into two groups, and the age at which the naming explosion was first recorded. There was also a relation between object permanence (e.g., finding an object that was hidden) and naming, which supports the discussion of Piaget's notion of object permanence in chapter 1.

Does this mean that children are categorizing here for the first time? A number of studies (Cohen and Strauss 1979; Ross 1980; Sherman 1985; Younger 1985) have found that children of about ten months of age form rather complex categories such as the category of stuffed animals. However, the technique used in these studies (the infant's habituation to a familiar instance) could involve the detection of a prototype rather than of distinct categories. Other studies which reveal qualitative changes in children's spontaneous sorting of objects could be interpreted as showing that infants have perceptual preferences for some objects rather than others (Sugarman 1982). Genuine active categorization therefore requires that children begin to sort objects into two spatially distinct groups; e.g., when faced with a mixture of balls and cubes, all the balls are placed in one pile, and all the cubes in another pile. May language be said to play a part in promoting this kind of categorizing?

The naming explosion described above inaugurates a new phase in the child's use of words. Prior to this change, the child appears to have caught onto the fact that words such as *gone* and *there* are about events, and can be used to communicate. The discovery that inaugurates the naming explosions (operationalized by Gopnik and Meltzoff as the first session in which more than ten new names were acquired) appears to be that the objects one names may be placed into distinct categories represented by the name. That is, the objects infants sort into piles at the same time that they display a naming explosion are not simply prototypes. They correspond to classes of objects which are set off as distinct from other classes of objects. How does this ability differ from the perception of prototypes?

In their discussion, Gopnik and Meltzoff (1987) note two aspects of this activity which distinguish it from the ability to form prototypes. In order to actively categorize objects, children must be able to consider the properties of the object independently of their immediate peceptions of those objects. Second, the general notion that all objects belong in some category cannot itself be defined in strictly perceptual terms. A child who relies upon an omnidimensional meaning system as described in Stern (1985) could not begin to categorize in this fashion without some rather drastic change in his or her approach to reality. The way in which a preverbal child computes a prototype is not subject to awareness or reflection. He or she cannot reason (in some nonverbal mentalese) that "this ball belongs in a separate area, 'cause it's different from the cube." He or she may note the difference as a feature of a particular setting, but may not refer to this difference as existing independently of what is perceived. To establish this independence, a marker (such as a word) that may be used independently of a setting, must be available so as to infer its existence independently of immediate perception. Objective categories (by this view) are therefore different from prototypes, as they require the existence of an independent system of signs (such as language). These signs in turn enable the child to classify objects in classes that are independent of the settings from which they derive their meaning.

Finally, these authors conclude that it is the "semantic rather than formal aspects of language development (which) are related to cognitive development" (Gopnik and Meltzoff 1987, 209). That is, children latch onto the possibilities of words as semantic markers before they have established the structure of language as a scaffolding for cognition. It is because words are equated by the child with very specific (in the noninformation theory sense) concepts that words initially establish a fixed reference for the child. It is within the context of this achievement that an information theory approach to meaning helps to envisage how words serve to anchor semantic contents, and to organize our meaning into hierarchical classes. The specific meanings referred to by Gopnik and Meltzoff are the opposite of the specificity of information theory. In the former, the child is equating the word with a specific task. In the latter, the semantic content emerges from a *dereification* of meaning; i.e., a reversing of the initial fixed reference of words. As noted above, this leads to a shift in the way children categorize which is of critical importance. As will be further described in the next section, this shift may be seen as largely responsible for the literalization of meaning, and the objectification of our world.

FROM BASIC CATEGORIES TO HIERARCHICAL STRUCTURES: HOW MEANING BECOMES DISTORTED WITH LANGUAGE

When an eight-year-old child who has adopted a language is shown a picture of a poodle and of a doberman, she or he will tell you that both are dogs; that dogs are animals; and that a poodle or a doberman are included in the class *dog*. The child will reason this way, thanks to the hierarchical system of class inclusion introduced by language. The preverbal child however will not reason this way. The superordinate concepts of *plant* and *animal* do not exist in particular settings, and so could not be referred to preverbally. Preverbal meanings are holistic and intuitive (as opposed to the linear-sequential, analytic mode imposed by language), and are not subject to being subdivided into hierarchical classes. If the poodle is to be related to the category *dog*, it is because it pertains to the prototype "dog," not because it is a sub-part of a class.

Meaning for the preverbal child may not be hierarchically structured, because it has only one level. This idea was presented in the previous section in terms of how we arrive at semantic contents. Without the structure of language, we lack a means of lifting a particular piece of information out of its setting. We therefore lack the means of establishing the hierarchical classes of meaning which are based upon this ability. To use the fishing analogy again, the preverbal child is like a fisherman who has only one line, and catches only one fish at a time. The net provided by language enables the verbal child to preselect a sequence of meanings in a way that is not possible for the preverbal child. For the child who has mastered language, parts relate to parts because they belong to a same file category. And parts relate to wholes because they are classified as subordinate to the whole as category. This enables the verbal child to draw upon settings that are not immediately present, since what belongs in a given category can be surmised from the words we use.

In contrast, the preverbal child has a very different way of grouping events. In a study reported by Stern (1985, 97), for example, Strauss (1979) has shown how infants establish prototypes of what they experience. He and his coworkers showed ten-month-old infants a series of schematic face drawings. Each face differed in terms of the length of the nose or the placement of the eyes or ears. The examiner could then determine which drawing best represented this series by noting which drawing was most quickly habituated to on a subsequent presentation. The drawing the infants selected was one which averaged the facial features of the series they had seen. That is, these ten-month-old infants were able to represent a prototype of the drawings based, not on what they had seen (since the prototype selected was never in fact seen), but on a kind of averaging out of their visual experience in terms of its overall organization.

The process identified for us by Strauss is creative. It arrives at a sense of events based upon an ability to average out different reactions. This process does not require a hierarchical structure of class inclusion to arrive at prototypical categories. The categories established are flexible and subject to renewal and growth. With language, the prototypes we communicate are in several ways preselected. First, to be communicated, they must subscribe to the rules of syntax and grammar. Second, the categories referred to are fixed by convention. Third, the prototypical generalities that arise with language are not functionally grounded in our experience. They require that we infer their meaning on the basis of our nonverbal grasp of a particular context, but we need not do so with any precision. As such, their increased efficacy as means of communicating is at the expense of the "lived" aspect of the basic categories of nonverbal meaning, as described earlier in the quote from Stern (p. 71 of this text).

But if the infant naturally thinks in terms of prototypes (as is shown in Strauss's study), why should the heirarchical classes we construct with language prove a problem? Shouldn't the child easily come to adapt these categories to the prototypes that are established naturally? The problem is that the verbal child no longer categorizes in the same way as the preverbal child. The linguistic sieve alluded to by Stern is the system of class inclusion, which becomes a sieve precisely because it works independently of specific episodes.

To illustrate why this switch (from global, omnidimensional perception to hierarchical class inclusion) is problematic for the child, I will quote some children's sayings from a collection assembled by Chukovsky (1963). The first states: "Can't you see? I'm barefoot all over!" This delightful expression, used by Friedrich (1979) as an example of poetic imagination, may also be described as an example of what is known as a "paleologic thought disorder" or "archaic logic." For Arieti (1955, 1967), (following Von Doramus 1944), children initially reason in this "archaic" way, because they establish equivalence on the basis of the compared items sharing a part. The example quoted above appears to demonstrate this archaic logic in that the child is basing her comparison on the fact that the foot (because it is bare) is the same as being bare; or being bare is the same as a bare foot "all over." Only gradually (for Arieti) does the child learn to establish equivalency based on the concept of comparing wholes; i.e., of saying (far less poetically) "My foot (taken as a whole) is bare, as when I'm bare all over."

Given the evidence cited in the Appendix, it is today clear that Arieti and Von Doramus are making a mistake in assuming that children reason in this way; that is, they are basing their conclusion on the verbal reports of children, without accounting for the role of language in these reports. The mistake is understandable (Piaget made it too), in that these assumptions predate the discoveries (e.g., Meltzoff and Borton 1979) described by Stern as to the child's amodal perception. That is, prior to the discovery that infants are attuned to the amodal patterns of events, it was thought that they must start with parts of events, until they learn how to integrate them as wholes, because that's what happens when children start using words.

The point being that the nonverbal child does not in fact determine classes in terms of common parts at all! The three-week-old infant who recognizes a nipple in a perceptual mode other than the one in which it was initially experienced is not comparing parts, as is claimed by Arieti and Von Doramus. He or she is comparing these experiences on the basis of their amodal meaning. In other words, Von Doramus and Arieti (and Piaget) notwithstanding, equivalency based upon the whole *comes first!* Only with words do children begin to classify on the basis of part to part. Indeed, the child who says, "Can't you see? I'm barefoot all over!" is making a logical point if this statement is understood nonverbally. In nonverbal meaning where the part is an experienced feature of the amodal whole, one could be "barefoot all over" since the "barefoot" is not a subclass, but a feature of the whole. With language however, the part loses its organic relatedness to the whole in order to become a subordinate class.

A second example from Chukovsky: "Please don't cut this pine tree . . . it makes the wind." Here, the child is apparently assuming causality on the basis of contiguity. Because the tree and the wind occur together, Piaget, Arieti, and Von Doramus would say, the child concludes that the tree "makes" the wind. But would a preverbal child be concerned with relating the wind with the tree? Or is language necessary to define something as causing something else? This is not to say that children do not sense causal connections. Bruner (1977) has enabled us to appreciate infants as inveterate hypothesis testers (of what goes with what). And as noted above, this is determined, not on the basis of paleologic comparisons, but of an innate ability to establish basic similarities. Only with language could wholes be reduced to parts and parts treated as wholes as in paleologic thought. And only then could contiguity become a basis for causality. That is, the predictability of language is largely a function of constraining meaning into containers which in turn serve to identify the items that fit into it.

What I am attempting to convey is a point that is critical to the entire thesis of this book. Namely, that the structuring of meaning by a language system into the empty slots of class inclusion results in the literalization of meaning.

HOW LANGUAGE LITERALIZES MEANING

Normally, a literal truth refers to something we might agree to from observation, as in: "Its a literal truth that water turns to ice when you place some water in the ice tray of your freezer." In this section however, the term *literal* will refer to a mistake we may make as the result of having assimilated a language system. The mistake in question (which may become a source of either creative discovery or pathological distortion) is that we may treat words as if they were the events they refer to. Stated in terms of the language as filing system metaphor, the mistake I allude to consists in treating the name of a particular file as if it were the file's content. The mistake in question, modest though it may appear, may be said to account for all of the mistakes recorded by Piaget and his followers from the spoken records of children, and attributed to the child's egocentrism.

For example, Piaget tells of a child who explained a large mountain and a small mountain by saying that the former existed for adults and the latter for children. He also describes how children tend to attribute causality to any two facets observed contiguously in time and space, as when a pebble which has sunk to the bottom of a tank of water is said to have done so because of its color, or the child quoted above who claims that a tree makes the wind. Relationships are seen between events where none exists, as in young children who report that their movements cause the movements of the moon. Words for children initially carry very literal connotations. The child is caught for a while between two systems for determining comparison, neither of which can work. The innate meaning of amodal wholes does not work verbally because it is being replaced by a system of hierarchical class inclusion that splits up the part-whole relationship of preverbal meaning. The part-whole relationship of class inclusion in turn can't work because the child has not yet mastered language's complex hierarchical structure, and because the child is still confusing the file aspect of language with its content.

Thus, when a child (as described in Piaget) claims that a large mountain is for adults and a small one is for children, he or she has literalized the relation of size as being a property of the word used, rather than a description of a relative dimension. Only if size is thought to literally belong to the words *large* and *small* could the large mountain and the large adult be for each other. Large as an expression of relative size has been literalized as a nonrelative attribute of adult "bigness." This "bigness" of large does not qualify the adult in relation to the child; it *is* the adult.

Similarly, a pebble could be said to sink to the bottom of a tank of water because of its color, or because of any quality that is named for the pebble. Only when a child has discovered that words are about possible meanings, will it occur to him or her to ask which attribute of a pebble must be referred to, to account for its sinking. Prior to this discovery, any attribute will do, because any attribute *is* the pebble, and sinking is what pebbles do. In these instances the attributes said by our language code to belong to the pebble (its size, color, shape) literally *are* the pebble, and therefore may be seen as causal agents for what the pebble does. These comparisons are made, not because of the paleologic assumption that a part is the same as a whole, but because of the literal understanding introduced by language, that the qualities referred to by a word belong to that word.

The literalization of the word—the belief that words are what they refer to—involves a literalization of the settings words partake of as well. When, for example, the child states that its movements control the moon, the moon is being linked to a setting where it is part of an event. In this event (one may assume), the child's movement has priority because it is under conscious control. Taken literally, the moon as a part of this setting, is therefore subordinate to, or dependent upon, the child's movement. Having conscious control assumes the literal significance of responsibility in a report which, if truly believed by the child, would suggest a serious thought disorder. There are however good reasons to distinguish between what the child says verbally, and what the child genuinely knows. In other words, the confusion introduced by language affects the way in which children express themselves, but not the way in which they actually perceive and understand nonverbally. Hence the inadvisability (in educating young children) of insisting upon consistency and "truthfulness" prematurely. For the moment I would stress that what is common to all these examples is not the inherent egocentrism of early thought presumed by Piaget. Rather, it is that the child goes through a period in the early assimilation of language where the innate meaning of perception is rigidly fixed to words, in a way that manifests a confusion of the word with its reference.

Several of the conditions under which we assimilate language may be seen as contributing to this phenomenon. First, words are initially adopted by the infant, not because they pertain to the infant's meaning system in any way that could make sense for the infant, but because of the adult caretaker's insistence that they belong to a particular setting. One must assume that a word is at first meaningless for the child. Words like *milk, leche,* or *lait* have meaning only because they are presented as signifying the white liquid which the infant drinks. Even then, the infant must go through an arduous guessing game as to what feature of a setting the word actually refers to. Mother must constantly correct her child as he or she comes to discover that most words are merely a subset of mother's possible meanings. The infant in turn is well-equipped to enter into this process. As noted earlier, the infant (as per Bruner) is an inveterate hypothesis tester. From almost the start, he or she operates by checking out the possibilities in a setting in terms of what works. In the case of language, however, the hypotheses as to how language works are tested out against the solutions provided by their caretakers. What must gradually be discovered is the relationship of language to the infant's innate meaning system. This discovery may be akin to that dramatic moment when the deaf and blind Helen Keller suddenly connected her teacher's hand sign to the experience of water; or it may sneak up on the child unawares, so that he or she never quite realizes the momentous change taking place. Either way, the child, in being told what things are named, could hardly avoid equating the name with the thing *named*. Short of having an intuitive grasp of the communicative nature of language, this is the only reasonable assumption one could make!

Because words are initially adopted on the caretakers say-so, they bypass the infant's normal means of generating meaning. That is, because words start off as induced labels, they are readily taken by the child as being the things they name, or as having the very qualities of the things they refer to. The child, in other words, has not yet learned that a language is essentially about itself, not in the literal sense of being what it represents, but in being about its possibilities for generating meaning. As it gradually begins to dawn upon the child that there is method to this madness of naming things, something approaching magic may be said to occur. At some point, the structure of the preverbal system must begin to resonate with that of the language system as the latter's syntax and grammar take shape. That is, there must at some point (to borrow Mead's term), be a *fusion* of the two systems, so that the meaning-engendering capacity of perception can be captured by language. The child has caught on to the principle enunciated by Grice, that when you hear a word, there must be a meaning that goes with it. But the meanings that initially go with words will be fixed to specific settings, and therefore literal in their inability to refer beyond those settings.

A critical difference has also been introduced. Prior to this fusion, the child has only one level of meaning; i.e., the meaning that is unconsciously generated in interaction. Suddenly, with the added level of language, those aspects of meaning that constitute the nonconscious ground of perception become part of communication. Just as a file enables one to classify kinds of events, so too may the child begin to speak of kinds of meaning that could not be expressed nonverbally. The child now has words to describe relations such as *big* and *small* which before could be known but not referred to. This last idea was expressed earlier in terms of seeing language as a filing system. That is, once you can file information under *big* and *small* the file itself becomes a category, and you can start to ignore the information that gets filed. The file as category takes on a life of its own.

Finally, the child initially has no way of distinguishing the language file from the content it classifies, since he or she cannot know that the words they are learning to use are not about events! Rather, they are about the way events may be classified for the purposes of predictable communication. The child, who's been repeatedly told which words correspond to which things, and who's had to bypass his or her own meaning system to adopt these words, quite naturally succumbs to the illusion that language is what it expresses. Thus, for the child who says that big mountains are for adults, the term *big* is equated to that which it qualifies (the adult), because no distinction can be made, as yet, between the word *big* as a file category, and the contents it refers to. Words assume a literal reality—they are what they describe—until the individual has developed the reflective ability to appreciate them as being *about* possibilities of meaning.

A critical result of this transformation is that within each individual's development words come to offer the option of being taken *literally* or *metaphorically*. By this view, a word is taken literally when it is taken to be the state or entity it refers to, as when the expression "I am an American" is taken to be a literal expression of identity, as opposed to an expression of affiliation. When reified in this manner, an identity is something that is literally possessed; i.e., that one might fight over, or feel proud of, or ashamed of. We could not literalize meaning in this way were it not for language.

A word is taken metaphoricaly when it is understood to be about a meaning, as when the expression "I am an American" is understood to summarize a vast array of characteristics pertaining to one's history, culture, geographic location, and so on. Understood metaphorically, an identity is something one has reason (or not) to attribute to one's self, and that one might value (or regret), in terms not of what it *is*, but of what it implies. In assimilating a language, the child has started the important process of reifying a common world of objective things; things which may then be understood as having an independent existence. Hence

LANGUAGE AND OBJECTIVITY

In order to convey a sense of how language objectifies meaning, I will present three different positions which purport to explain how we either establish or deconstruct an objective reality. The phenomenology of Alfred Schutz, the deconstructive strategies of Jacques Derrida, and our current view of objective reality in science may all be seen as shedding light upon the role language plays in the objectification of our world.

Alfred Schutz

In *The Phenomenology of the Social World* (1967), Alfred Schutz describes objectivity as a state in which the interpreter's own processes of understanding are ignored. That is, in objective thought, we attend to our experience, but not to what we might know about that experience reflectively. In this discussion, I will substitute the term *reification* for *objectivity*, as has been done in Thomason's (1982) presentation of Schutz's work. That is, the term *reification* will be used to refer to the "thingification" Schutz attributes to objectivity; i.e., the attribution of "thing" qualities such as concreteness, autonomy, impersonality, and externality, that generally come under the rubric of objectivity.

Schutz describes the process whereby we reify an objective world as follows:

> I leave out of my awareness the intentional operations of my consciousness within which their meanings have already been constituted. At such times I have before me a world of real and ideal objects, and I can assert that this world is meaningful not only for me but for you, for us, and for every one. This is precisely because I am attending not to those acts of consciousness which once gave them meaning but because I already presuppose, as given without question, a series of highly complex meaning-contents. The meaning structure thus abstracted from its genesis is something that I can regard as having an objective meaning, as being meaningful in itself, just as the proposition $2 \times 2 = 4$ is meaningful regardless of where, when, or by whom it is asserted. (35–36)

We come to establish an objective reality that is the same for you as it is for me, states Schutz, because the meaning of our experience may become a *taken for granted* meaning. One justification he offers for this interpretation, is the fact that in most instances the process is reversible. That is, reifications may also be " 'unfrozen' and brought back to their original active state" (ibid., 77). For example, once I have learned how to read a calendar by identifying the months, weeks, and days of each season, I may set aside what went into this construction, and take it for granted as an unquestioned feature of my existence. Only if I forget how it works will I be obliged to reflect upon what I know, so as to correct my grasp of what is otherwise taken to be an unquestioned fact. In Schutz's words, when I reflect,

> I no longer have before me a complete and constituted world but one which only now is being constituted and which is ever being constituted anew in the stream of my enduring ego: not a world of being, but a world that is at every moment one of becoming and passing away—or better, an emerging world. (ibid., 36)

In contrast to the existentialist's condemnation of the reification of our fellow man (e.g., Heidegger's *"das man,"* Sartre's "bad faith"), Schutz sees the reification of our experience as essential to our social reality. Without it, we would lack the common ground of a shared frame of reference. As described by Thomason, the flux of pure becoming "must be ordered, and the uniqueness and diversity of life must be suppressed" (1982, 94). What is the basis for adopting an objective as opposed to a subjective mode of interpretation? How is it that we come to reify and dereify the experience we have of our reality? Schutz approaches this issue in terms of the notion of "typification." For Schutz, we organize our experience according to its familiarity. The typifications that arise out of familiarity compose "meaning complexes," which enable us to make sense of our experience; i.e., they permit us to grasp that experience "in its structurization according to types and typical relations of types" (Schutz 1962, 285). Typification therefore refers to our cognitive ability to discern what is invariant in our experience, across contexts. This capacity then allows us to understand particular events as examples of more general meaning. For Schutz, these typifications come to mold human action and therefore assume a "determining influence." That is, these ways of anticipating our reality establish "thought objects" which are ways of preselecting and pre-interpreting our reality. As described by Thomason:

Once aspects of experience are typified, they can be grasped as the "same," or at least "similar," and yet these typifications do tend to take on that autonomy, independence and externality which reification also ascribes. A degree of reification seems to exist, then, even in such entirely normal processes as our use of language. When we "name" various objects of experience, we tend to grant those objects a certain autonomy and independence. Without doing so, it is questionable whether we could successfully recognize the "sameness" which things with the same name share. (1982, 96)

This quote from Thomason brings out an omission on Schutz's part, that is critical to his thesis. He failed to distinguish between the typification of preverbal meaning and the reification of language. He was therefore fated (as was Piaget) to attribute to preverbal meaning, a process of reification that could only arise with language. For example, nothing in the explanation quoted above, has a bearing upon how typifications assume an external, objective "thinglike" quality. That is, the ability to note similarities and differences and to establish a sense of what is typical in a particular context, says nothing about how we come to *reify* that context as something that is impersonal and external to the self. When Thomason says, "When we 'name' various objects of experience, we tend to grant those objects a certain autonomy and independence," the very thing one would explain—the autonomy and independence we grant to objects—is presumed as a tendency we have when we name, that merely reflects the preverbal tendency to typify. Schutz and Thomason are assuming that to find an analogy between events is to discover their independence. The infant who recognizes a particular rubber nipple at the age of three weeks, is not conscious of his or her separateness from the nipple. The ability to make this distinction, one must assume, is innate. It need not, and indeed could not be derived form the ability to categorize objectively as it must precede such an ability. The fact that infants differentiate the intrinsic from the extrinsic does not suffice to establish their independence from what is extrinsic, as the two are in fact (according to the evidence cited in the Appendix) *not* independent.

Further on, Thomason says that reification occurs when:

We forget that we have played any significant part in negotiating the experienced sameness of the world. We begin to reify whenever we treat the "sameness" of objects in our world as somehow independent of our own inclinations to *treat them* as the "same." Likewise, we are *able* to treat elements of experience as the same because we regard them as (independently, externally, objectively) *already* the same before and apart from how we "treat" them. (97)

One is tempted at one and the same time to say amen to this phenomenological description of what it means to reify (for this feature of our experience is rarely noted) while crying out in alarm that a description should not be confused with an explanation! We do indeed forget that we play a part in creating the meaning of our world, just as we tend to treat objects in our world as independent of our experience. But pointing this out does not of itself *explain* how we come to do so. Without wishing to deny the paramount importance of Schutz's work, it must be said that Schutz ignored two critical aspects of our development which had been pointed out by another prominent social psychologist, George Herbert Mead (1934). First, that the establishment of an objective sense of reality that is conceived of as being independent of one's experience presupposes the establishment of an objective self. That is, until I have begun to conceive of myself as existing independently of the particular settings I experience, I will not be capable of reflecting upon the fact that objects exist independently of my experience. What I experience will not be *mine* in the reflective sense of belonging to a *me*.

Second, the emergence of a reflective, self-conscious self, is unimaginable without language. For reasons which are addressed in chapters 3, 4, and 5, the ability I have to reflect self-consciously upon what *I* felt in a particular context, or upon what it means to be the particular person *I* am, could not exist without the reflective ability we attain with language. Furthermore, aspects of what Schutz attributes to the "thingification" of our reality—its autonomy and impersonality—are properties that are lent to our experience by language; i.e., they are a function of the literalization of meaning with words, when we confuse the word with the meaning it refers to. Hence the phenomenon of the child who believes that the word is the thing it refers to (rather than an aspect of its meaning), and then takes the word as objective reality. Trifle with a child's name (up to a certain age) and you will normally cause considerable distress. To say that this child's reality is objective *because* it may be taken for granted, is to deny the relevance of language to the way we realize meaning. If we must affirm the objective limits of our reality, it is ultimately so as to permit the emergence of new limits. Otherwise, why would we ever question what we know?

Jacques Derrida

In an approach that owes as much to the dialectical tradition of Hegel as to the "anti-reason" of Rousseau and Nietzsche, Jacques Derrida (1981) has evolved *"une stratégie générale de la déconstruction"* (a general strategy of deconstruction) which he describes as follows: "In a traditional philosophical opposition we have not a peaceful coexistence of facing terms but a violent hierarchy. One of the terms dominates the other (axiologically, logically, etc.), occupies the truth commanding position. To deconstruct the opposition is above all, at a particular moment, to reverse the hierarchy" (41).

In other words, the pursuit of objectivity does not (by this view) consist in looking for an extrinsic reality, but for the flaws in our ways of expressing what we take to be real. As for this text, truth is something we may only approximate in the course of our attempts to express what we know. To promote the renewal and growth of our concepts, according to Derrida, one must stand them on their head; i.e., one must "reverse the hierarchy." The literary critic Jonathan Culler (1982) points out that there are at least three other steps in this process. To *displace* the system, since deconstruction works within the terms of the system in order to breach it; to determine what the system in the course of being constituted has had to *conceal* or *exclude;* and to identify the *rhetorical operations* that support the arguments of the system. Applied to Piaget's theory for example, the terms of the system include an innate egocentrism, and a gradual differentiation of the subjective from the objective. What the system excludes is the role of language in cognitive development. Piaget's notion of egocentrism (as discussed in chapter 1) constitutes the reified foundation term of his discourse; i.e., it constitutes a taken-for-granted premise. For Derrida, these foundation terms are not analyzable until one has wrested free the implications frozen in this reification, so as to reconstitute the free play of differences that permit the expansion of meaning. For this reason, a rhetorical operation is viewed here not merely as a device for concealing or confusing what cannot be reconciled with one's system. Rhetorical operations may also be said to constitute the living edge of one's discourse, since the parts that are concealed or excluded by these reified foundation terms are the very elements that are needed to challenge the system in the direction of growth. The work of the deconstructionist may therefore be compared to the mechanic who, in cleaning our spark plugs and clearing our filter, enables our vehicle to get moving again.

The notion of deconstruction may therefore be seen to fit in quite well with the thesis of this book; i.e., that the concepts of language which we use to present our reality must undergo a continuous process of dereification if they are to be viewed as objective. Objectivity by this view is not an end in itself, but a continuous process of defining our reality. Yet Derrida makes no mention of language in this process! Indeed, his general strategy is directed not at language but at what he himself has termed the logocentrism of Western thought. The logocentrism condemned by Derrida is what he perceives to be the Western philosophical presumption that meaning exists in itself, as a foundation for all that follows. Hence Derrida's (1978) description of Western philosophy as a "metaphysics of presence"; "It could be shown that all names related to fundamentals, to principles, or to the center have always designated the constant of a *presence*" (279). [And earlier] "Logocentrism would thus be bound up in the determination of the being of the existent as *presence*" (12, my emphasis).

In other words, the logocentrism of Western philosophy is attributed to how basic terms are presented as literal presences that determine meaning. For Derrida, *presence* institutes a grounding principle, as is found in opositions such as meaning-form, soul-body, literal-metaphorical; i.e., terms which define a heirarchy when, for example, the initial term assumes priority. Among the familiar concepts that reveal this determining presence, Culler mentions the presumption of the immediacy of sensation, or the presence of ultimate truths to a divine consciousness, or the effective presence of an origin in a historical development, or a spontaneous or unmediated intuition, and so on (Culler 1982, 93–94). Presence, in other words, establishes a stance that is taken as objective when in fact it includes a complex construction that has yet to be spelled out. That is, it treats the present as a simple, indecomposable absolute when it is in fact a product of the relation between past and future. Derrida's presence may therefore be equated with Schutz's reification, as constituting the objectification of our thought. But whereas Schutz sees this as necessary to the construction of a taken-for-granted reality, Derrida ascribes this process to the presumptions of logocentrism, which block the growth of understanding. Presence not only ascribes literal attributes to our experience, such as the topological priority of an origin in historical development; presence also blocks the realization of meaning insofar as the assumptions that support its meaning may not be reflectively known; i.e., they have yet to be made explicit so as to be reflected upon.

Derrida's own interpretation of the work of Ferdinand de Saussure offers a good example of how he uses this idea, and of its limitations. Saussure was among the first (with Peirce), to insist upon the purely relational nature of a linguistic system: "In the linguistic system, there are only differences, without positive terms" (1959, 120). Since each element in a language system is said to be constituted by its relation to other elements of the system, there is no possibility of the logocentrism decried by Derrida, as no term has priority. Yet Derrida claims to have ferreted out a logocentric assumption at the very heart of Saussure's system—the concept of the sign itself!

Saussure's starting point is based upon a distinction between the sensible and the conceptual. The sensorial signifier (what is heard or seen), exists to give access to the signified (what is conceived). The signifier is therefore seen (by Derrida) as having been subordinated (by Saussure) to the concept it communicates. An important consequence of this logocentric prioritizing (Derrida claims), is that while speech is viewed as natural communication, writing is seen as an artificial and oblique representation of a representation. In a moral fervor which for Derrida betrays an unconscious agenda, Saussure speaks of the "danger" and "tyranny" of writing, which "usurps" and "corrupts" the role of speech. The logocentrism at the heart of Saussure's linguistic theory is therefore seen to be identical to the logocentrism that lies at the heart of philosophical metaphysics in general.

The problem with this analysis of Saussure, is that if (as Derrida has argued), Saussure does in fact objectify or give presence to the concept as existing prior to the signifier, this need not be only because he wishes to devalue the written sign. Rather, Saussure lacks an explanation as to *how* conceptualization becomes linked to a signifier in the first place. The terms *signifier* and *signified* are foundation terms which, in not being capable of being further analyzed, stand as rhetorical operations. That is, there was not (and there still is not) a means of explaining how an acoustical image lends itself to this kind of fusion. The basic terms in Saussure's discourse could not, therefore, be further analyzed or reflected upon. The logocentric assumption which then slips in (that writing corrupts the role of speech) is seen here as resulting from the inevitable reification of the notion of the conceptual aspect of the sign as a source of meaning.

In support of this analysis, it should be added that for Saussure, the signifier and the signified are indivisible aspects of a single unit. Saussure in other words, understood that this distinction should be maintained without collapsing one of its terms in favor of the other; i.e., without asserting (as in logocentrism), that one term constitutes or substitutes for the other. As noted by Derrida, however, he was not (in his view of writing) always true to this insight.

Derrida's interpretation of Saussure may therefore be seen in the light of his own failure to appreciate the limits of one's discourse as an inevitable feature of the reification of language. Given this failure, one must question the rhetorical operation at the heart of Derrida's notion of logocentrism. As a foundation term, logocentrism fails to account for the reification of meaning with language which is responsible for the literalness of logocentrism. The notion of logocentrism must in turn be deconstructed so as to uncover the neglected aspect that underlies this term; i.e., the reification of meaning that occurs with language. The final section of this chapter examines these issues within the context of the philosophy of science. How do today's scientists respond to the question, What is objective evidence?

OBJECTIVITY IN SCIENTIFIC INQUIRY

If we go by the arguments made in the previous two sections, any explicit (verbalized) meaning system—be it a philosophical system, or a scientific paradigm—is inevitably grounded in basic foundation terms which are in fact reified beliefs. These beliefs stand at the limits of a theoretical discourse, and correspond to what we *take to be objective*. The term *objective* is therefore distinguished from *objectivity,* the latter being understood in this text as a process that inheres in one's willingness to question one's beliefs so as to think beyond them. How does this position compare to the commonsense notion that the ultimate arbiter in science is that which we perceive with our senses? If the truth of a scientific statement depends upon the verification of what can be directly experienced, how could the objectivity of scientific theories be due to our being capable of thinking beyond them?

Until recently, a basic assumption as to what constitutes objective scientific inquiry has been the presumption that signs owe their meaning to the objects they refer to. Granted, the assumption that words work by referring us to things, and are therefore verified in relation to those things has not been totally taken for granted. Philosophers were well aware of the fact that many of our theoretical terms such as *atoms* and *force fields* are unobservable. One approach to this difficulty was to define these unobservables in terms of observable statements; i.e., statements which describe the procedures used to define the variable in question. Thus for example, a force field can be defined in terms of the observable acceleration of material bodies. As brought out by Papineau (1979) however, there are two serious problems with this solution. First, when we specify the observable features that would be displayed if certain circumstances were to obtain, we find that our terms are invariably *underdefined*. For example, we cannot really say what having a temperature would mean if a thermometer is absent, since the term *temperature* only has meaning in terms of the procedure that defines it.

A second problem with observationally related theoretical terms is that they also tend to be *overdefined*. Since the term is defined by the procedure used to infer it (e.g., using a thermometer), each procedure would have to define a separate term. Temperature for example may be measured by a host of different devices, each of which will provide a slightly different reading. Yet there is no basis for selecting one of these readings as providing us with the meaning of temperature.

Having failed with the attempt to define unobservables in terms of what could be experienced, our philosophers of science next turned to a "double language" model of verification (e.g., Nagel 1961). Theoretical language (it was now said) is related to observational language via *correspondence rules*, which tell you how to infer the nonobservable from the observable. Correspondence rules would specify what observations should be made for maintaining the presence of a theoretical state. The problem with this approach is that it offers no way of deciding how correspondence rules are to be revised when they conflict. And it offers no basis for deciding what is to be said when none of the test conditions specified by the correspondence rules obtain.

After decades of attempting to salvage verification theory, we have come to a realization as to why this kind of verification won't work. It is highly unlikely that we will ever devise an observation language that is not to some extent theoretical! That is, empirical evidence continues to be essential in that it may conflict with the predictions of a particular theory. But (and here is the critical point), what we *say* in response to our experience cannot be independent of the theory (and the language) we use to give our terms meaning.

With today's emphasis upon the importance of language, it has become clear that the experience we use to validate our theories will only have meaning in terms of some interpretive frame of reference. Hence the questions raised by Kuhn (1970) and Feyerabend (1975), over the very feasibility of making objective choices between scientific terms and the theories they depend upon for their meaning. For these authors, the meaning of a scientific term depends upon the surrounding context of scientific theory. Since this would also apply to the terms used to make observations, we have (it would seem) no way of showing how the terms of one theory are any more objective than those of another. That is, we have no way of deciding how the terms of a theory are to be used, other than the theoretical context that gives them meaning.

Hence the replacement of the traditional empiricist position with the "meaning holism" of Quine (1960), Dummett (1974), and Putnam (1988), among others. According to meaning holism, words have meaning in terms of the assumptions we make in using them, and not in terms of the sensations they refer to. The critical difference introduced by this assumption, is that we may no longer assume that what we take to be objective about our reality corresponds to something "out there," i.e., that is independent of how we perceive it. Rather, our objectivity will always be a function of how we define that reality. In this vein, Papineau (1979) has argued that we might think of theories as more or less successful attempts to picture reality. Our theories could therefore be deemed more or less appropriate creations of reality, not in terms of some photographic likeness, but of the overall coherence and integrity of the work. Theories might then be compared based upon their "programmatic promise"; i.e., their ability to predict lawful relations, and their freedom from conflicting generalizations.

Among the problems that have been identified for meaning holism is the following: If words have meaning only in terms of the assumptions we make in using them, how are we to challenge a particular assumption made by a theory, without altering the entire theory: In mainstream psychoanalysis for example, the meaning of terms like *instinct, repression,* and *cathexes* are intimately linked. You could not alter one, without altering the entire system. How is it possible then to deepen one's understanding of a particular domain, without altering one's beliefs at each step of discovery?

Papineau's response to this dilemma is to point out that there is nothing in a holist view to stop us from accepting some generalities as being more central than others. That is, a group of scientists working in a given area can be expected to differ in some respects regarding their assumptions about the subject matter. Yet at some level of centrality, they may be expected to share certain basic assumptions such as the conservation of energy, for example. For assumptions of a lesser degree of centrality, the adherents might share less in common, and split into a small number of camps. At the extreme of least central generalizations, it would be unlikely to find full agreement between any two scientists. Typically, once a basic paradigm has been accepted by a group of scientific practitioners, they will preserve continuity by accepting some basic level while following different lines of research at less basic levels. Papineau likens this process to a tree where the tree trunk consists of those basic assumptions that are common to all scientists in the field; the first branching of the trunk to those more basic points of initial disagreement which divide the community, and so on. If the trunk itself is discarded in favor of an alternative, one has what Kuhn refers to as a scientific revolution.

We are still in the dark however, as to how agreement is to be reached by the members of a scientific community. If our theories do not refer us to the natural elements of an external reality, on what basis are we to accept or reject the assumptions being made? For example, there is a contradiction at the heart of mainstream psychoanalytic theory. Whereas the theory's metaphor of the mind is deterministic in that its structure is strictly determined by instinctual energy, the practice of psychoanalysis relies upon the individual's capacity for free choice. One could not ask for a clearer contradiction, yet it has not in any way caused the adherents to mainstream psychoanalysis to alter their theory or their practice. Thus, the fact that the generalizations one makes may contradict each other, and yet remain as parts of one's theory seems to belie Papineau's optimistic stance.

A counter to this last point would be that Papineau is addressing scientific theories which have achieved a common ground or accepted paradigm (what Kuhn refers to as "normal science") within the community of researchers. Psychoanalysis, and indeed the very discipline of psychology itself, have yet to settle upon a common view of the mind that is accepted as basic assumption by this community. And yet one would still want a sense of how such an agreement might be reached. A sense of how this would work will be discussed in terms of imagining how new theories emerge.

If the discovery of new meaning is largely a function of drawing analogies between what we already know and what we are discovering, then the metaphor is crucial to the realization of new theories. Lakoff and Johnson (1980) have described how metaphors enable us to call upon familiar events in our lives so as to explore more abstract realms of meaning. Having equated time with money for example, I may then describe time as something that may be spent, saved, borrowed, or stolen. If I view the metaphor "time is money" as a way of explaining the meaning of time, I may be said to have a theory. That is, I have a scheme (time as a commodity of exchange) that I may use to explain an abstract domain (time). With this scheme, I may infer other qualities about time (that it can be saved, begged, borrowed, and stolen) that I would not otherwise have thought of. The limits of my scheme become apparent when I discover qualities of time that are not reflected in my time is money scheme. The notion of quality time is already difficult to reconcile with time is money." The notion "Time may not be owned" flatly contradicts it.

This use of the time is money metaphor is not substantially different from the psychoanalytic metaphor "Meaning is energy."

Chapter 1 describes the ways in which Rapaport's (1951) sophisticated elaboration of this metaphor as a theory of thinking does not work. That is, much of what Rapaport attributes to the mind on the basis of his energy distribution metaphor is in fact a function of adopting a language. This kind of anomaly—that reflection and impulse control require language, yet are explained only on the basis of a hypothetical system of energy distributions—seems important on several counts. First, it points to a limitation of this metaphor in terms of an area of functioning (linguistic behavior) that it does not consider. Second, it highlights the process whereby we build metaphorical explanations of our reality; i.e., that ultimately agreement will depend upon the degree to which a metaphorical projection succeeds in accounting for what we know about a particular domain when not viewed from the perspective of the metaphor in question. That is, the fact that the basic terms of a theory will determine what may meaningfuly be dealt with by that theory does not preclude our questioning it (*à la* Derrida) on the basis of what its terms exclude.

Thus, while the positivistic notions of verifiability today have lost their plausibility, this need not deny us the pursuit of valid theories, or keep us from applying criteria for the usefulness of a theory based upon an appreciation of how theories work. From the perspective of this book, this criteria would include a theory's ability to explain a heretofore unquestioned aspect of our reality; and the theory's ability to expand in response to challenge, in a way that deepens and thereby alters the reified terms it is based upon. Finally, the usefulness of a theory also depends upon the integrity of those who practice it. If a community is led by a priestly cast that considers itself to be above the constraints of accountability, the theory will suffer stagnation.

Once someone comes up with a metaphor which captures the imagination of a community or practitioners, the metaphor's usefulness may only be gauged by stretching its plausibility to the limit. It is in the course of this exploration that one has the opportunity to deliteralize its terms and clarify its premises. Only when a theory's usefulness has been exhausted in this manner, might it yield the seeds of its own destruction. That is, once a theory reveals its limitations in the deliteralization of its basic terms, one is permitted to see beyond its limits. Ultimately however, the full limitations of a particular theory will only emerge once you come up with a better theory.

In this chapter, I have argued that objective knowledge is not a function of discovering something "out there" which exists independently of how we perceive it. Objectivity (as defined in this text) is a function of one's willingness to question the assumptions that ground one's beliefs so as to see beyond them. Objectivity is therefore a quality, not of the object of one's quest, but of the quest itself. To objectify one's reality however (by this view) is to accept one's beliefs without question. Were it not for the literalization of meaning with words, we would not objectify a reality as existing independently of how we perceive it. Conversely, were it not for the opportunity language brings to reflect upon meaning, we could not undo these objectifications. The next chapter examines the role of language in reflection.

5.
LANGUAGE AND REFLECTION

Perhaps the most important function introduced by language (aside from the vast improvement in our ability to communicate) is the fact that it permits conscious reflection. This ability as viewed here is not only responsible for the emergence of a self-conscious self; it is also seen as the principal means we have at our disposal for gradually dispelling the literalness of early verbal thought, and for reintroducing some of the richness of nonverbal meaning that was sacrificed to the incursion of language.

Before looking at how language promotes reflection, I will have to defend the view that a phenomenon such as reflection or introspection in fact exists. Because a number of language philosophers (Ayer, Ryle) have questioned the existence of reflection, I will first outline the role reflection has played in the history of our thought, and then describe why its existence has been questioned. I will conclude that the questions raised about reflection stem from a lack of awareness of the role played by language in reflective awareness.

A HISTORICAL REVIEW OF THE NOTION OF REFLECTION

The act of reflection (as a reflexive looking within) has traditionally been related to the ways in which we are said to use reason. One capacity attributed to reflection has been that it enables us to capture the *conditions* of our use of reason. For example, I observe that every time I touch a hot stove, I feel pain. I might then reflect upon this observation, and question the conditions under which I came to this knowledge; i.e., that my pain informs me of this aspect of hot stoves.

A second meaning that has traditionally been associated with the act of reflection has to do with its emancipatory function. Having reflected upon the effects of hot stoves, I may make an explicit note to myself that hot stoves burn my skin, and conclude that knowledge depends upon paying attention to the consequences of my behavior. I might then question earlier assumptions, such as the belief that hot stoves are inhabited by evil spirits, or that the pain I felt was caused by my irreverent thoughts. I do not wish to imply that these examples describe how we in fact come to this understanding. If the notion that hot stoves contain evil spirits is held in place by a reified belief system, it will be immune to challenge. I wish only to illustrate how reflection is traditionally understood to permit the theoretical and practical understanding of events; and is seen as enabling us to specify what must be done, once we have grasped the nature and limits of reason, to achieve enlightenment. In one of the earliest classical accounts of introspection, Augustine (354–430) alluded to both of the meanings described above when he interpreted the Socratic "know thyself" as meaning that the mind should reflect upon itself. Augustine is herein announcing a theme that will endure for the next fourteen centuries of philosophical thought: that we may perceive internal events through a process of inner observation; and that this process provides us with *indubitable* knowledge. This is not to say that introspection was confused with perception. In the *Summa,* Aquinas (1225–1274) quoted Augustine to support the view that the mind perceives itself. But he attributed to introspection the subsidiary role of sorting and understanding the data provided by perception.

When (in the time of Descartes) perception came to be viewed as a source of error, reflective consciousness was seen as our only basis for uncovering truth. Reflection therefore became not merely a means of dispelling error, but our principle method for discovering ideas. In this vein, Hobbes (1588–1679) saw reflection not only as a source of knowledge about human psychology, but about political and social man as well, since "whosoever looketh into himself will know the thoughts and passions of all other men" (1958 [1654]). One example of the way in which reflection was thought to work is described by Locke (1959, [1690] 1:2.1.24). By his view, we get ideas from our sensations. The mind then comes to reflect upon its own operations in relation to these ideas, which become what Locke called "ideas of reflection." Reflection therefore accounted for our awareness of how we come to understand the operation of the mind itself, based on the sensations conveyed by our experience. Not much, however, was said about how reflection works as a process. These questions had to await the emergence of experimental psychology which, ironically, led to the temporary demise of introspection as scientific method.

In his book *Psychology from an Empirical Standpoint* first published in 1874, Brentano (1973) declared that the chief method of psychology was "inner perception," which he distinguished from "inner observation." By this view, a first order of mental events has to do with the direct experience of thoughts, feelings, and volitions. We may not however *observe* this first order without destroying what we wish to observe. The direct level has to be perceived indirectly, by a kind of reflective awareness that is not the same as direct observation. This indirect noticing of mental events nonetheless was viewed as our only means of noting the operations of the mind. The psychologist Wilhelm Wundt (1912) endorsed Brentano's version of introspection. He felt however that inner perception could become a scientific method only by controlling its conditions. This amounted to controlling the stimuli thought to cause the content of our perception, which could then be passively observed by a trained observer. Wundt was in effect presuming what he would explain by presenting subjects with what he thought would produce primary sensations (e.g., simple colored shapes); and by limiting the reports to questions of size, intensity, and duration. In the course of making introspection "scientific," his laboratory produced a number of technical innovations still in use, such as the tachistascope and the chronograph. These may hardly be said to have justified the enormous waste in time and energy that came of having adopted a reified notion of the mind that was never questioned. The metaphor of the mind (adopted from British empiricism) as a container of sensations, was to be pursued to its dogmatic limits.

For the American pragmatist William James (1950), the subject of psychology in his famous *Principles* [1890] was not sensations, but the phenomenal "stream of consciousness" we have access to via reflection. The psychologist's role was to relate this stream of consciousness to neurological phenomena, insofar as James presumed a one-to-one correspondence to exist between this stream and physiological events in the brain. Before this could be done, however, a thorough mapping of the stream was required, and could only be accomplished by introspection. Auguste Comte (1789–1857), the founder of positivistic philosophy, had objected to what he deemed to be the logical absurdity of claiming that we could split ourselves in two by being aware of our awareness. An awareness that provides us with awareness of events cannot treat itself like an event. James's response was to endorse Mill's notion that in reflection we are reflecting, not upon our awareness per se, but upon our *memory* of that awareness. The point is that there was in fact no basis to either confirm or deny this assumption, for we as yet had nothing to put our finger on as to what was really involved. As long as we lacked some measurable correlate of what introspection was thought to be, not to mention a model as to how it operates, any plausible account would do. There was as yet no basis to rule it out.

What the various accounts of introspection were missing up to this point was a grasp of the role of language in this process. The importance of language had not escaped the British empiricists, who thought that analyzing language would explain how you get from impressions to ideas. But just what language contributes to ideas was not yet questioned, as language was still viewed as a simple conveyor of ideas. Elsewhere, Wilhelm von Humboldt (1767–1835) was formulating a view of language as characterizing a world outlook that presaged the Sapir-Worf hypothesis. But it was left to George Herbert Mead to relate language to reflection, for a reason which must today seem obvious once it is stated, but had not till then been noted. Namely, that in order to reflect upon the self's experience as being something that happens to the self, there must be an objective self to refer to. That is, one must have access to a *me* that is conceived as existing independently of one's experience; which is to say a *me* as it exists for the other. In true deconstructive fashion, Mead had turned the entire enterprise on its head, by describing reflection, not as an act of inner observation, but as a particular kind of relationship between aspects of the self. The relationship in question is the result of how assimilating a language splits the mind into an experiential *I* and a social self-conscious *me*.

From the perspective of this book (which follows Mead's seminal account), the objective level of meaning introduced by language enables us to literalize our reality and to thereby relate to it (and to our objectified *me*) as being independent of what we experience. The quality of self-observation we attribute to reflection is not (by this view) a function of observing what goes on inside, or of turning reflexively on the self; rather, it is a function of deliteralizing (or dereifying) the meanings which have been captured by language. Needless to say, Mead's account was not appreciated by the mainstream academics of his day; indeed, to this day, his view of language has yet to receive the attention it merits.

With the advent of behaviorism, introspection came to be seen as an unreliable method of investigation (principally because it was so thoroughly misunderstood!). As long as introspection is taken to be a method for observing pre-existing contents of the mind, one may not appreciate its function as our principal means (as had been intuited since Augustine) of discovering reality. Since experimental psychology took reflection to be a method not of discovery, but of observation, these observations gave rise to fruitless debates. Thus for example, the debate between Titchener at Cornell, and the members of the Würzberg school in Germany, over the existence of nonsensory conscious thought. The method of introspection had become so hedged in with rules and regulations (to assure its scientific purity!) that the rules themselves determined what you could find, not the act of reflection per se. As a result, introspection came to be seen as an unreliable source of psychological data, and the way was cleared for Watson's behaviorism. Not only introspection, but the very idea of consciousness had become "unscientific" in our approach to understanding the mind.

Henceforth, we would limit our enquiry to what we could observe. When referred to at all, consciousness was explained (e.g., Lashley 1923) as a subvocal activation of the mechanisms involved in speech that stopped short of producing speech. Introspection was seen as a kind of aberration of the mind similar to astigmatism; i.e., as providing a partial and distorted view of what is better left to ordinary observation. I will not in what follows consider the contribution phenomenology has made to our understanding of reflection. In 1902, Peirce noted that an analysis of the contents of awareness constituted a first phenomenological step in philosophical analysis. But it was Husserl (1859–1938) whose 1913 work *Ideas Toward a Pure Phenomenology and Phenomenological Philosophy* (1969), cast reflection into the form of "bracketing" our experience so as to explore the essences of phenomena. In this survey, my concern will be with positions which have denied the relevance of a reflective process to meaning. That is, I will address a premise that is common to what the English psychologist Mace (1948) calls "analytical behaviorism" (as opposed to the "metaphysical behaviorism" which denies the existence of conscious states or processes) and to the linguistic philosophy of Ayer and Ryle. Namely, that statements about mind or consciousness turn out on analysis to be statements about the behavior of material things. That is (borrowing Mundle's amendment to Mace's formulation [1979, 53]), statements ascribing any state of mind (mind predicates) to a person can be analyzed into statements about what other people can or could observe this person doing. My objection to this premise is that it ignores the most characteristic feature of reflection; namely, that it is not directly subject to consensual observation, yet constitutes a critical stage in the realization of meaning.

The concerns of behaviorism in the United States were not dissimilar to the ones being expressed by the Vienna circle in Austria. Both sought means of verifying one's assumptions based upon what could be observed. The Vienna circle had adopted a position which states that the meaning of a proposition is the method of its verification. As is noted in chapter 4 of this text, this idea has since been discarded. Its importance is seen here in the fact that it inspired a book (Ayer's *Language, Truth and Logic*, 1946) which first appeared just before World War II, and which, as one of the main intellectual influences upon English-speaking philosophers of that period, prepared the way for linguistic philosophy.

For the Ayer of this early work, the philosopher is not directly concerned with the physical property of things, but only with the way in which we speak about them. As described by Ayer, "the propositions of philosophy are not factual but linguistic in character—that is, they do not describe the behavior of physical, or even mental objects; they express definitions, or the formal consequences of definitions" (ibid., 57).

As noted in Mundle (1979), Ayer's principle concern—the basis upon which what we say has meaning—is itself based upon the questionable identification of meaning with evidence. To determine how statements have meaning, Ayer proposed a verification principle (VP), whereby what a person says is meaningful when it is verifiable in terms of the "sense data" of what can be directly experienced. The problem with this condition (states Mundle) is that sentences are used to assert propositions. Propositions are what we assert when we use sentences. By definition, propositions are either true or false, else they would not *be* propositions. It would be self-contradictory to speak of a meaningless proposition, since a proposition is the meaning we attach to a sentence. The question "Is it meaningful?" should therefore be asked only about sentences or symbols. And the question "Is it verifiable?" should be asked *only* about propositions. A sentence as such is not true or false, and therefore not capable of being verified. As stated by Mundle, "the predicates 'meaningful' and 'meaningless' are applicable to sentences but not to propositions and the predicates 'verifiable' and 'unverifiable' are applicable to propositions but not to sentences as such" (ibid., 258). The distinction drawn by Mundle between meaning and proposition is the same distinction made in this text in terms of the metaphor of language as a filing system. In this analogy, the meaning of a sentence is represented by the filing system that organizes the information in the file, whereas its propositional truth is represented by the information a file stores.

Having (by this view) confused meaning with evidence, Ayer is then led to reject a good deal of what we normally accept as meaningful, because it does not subscribe to his VP. For example, a deduction Ayer draws from his verification principle is that metaphysical statements are literally meaningless; i.e., a metaphysical sentence purports to express a genuine proposition, but in fact does not. But, (as noted by Mundle), if metaphysics may be understood as a concern for questions about what exists, then Ayer's thesis is eminently metaphysical! That is, the claim that all empirical statements are really about a person's own sense data, is clearly metaphysical. Ayer merely redefines metaphysics so as to make it applicable only to metaphysical theories other than his own.

For Mundle, this mistake is not accidental, but results from a misuse of the word *concept* in linguistic philosophy. According to Mundle, a legitimate way of using "concept" is when the "concept of A" for example is a way of mentioning "A," of talking about the use of the expression "A"— and of other expressions which have the same use. If however, the "concept of A" is used to talk about the things called "A" or about the properties of these things which cause us to call them "A," this would be a misleading way of using the expression "A." Mundle's point (from the perspective of this book) refers to the *literalization* of meaning; i.e., to confusing the meaning of "A" as file definition (in terms of the language as file metaphor) with the contents of that file. That is, Mundle's emphasis is upon the misleading nature of talking about an expression as if it were the thing itself. A similar kind of confusion (of the name with the thing it names) may be seen in what Ryle refers to (in his influential *Concept of Mind*, 1949) as a category mistake.

For Gilbert Ryle (1900–1976) the task of philosophy is to rescue the world at large from conceptual confusion. And since the conceptual mistakes we make result from the misuse of ordinary language, then philosophy (as with Ayer) is concerned mainly with language. One falls into confusion, for example, when grammatical similarities and differences are construed to be logical similarities and differences. Or when one explains one concept in terms of one sort of category when it should be consigned to another. Or when a word designating a part is mistakenly related with a word designating a whole. Most of his examples are of this last type, such as the person who took the University of Oxford to refer to an institution of the same kind as does (its part) Christ Church; or who took a division to refer to a military unit that is distinct from the battalions which comprise it.

In this vein, Ryle claims that all sentences which bring together terms like "body" and "mind" or "mental" and "physical" are category mistakes. This stems from his belief that the notion of an immaterial mind is itself a category mistake; i.e., it attributes a nonphysical substance (the mind) to a physical category (the body). For Ryle, the correct category for alleged mental items, operations, and products is *behavioral dispositions*. To avoid these category mistakes, one must refuse any account of psychological concepts that refer to inner events. Introspection by this view is nothing more than our ordinary perception of ongoing behavior, or the recall for consideration of past behavior from memory. In introspection (for Ryle), we "catch ourselves doing so and so." As a result of these assumptions, Ryle ends up treating as senseless many sentences which are commonly used and understood. For example, sentences like "His behavior had both mental and physical causes," are condemned by Ryle as "not proper," "absurd," and "makes no sense" (1949, 22).

Ryle has two ways of justifying this position. First, he states that the logical regulations he refers to are in keeping with normal English usage; i.e., that statements using dispositional words have been misinterpreted as reports about private episodes. As noted by Mundle, this amounts to appealing to normal usage, and then condemning normally used sentences as mistakes. Ryle, however, also claims that these mistakes are "breaches of logical rules" (ibid., 8). The rule in question is that you may not say something about a concept belonging to one category, that should properly be said about a concept of a different category. But such a rule presupposes that you have a further rule for assigning concepts to the same or to different categories. The only guidance Ryle offers in this regard is to say, "When two terms belong to the same category, it is proper to construct conjunctive propositions embodying them" (ibid., 22). This would imply that terms are of a different category when it is improper to construct a conjunctive proposition embodying them. But as noted by Mundle, this rule could not be applied without an independent way of showing when a conjunctive sentence is improper. Such a rule does not in fact exist.

There is a good reason for the nonexistence of this rule. The bringing together of different realms of linguistic meaning does not, of itself, constitute a mistake. Rather, what Ryle is drawing our attention to, is the fact that we may literalize our meaning with words. If for example, I describe the concept of an ego as something *in* the person's mind, the problem is not that I have joined two categories that don't belong together, since the expression "The ego in his head must be bursting!" may sound awkward, but it does not strike us a wrong. Rather, the problem is that I may then literalize the word *ego*. That is, I may then confuse the word with what it refers to, and treat it as having physical properties. The confusion therefore is not between verbal categories per se, but between a verbal category and what the category refers to (i.e., between the file and its content).

Words by their nature are meaningful statements *about* something. The things they are about can be taken *literally* and *metaphorically*. That is, the reference of a word can be reified as a property of the word, or can be understood as what the word is about. That words may be taken literally should not be seen as a mistake. Rather, the mistake would be in taking words literally when their context implies that they are to be understood metaphorically. When the swimming coach says "Jump!" as a command, you do not (if poised expectantly on the edge of a swimming pool) pause to ponder what the command is about. Rather, you take the command literally as an unquestioned prod to action. Later, if asked to reflect upon what it was like to hear this command, it would be quite inappropriate to get up and jump. Missing this piece of the puzzle, Ryle attempted to make up for this gap by inventing rules of his own. In doing so however, he collapsed his discourse in the direction of attributing all meaning to language.

The problem with Ryle's argument becomes clearly apparent when he attempts to account for the realization of new meaning. For Ryle, our thought processes and the images of our imagination are in fact a "silent soliloquy," or a "talking to oneself." By his view, we become aware of our own thoughts in the same way that we convey them to others—by paraphrasing them. What is not at all clear is why paraphrasing thoughts we already understand should lead us to new thoughts. The implication is that the novelty already exists in the sentences one paraphrases; an assumption which (once again) ignores the idea that sentences are *about* meaning, and not the meaning itself.

I conclude this section with a critique of a position which complements Ryle's; i.e., it reduces meaning not to language, but to perception. That is, it fails to concede a role to language in the elaboration of meaning. Most importantly for the purposes of this essay, it explains away the act of reflection by attributing it entirely to perception and memory.

In *The Disappearance of Introspection* (1986), Lyons starts with the observation that our assumptions about introspection depend upon our having presumed a world "outside" our epidermis and a world "inside". Once you assume that we perceive "external" objects thanks to the "internal" images we form of those objects, you have to invent an operation for this internal sense, which is called introspection. What is radically wrong with this notion (for Lyons) is the idea that a "second-level" process of observation or scanning must be applied to a "first-order" process of perception. This is not to claim (as did Ryle) that we lack privileged access to these processes; rather, it is to assert that there is only one level to be aware of, and that our awareness of this level is no different from the kind of awareness we bring to any other kind of observation.

To support his position, Lyons appeals to the (by now) well-accepted fact that the procedures of the mind/brain that result in meaningful perception are not, and may not be, directly known by us. That is, whatever goes on under the label of introspection cannot be an internal perceiving, sensing, or scanning of internal cognitive and brain processes or events. Our awareness does not, states Lyons (quite correctly, I believe), have access to physiological events in the brain, any more than we have access to the information conveyed by the brain to the mind. All we have access to is the result of this process. Therefore, when we claim to be introspecting, what we have access to is "more like the formation of or reference to some already formed, stereotyped culture-tinged model or version or rationalization of what we believe to be our inner cognitive and appetitive processes in particular circumstances" (ibid., 152).

In other words, the raw data of perception is by no means "raw." If we have till now presumed that we could reflect upon the elements that contribute to our perception, it is because we have presumed an extrinsic reality that is fully formed, and that we must learn to reflect in the mind so as to duplicate it in our perception. The fact of the matter however (for Lyons), is that when we reflect, we are acting like scientists. That is, we are constructing models or theories of how this reality we have access to comes into being. We do not however perform like very good scientists, as we are mostly intent upon fitting our perception to culturally stereotyped explanations so as to make sense of the situations we find ourselves in. As described by Lyons:

> What we do [when we introspect] is fashion models of particular cognitive or appetitive episodes by abstracting them from perceived overt cognitive acts and "replay" them by means of perceptual memory and imagination. We do not introspect; we internally reconstruct—at least in outline or in edited or dramatized or surmised versions—overt intelligent performances. These will usually be in term of some language, code, or calculus but need not be. (152–53)

Lyons marshals a good deal of empirical evidence to support this position, and to challenge the view of reflection as a special ability of the mind. Defined as "the awareness and verbalization of one's own thought process" (Ginsburg and Opper 1979), reflection does not appear in the child until about the age of eight. According to one researcher, we learn to express our reactions "as we gradually attain a better knowledge of the behavior of things outside us" (Johnson 1982). The available evidence therefore suggests that children (when they reflect) are learning to use already existing abilities in a more sophisticated way, rather than a special faculty of the mind.

Lyons's main and most telling point, however, is that much of our ability to attend to our "sensory receivers" has been found to be severely limited. That is, the accounts and rationales provided by subjects when they reflect upon their perception (as reported for example, in Nisbett and Wilson [1977]), are notoriously inaccurate. This is not to say that we lack access to our feelings, or to what we see, taste, and smell. Rather, it is to deny that this access has anything to do with "sense data" or with the manner in which we synthesize what we perceive.

What, then, of the reflexive nature of our introspective reports; i.e., the sense we have that our awareness (in reflection) is turned on itself? For Lyons, perceiving and attending to one's perception are not distinct processes. One can perceive, and one can do so attentively, so that the awareness of what we are doing is a part of the perception itself. The point being that we have access (by this view) only to the results of how the mind brain put together a reality. The rest lies hidden in the brain. What we may do, however, is to replay these occurrences so as to attend to them more carefully, or interpretively, which (for Lyons) is what we call reflection.

In support of this last point, Lyons cites evidence to the effect that the visual imagery of imagination, dreaming, and perceptual memory are intimately connected to seeing, and must therefore be derived from perception. To introspect is therefore to replay our perceptions so as to attend to them more closely. The explanations we provide as a result of this closer attention, however, have little to do with its actual content. The models we construct pertain to events which never reach our experience. As such, they (the models) conform not to the way meaning is realized, but to the folk psychology of our particular culture; i.e., to the culture's assumptions as to how meaning is realized. These assumptions have to do with a culture's view of how we function, and range from the best ways we learn, to how we should account for human frailties, and so on.

But is it true that the awareness we have in introspection is no different from the awareness of perception? One obvious difference is that the content of introspection must be verbally mediated. Whereas we perceive without putting our perception into words, we do not normally introspect (as an act of reflection) without words. As Lyons fails to consider this point, one must conclude that for him, language has no influence upon the quality of our awareness; our words simply report states which are unaffected by the act of conceptualizing and reporting with words. Lyons therefore disregards the critical differences that exist between verbal and nonverbal meaning described in this text. Another feature of language ignored by Lyons is that it structures meaning in the form of a linear-sequential array. Were this not possible, we would be unable to compare different meanings so as to say what their similarities and differences are, or further clarify their meaning. Finally, because language predetermines the categories we bring to our experience, we are able to reflect upon their meaning by using language to hold these experiences in our awareness. Language brings to our experience the reflexive quality which makes it seem as if our thoughts are turning upon themselves; and it also structures our experience in a way that makes it seem internal so that when we use language to reflect, we appear to be "in" our thoughts. Given this involvement of language with the act of reflection, and the critical differences that exist between verbal and nonverbal meaning, reflection (it is maintained here) may not be equated with perception.

A further question raised by Lyons's thesis has to do with the folk psychology he claims we use so as to interpret our perceptions in terms of stereotyped models. How do these folk models of the mind arise? One possibility is that it is our perceptual understanding that is projected onto these systems as models. This would be a way of explaining how our reflections are but ways of casting what we know in the form of different meaning systems. But we would then have to account for how these systems arise in the first place. And we would need a sense of how they change. In this book, I offer a view of how language plays a critical role in the creation of new meaning, which includes reflection as an important part of this process.

What I hope to show in the section which follows is that the traditional view of reflection described above is correct in its assumptions about what is accomplished by reflection. Far from having disappeared, introspection remains our principal means for creative discovery. What the traditional view lacked (prior to Mead), and what authors such as Lyons still lose sight of to this day, is how language permits this process to take place. Stated in terms of the language as filing system metaphor, the act of reflection depends upon the fact that language (like a file) enables us to hold its contents. As noted by Mead, language makes it possible for us "to pick out responses and hold them" (1934, 97). How language does this is probably due to its independence as structure, and to its hierarchial organization, both of which enable us to use language as a kind of scaffolding. In the next section, I elaborate upon some of the characteristics of reflection, as seen from the perspective of language.

ASPECTS OF REFLECTION

Because a first, preverbal level determines meaning, language as a second, superimposed level may determine the conditions for communicating that meaning, while remaining independent of what is communicated (as in the analogy of the fishnet that can be used in any waters). Under normal conditions, the fish may not be abstracted out of its ecological niche. You would have trouble catching a fish and holding it with your bare hands. With a fishnet however, catching and holding a fish for inspection becomes commonplace. In a similar vein, language's ability to define things was ascribed above to the fact that, like a net, it operates in a way that is independent of the setting to which it is applied, and may therefore establish empty categories which define the general category of contents that are to fit into these slots; slots which may then be used to hold a particular content for reflection.

In nonverbal meaning, the content of a gesture depends upon an actual (physical) setting for its meaning. If I wish to communicate my anger, my gesture will be a part of the setting I am communicating, and will only have meaning within that setting. Furthermore, when I draw an analogy to communicate my anger, the analogy is a complete expression of what I feel. If I break a dish to convey my frustration, the broken dish *is* the anger I wish to convey.

With language, the medium I use is independent of, and therefore neutral with regard to the context I communicate. I may say "anger" without at all being in that state. Words (being neutral in this way) permit us to designate states we do not for the moment experience, or to even lie about a state, in a way that would not be possible nonverbally. Furthermore, with language I may select comparable parts out of context, so as to draw an analogy, in a way that is not possible nonverbally. That is, language permits us to designate parts of things, and to draw analogies between these things. The simile "my love is like a red red rose" for example, does not also imply that my love has a thorny stem, as it would if the two were compared nonverbally. In nonverbal meaning, a likeness may not be based upon a selection of shared properties, since the properties *are* the meaning in question. In making this analogy verbally, it is understood that the words *my love* and *rose,* however alike, denote separate entities. The fact that words enable us to do this also permits us to express meanings *about* meanings. When I say, "my love is *like* a rose," I am relating how the meaning *rose* can be about *my love;* and I am also saying that words are about themselves and about their relationship to other words.

Two important features follow from this reflective aspect of language. First, because language permits us to say what something is like in its various aspects, it allows us to reintroduce some of the particular features of "life as lived" that pass through the linguistic sieve of class inclusion (in a manner to be described shortly). Second, if language allows us to reintroduce aspects of nonverbal meaning, it is because it permits a form of understanding not possible preverbally. In nonverbal meaning, one lacks a means of examining a content outside of its setting, or even in its setting for any length of time. Returning to the net analogy, without some instrument with which to capture a fish, you could not seize a fish long enough to examine it in any detail. Having communicated your anger, you would not then pause to wonder what the anger was about, unless you had a language with which to reflect upon the state you were just in. Just as a net permits you to examine what you catch because it is held by the net, so too with language. That is, the structure of language holds the meanings it constrains, much as the harness holds the horse it is attached to. In this manner, language enables us to reflect upon or muse on the experienced content of that meaning, and to then describe what the experience is like. In terms of the file metaphor for language, in reflection we take the opportunity to open a particular file in order to examine its contents. If for example I ask myself, What was I angry about? I might then reflect upon a specific episode and summon the attending emotion.

Another approach to understanding how language performs this function is to contrast the holistic and relational nature of nonverbal meaning to the linear-sequential, abstracting nature of language. The advantage of language's sequential array is that the entities it delineates are then in a position to be contrasted and compared. Contrasting and comparing different meanings may therefore be undertaken purposefully, so as to discover new joinings and differences that had not been appreciated before. It is this act of being able to contrast and compare different meanings—an act made possible by the holding function of language, and its linear-sequential array—that is referred to in this essay as an act of reflection. Reflection by this view is not therefore an act of inner observation, which would require the infinite regress of a little person observing a little person, and so on. Rather, reflection corresponds to an ability permitted by the structure of language, whereby we may muse upon and thereby deepen (in the juxtaposition of disparate experiences), our grasp of a particular experience. If, for example, having tasted a pomegranate for the first time, I wish to define this as yet ineffable experience, I will probably come to the following: having identified the acidity of its bitter aspect, I will set this off against its sweetness, and come to articulate its bittersweet quality. In the process, I will have increased the possible meaning of these terms, and thereby deliteralized their meaning to some extent by expanding their significance. In this example, the juxtaposition of these two disparate responses (bitterness and sweetness) is not something made possible by reflection: it *is* reflection.

The act of reflection is therefore seen in this text as a creative act in which one gradually undoes the reifications of language so as to slowly integrate those parts of nonverbal meaning that are sacrificed to language, or (as in the novelty of the pomegranate), are newly discovered. The ability to reflect is therefore seen as a core feature of what it means to be a human being. Without reflection, we would lack a means of further integrating the nonverbal with the verbal; i.e. of bringing the innate understanding of our biological self to the task of broadening the literal constraints of our language system.

The role of reflection may also be understood in terms of the two principal modes of the self introduced by language: the *reified self*, and the *reflective self* (corresponding to what was referred to earlier as the literal and the metaphorical use of language). The reified self is the objectified self; i.e., the self taken literally, that can be pointed to and treated as a distinct independent identity. That is, while the self as identity is not a thing of substance, in the sense that a rock has substance, the literal use of language allows us to treat the self as a thing. In this mode, the reified self can be held responsible for what the self does, in that both status and blame can be ascribed as belonging to it. The initial reification of the self is therefore an essential stage of becoming socialized; i.e., it is basic to our belonging and to our wanting to belong, insofar as these states initially literalize the relationship, as when one's prestige is tied to the country club one belongs to. In reification, the content of communication is closed; it assumes a literal, determinate quality. Words in this mode are objectified as referring to literal things; they stand for something irrevocably, and may not be appreciated as being about meaning. In terms of clinical examples, it is in this mode that children may take on parental attitudes literally, as when "You're bad!" becomes an identity that may not be challenged.

The reflective self is the self taken as metaphor. In reflection, the content of communication is open in that it is understood that words may also operate reflectively. That is, in reflection, the content of a word is not immutably fixed, but may expand in relation to other meanings when mused upon reflectively. The reflective self is therefore in a position to challenge the literal assumptions of the reified self. As described above, the child's initial use of words is quite literal. A means must therefore exist for *de*-literalizing or *de*-reifying words if psychological growth is to occur; i.e. if the verbal is to be integrated with the nonverbal. Hence the assumption proposed by this essay that the literal meanings imposed by language must (in health) be continuously challenged so as to yield to an ongoing enrichment of our reflective awareness. In other words, the objectification of the self which is essential to becoming a socially responsible being cannot be an end in itself. It must be worked through reflectively toward a position of personal integrity, if the individual is to become a responsible human being.

Having presented the data upon which the thesis of this book rests, I will now pause in this presentation to consider what has been accomplished. In these last three chapters I have presented a view of language functioning that attempts to account for issues raised by Quine and Putnam; to explain why children literalize meaning with words; to offer a view of what reflection is, without appealing to a little observer in the brain; and to try to account for the objectification of meaning with words (and explain what objectification means). Three further points round out the argument. The Piagetian and psychoanalytic explanations as to why children distort meaning are of questionable value. The criticisms that have been recently leveled against the traditional notion of reflection are far from conclusive. And recent attempts to explain the nature of objective reality falter in their failure to account for the role of language. Finally, any attempt to explain language must take account (as does this text) not only of the pragmatics of natural language understanding; but of what must rank as one of the most momentous discoveries of our era: the amodal nature of the infants perception described in the Appendix.

My argument starts with the assumption that, given the innate nature of preverbal thought, the preverbal and the verbal must be continuous; i.e., the verbal must capture the preverbal so as to have meaning itself. If you don't make this assumption, then you have to explain how language generates meaning on its own, which no one (to my knowledge) has seriously attempted to do, recently. The language as file metaphor used to describe how this would work, rests upon several areas of evidence: that the preverbal content of the file already has meaning; that the categories of language generalize meaning; that words evolve in what they refer to, while remaining constant in what they mean; that children literalize meaning with words; and that following Grice's cooperative principle, meanings are ascribed to words because they are *supposed* to have meaning.

Other observations such as the independence of language as a system, the role of felt meaning in recovering a lost word, the digital relationship of the verbal to the nonverbal, and the fact that Arieti, Von Doramus, and Piaget were wrong about the thought disorder of preverbal infants; all are independent of the thesis of this book concerning the relationship of the mind to language (adopted from Mead), and are therefore taken as valid evidence. Finally, the view of reflection as arising out of the juxtaposition of disparate meanings is an idea that is familiar to the readers of poetry (Culler 1975) but has yet to receive the attention it deserves from those interested in language. Not only is this idea one of our only ways of accounting for creative discovery (that does not reify reality); it solves the homunculus problem of how you could have an inner perception, without assuming a little observer in the brain.

A more detailed view of how we distort and create meaning will be addressed in the next two chapters. What I have described so far is a theory of how we represent reality. The Freudian metaphor may be said to have failed in this attempt, because it missed the principal ingredient of any representational system that is superimposed upon our innate meaning system; i.e., that (as per Mead) these systems are reflexive, which is taken here to mean that as communications systems, they are about themselves and the beliefs that support their function. That is, a language as representation system is not about what it (as system) represents. It is about its ability to communicate meaning. Hence (in this text) the notion that a language as filing system is about *how* to communicate, and only implicitly about *what* to communicate.

A further implication of this point is that the term *representation* as used in this text is something of a misnomer. That is, it refers, not to the duplication of an "outside reality" the way you would with a camera; rather, it refers to how a meaning is realized, within a particular representational system. It follows from this view that the self (a fairly recent notion among mainstream psychoanalysts) is best understood as a representational system. This I believe was Mead's point in presenting the self as a dialectic between a nonverbal *I* and a verbal *me*. The implications of this last point are developed in chapter 8.

The reader might still ask how this view of language makes a theory of meaning more capable of being challenged. If the way language structures nonverbal meaning (and distorts it, and establishes a basis for the self) is a function of how language works, then the ways in which language literalizes meaning in childhood, or allows for the deliteralization of meaning (as in a psychoanalysis) are eminently observable. These observations in turn would allow one to challenge or expand upon the thesis of this text, as will be described in chapter 7.

Finally, lest the description of the self as representational system sound too far removed from what is most genuine about our human condition, I would point out that the presumed purpose of this system is to continuously reconcile and creatively resolve the ongoing conflict between the biological self and the social self-conscious self described in chapter 2. Given these assumptions, the way in which the self creates and distorts its reality could not pertain to biological energy or instinctual aims per se. It would have to pertain to how we represent our reality with language. That is, the distortion and creation of meaning would have to be understood in terms of how meaning is realized within the representational system that is taken here to be the self. It is to these questions that we will now turn.

6.
HOW LANGUAGE PROMOTES THE DISTORTION OF MEANING

Insofar as this chapter has to do with distortion, I will start by outlining the main thesis of this book (which pertains to how meaning gets distorted), as it grows out of the descriptions in the last chapter on language. Following Mead, not only is language necessary if we are to share in another's perspective; we need language in order to consider and reflectively care about the needs of others, to become reflectively aware of who we are, and to share in the communal responsibilities that go beyond instinctual levels of conduct. Without language, we would be severely limited in our ability to transcend the particular contexts of our experience; i.e., we would be trapped in our private worlds. Mead saw language not merely as an instrument with which to communicate, but as a functional feature of the self; i.e., as an essential feature of what it means to be a person.

Mead was also an incurable optimist. He believed for example, that the salvation of our nation lay in the hands of the American engineer. Perhaps for this reason (i.e., his optimism), he failed to attend to the darker side of language. While language enables us to forge a social world, it is also responsible for much of what ails mankind. There could not (by the view proposed here) be any functional (nonorganic) pathology of the mind without language. Our phobias, anxieties, manic and depressive states; our neuroses and psychoses, are all to some degree related to the symbolic function introduced by language.

What Mead did emphasize (and we owe this understanding primarily to him), is the fact that language is necessary for the development of an objective sense of self. For Mead, only with language do we come to conceive of ourselves and of others as separate, independent beings, and to reflect upon our experience as a conscious self. Language is therefore critical to the development of qualities which distinguish the human being from other mammals; i.e., the ability to share in another's perspective; to understand consciously and care for who that other person happens to be; to consider and reflect upon the needs of others. This is emphatically *not* to say that infants need language to make sense of their world! Today, it is quite clear that infants are exquisitely attuned to their reality from the start. Based upon the studies referred to in the Appendix, infants have an inherent capacity to detect similarities and differences; to latch on to what is invariant beneath the flux of change; to intuit the relationship of a part to its whole without confusing the one with the other.

With the assimilation of language, the innately given power of the mind described above persists at the nonverbal level of experience, but undergoes a critical transformation in being taken over by the structure of language. On the one hand, the structure of language must capture this ability in order to become meaningful itself. Yet the communication constraints of a language system are for the most part learned by the child as a system of conventions and codes that are (initially at least) extrinsic to the self. In verbal meaning therefore, the child's ability to relate the elements of his or her world shifts from being an inherent property of the mind, to something which must conform to the extrinsic rules of language.

A useful analogy to imagine this process is to picture what it must be like to suddenly have to wear a harness. The purpose of this harness however (in contradistinction to the analogy being drawn) is not to yoke you to a carriage or plow; rather, it is to constrain your awareness so as to be able to communicate with others. That is, what was an intrinsic function becomes something that is (until language has been assimilated) imposed from the outside. The child is in the position of the person who, though he or she knows the lay of the land by heart, must nonetheless learn to read a map so as to convey that understanding to others.

With this change comes a further critical transformation. The linear-sequential mode of language places a new kind of constraint upon the child's preverbal mode of understanding. With language, the part-whole relationship of preverbal thought gives way to a wholly different way of relating the part to the whole. Whereas in the nonverbal mode of drawing I might (for example) intuit the structural relatedness of a branch to its tree, in the verbal mode branches belong to trees because they belong to a class of objects that is subordinate to the class *tree*. Preverbal meaning organizes our reality in terms of natural categories (e.g., *dogs, trees*) which precede the development (with language) of superordinate and subordinate classes *(animals-doberman, furniture-side table)*.

This shift does not occur smoothly for the child, but in fact generates a particular kind of error that may have far-reaching consequences. In order to start classifying objects in terms of where they belong in the vast hierarchy of class inclusions, the child must build an internal scaffolding, so to speak, within which to classify these objects and their parts, and this takes some time. The child in other words must shift from a *functional* mode of classifying events (how things work in a particular context), to an objectified mode of classifying events (according to the definitions established by language). What happens then is that the child continues to use his or her nonverbal means of identifying objects and events, but reports those events in a literal way. The term *literal* is taken in this text to refer to a kind of confusion that is only possible with language. In its broadest sense, *literal* will refer to those verbal definitions and categories which a particular culture takes for granted. More specifically, *literal* will also refer to when the word is taken to be the thing or quality it refers to, as when the child treats a name as if it were the thing named.

In treating a name as if it were the thing named, the child is by this view substituting a verbal symbol for the setting it stands for, in a fixed way. The word *milk* for example, will stand for the feeding context in the sense that (for the child) it *is* that context. That is, the assumptions the child brings (as amodal understanding) to the word *milk,* and to the context it refers to, are the same. The word *milk* may not yet be appreciated as an empty slot that will eventually be filled by a variety of semantic markers, i.e., milk as nutrition, as commodity, as symbol of dependence, and so on. The digital representation of words starts as standing for assumptions which are then imposed upon particular contexts, as when the word *milk* summons an expectation of feeding. For this reason, words are interpreted literally, as being what they refer to. Fortunately, the child does not (by this view) operate on the basis of these literal expectations alone. In terms of the analogy drawn earlier, it is as if the child continues to go by his or her inherent knowledge of the lay of the land, while only pretending to use a map. That is, the child continues to use his or her inherent understanding to make sense of events, but reports these events in ways which treat the word as if it were the thing referred to. What this says in essence, is that in transferring the inherent meaning engendering capacity of the preverbal mind to the definitions imposed by language, the child must digitalize meaning. Following Dretske's description of this process, the word selects one component of an information context as a marker that is then featured to the exclusion of all else. During this transition, the child takes a while to discover the most general feature of a meaning (as used by the linguistic community), which (as per Dretske) must eventually be adopted as the semantic content. Thus, when the child endows a word with the lived specificity of nonverbal meaning (as in the child who says, "I'm barefoot all over!"), the process of building a common world of objective meanings has begun. In being yoked to the structure of language, the meaning that is inherent in the child's relationship to its environment infuses that structure with meaning, at the cost of initially literalizing the child's reality. Not only is the word itself taken to be the thing it represents (rather than a feature of its meaning), but attributes like color or size are equated with the things they characterize, as when a pebble which has sunk to the bottom of a tank of water is said to have done so because of its color. Similarly, relationships are seen between events when none exist, as in the fact that till age four or five, children tend to report not only that the moon follows them, but that it is their own movement which forces the movements of the moon.

Fortunately, the nonverbal mode of establishing meaning does not disappear with the incursion of language, else we would all be in a terrible fix! Nonverbal meaning continues to ground the child in a meaningful (nonliteralized) world. Language therefore introduces a split at the very core of our being, where a functionally related self maintains an unconscious sense of relatedness to an inherently meaningful world, while a verbal self becomes the spokesperson for what may be reflectively known and communicated.

This last point has been nicely illustrated by an ingenious experiment conducted by Bower (1978). Bower set out to question Piaget's assumption that children only achieve a sense of the conservation of weight (i.e., the knowledge that changing the shape of a piece of clay does not effect its weight), when they are able to express this understanding in words. Up to a certain age, when a child is shown a lump of clay that is first rolled into a long string and then into a fat ball (in the child's presence), the child will claim that the ball version (of the same amount of clay) is heavier. Should this mistake be attributed to a lack of understanding? Or might it be due to the fact that the literalizing effect of language makes it difficult for the child to express an understanding he or she already has?

Using a high-speed camera, Bower showed that in being handed first the thin version of clay, then the ball, the child's hand did not rise up upon receiving the ball. If the child were genuinely expecting the ball to be heavier, the muscles of his or her arm would tense up to compensate for the difference. Bower concluded that there is a lag between the nonverbal conservation of weight and the child's ability to express this knowledge verbally. In the terms of this essay, the child's verbal grasp of the relationship of length and width to volume is at first literalized; i.e., the contrasting dimensions are seen as disjunctive rather than as related. Long thin objects cannot initially be described as sharing a common context with round fat objects, as these qualities stand in a fixed relationship to the words that describe them. Borrowing Piaget's term, the words and their reference must be "decentered" (i.e., deliteralized) so that they might be appreciated as depending (for their meaning) upon each other. That is, the assumptions one makes in using words must shift from the actual contexts which initially lend them their meaning, to the words themselves as being about meaning. The context we assume in using words (the assumption we make as to their reference) must not only become selective (as per Dretske) so as to mark a specific semantic content; they must also acquire the flexibility of empty slots; of categories that apply to a variety of contexts, depending upon the assumptions being shared by the communicants. Only in this way will words come to modify their meaning in relation to each other (to decenter their literalness), so as to recapture the contextual relations that were sacrificed to the digitalization of language.

Given this grasp of how language works, it becomes possible to understand both the distortion and the creation of meaning in terms of the kinds of assumptions we bring to the use of language. By this view, the use of language (in health) must undergo a continuous process of dereification. That is, the words we use must gradually be freed of the specific contexts they initially refer to, so as to partake of the definitions imposed by the structure of language as a system of communication. Freed in this manner, words may participate in the free play of differences that is the source of creative discovery, as will be described in the next chapter. In this chapter, I will describe a number of ways in which the dereification of language may be blocked. When first adopted by the child, words are taken literally. When blocked in their literalness, words carry distorted meanings, insofar as literal meanings are usually discordant with the setting in which they are used. That is, because literal meanings adhere rigidly to a particular context, they fail to account for the full implications of the settings they are applied to. Finally, once we have adopted a language, a further problem emerges. Because language enables us to adopt categories of meaning (semantic contents) which need not correspond to personally experienced settings, we become capable of assuming beliefs about ourselves that have little basis in fact. It is to these aspects of our symbolic lives that we shall now turn.

THE NEGLECT OF LANGUAGE IN THE PSYCHOANALYTIC THEORY OF DISTORTION

Given the time, difficulty and expense of a psychoanalysis, few people undertake this process out of sheer curiosity. Usually, it is undertaken (short of being a training candidate) because of a presenting symptom that is discomforting enough to warrant entering into this demanding procedure. Symptoms in turn may range from phobic-like fears which interfere with normal functioning—the fear of heights, of enclosures, or of sexuality, for example—to the "personality disorders," so called because they appear to pertain to some core personality issue, as when an individual is unable to give order or direction to his or her life, or to engage in the long-term intimacy of a responsible involvement, or is chronically subject to the painful reproaches of irrational self-doubt.

Psychoanalysis and psychoanalytically oriented psychotherapy have not been at a loss to suggest explanations for these kinds of disorders. Indeed, for these therapeutic modes, an understanding of the genesis of the problem is considered to be one of the important ingredients of a cure. If you know why you are having a particular problem, by this view you are on your way to solving it. Thus, for example, a symptom might be understood in terms of a specific, traumatic event, as when a pigeon phobia is related to the trauma of having witnessed a primal scene (the psychoanalytic term for catching your parents in the sex act); an understanding which (it is claimed) must be grasped if the symptom is to disappear. Or a symptom might be understood in terms of the nature of one's upbringing, as when the inability to give order or direction to one's life is related to an absence of the kind of structure and care that are deemed necessary to instill meaningful constraints and self-discipline in a child. Or the individual's self-doubts and depressive episodes are related to a failure of the preoedipal mirroring phase, in which the loving attention of a caretaker is said to give birth to a sense of self; or to the ambivalence born of not having resolved the oedipal phase of development.

I will not at this point inquire further into these possible explanations, however, useful and efficacious they may be as therapeutic metaphors, as I will, in what follows, be addressing a different level of understanding. That is, I will be questioning whether we might consider not merely the conditions under which development goes astray, but the actual process of distortion in a way that could account for the "what" of what gets distorted, and the "how" of how this occurs intrapsychically. To explain how these pathological developments arise, one would need not only a sense of what occurs under optimal conditions, or of what conditions must exist for a development to become pathological, one must also have a sense of the process whereby a mind is shaped, in a way which will permit one to specify which parts of the process are affected, and under what conditions.

For example, if a certain kind of caring support is deemed essential for the development of discipline and self control in a child, how is one to appreciate the effects of such a milieu upon the formation of the individual's psyche or personality? To offer such an explanation, one must have some means of imagining and describing how the mind takes shape. Among our developmental theories (described in chapter 1) various attempts have been made to account for how the child comes to think, and to distort meaning. We have, however, only one clinical theory (i.e., geared to the practice of psychotherapy) which addresses the development of the self at this process level; namely, mainstream psychoanalysis. The term *mainstream* is used to distinguish psychoanalysts who subscribe to the traditional energy/drive model of the mind described in chapter 1, from the interpersonalists, humanists, and existentialists who shun this model, but also refer to themselves as psychoanalysts; or the Jungians who simply refer to themselves as analysts.

Other clinical theories offer a kind of catalogue of the competencies and possible failures one must attribute to the self to account for its development. For example, Sullivan's (1953) interpersonal theory of the self attributes dynamisms and security operations to a self that comes to embody the individual's significant relations with others. Philosphically,

Sullivan's theory is aligned with the pragmatism of Peirce and Mead, and is therefore in keeping with the premises that constitute the philosophical ground of this book. Unfortunately, Sullivan did not attempt to convey a sense of the intrapsychic process of building a mind, in the sense of describing how these structures are thought to arise, *qua* structures. Hence (I believe) the enormous influence mainstream psychoanalytic theory has had upon the professions which train psychotherapists (the psychiatrist, the psychologist, the social worker, the counselor for example) —those clinicians who require some sense of the genesis of emotional security in the child, and of how this security may be interfered with, in order to do their work.

In presenting Rapaport's systematization of the psychoanalytic metaphor in chapter 1, I described how the structure of the psyche arises in psychoanalytic theory. Psychic structure (by this view) is largely a function of the countercathecting energies which constrain the building up of tension in the organism. Given this assumption, it becomes possible to envision two broad areas of possible dysfunction. Assuming (as have the Object Relations analysts), that an infant's parents must provide what Winnicott (1965) has described as a "facilitating environment," then the parental environment may also interfere with this inherent unfolding. This would occur for example, when parents fail to provide support or provide the wrong kind of support. The infant's mind may then develop in a variety of dysfunctional ways, depending upon how this kind of deprivation/frustration affects the overall development of the individual's ego. This relatively simple metaphor of the mind (though subjected to a plethora of elaborations!) has provided a useful framework within which to organize and understand the course of a psychoanalysis or a psychotherapy for most of this century. Today, however, the Freudian metaphor reveals the shortcomings that of necessity come to light in any mature metaphor, when it has been diligently believed in by its adherents over a sufficiently long period. In what follows, having given due credit to the fact that mainstream psychoanalysis is virtually alone in having systematically developed its metaphor at this level of understanding, I will focus upon a shortcoming which sheds light upon what must be addressed in a theory of distorted meaning.

In pursuing the limits of *any* metaphor, one must find that the data to be accounted for cannot completely conform to the assumptions of the metaphor. From the perspective of this essay, the Freudian metaphor fails to account for the role of language in the distortion of meaning. For example, chronic self-doubt is a distortion in the sense that the self's viability is constantly being scrutinized when there is little or no reason to do so. This state may, from a Freudian perspective, be interpreted in terms of a fear that unacceptable impulses are perpetually on the verge of breaking through. And yet the very existence of self-doubt requires an act of reflection, and that act is made possible only by language. Surely then, the structure of language must play some part in how self-doubt arises. Yet the biological metaphor of psychoanalysis says nothing about this role. Indeed, the critical notion of *defenses* (as elaborated from within the psychoanalytic metaphor to account for the ways in which we fend off unacceptable impulses) refers to a phenomenon which requires a language in order to exist. One could not, for example, repress the reality of an event, were it not for the fact that to be subject to conscious reflection, it must be named. Only if you can name an event, might you (in repression) *fail* to name it. Only with language (it is claimed here) might we distort the inherent authenticity of the way in which we create our reality—a point which would also be true of the other defenses of psychoanalytic theory, such as denial, dissociation, reaction formation, and the like. This point has been taken up by at least one psychoanalytic author (Basch 1983) who describes how language is necessary for the disowning, disavowing, and repression of meaning. Basch has not, however, speculated as to how language enters into or permits these defenses.

There is a further dimension to this issue. In adopting the psychoanalytic metaphor, one assumes a view of the human mind as a homeostatic mechanism. The question then becomes, how well does this metaphor account for what it means to be a human being? Many have argued that it does not. Murray (1962) for example argues that the psychoanalytic metaphor is not only a reduction *psychologem,* but a reduction ad absurdem. Chein (1962), anticipating the ego psychologists, points out that this view of human beings as helpless, powerless reagents neglects the equally probable view of human beings as active, responsible agents. Indeed, it is this view of people as conscious moral agents that led to the existential psychotherapist's perspective (e.g., for Boss, Binswanger, Minkowski, May, and Frankl). The objections raised by Murray, Chein, and the existentialists are (I believe) reducible to the absence, in mainstream theory, of the symbolic dimension of our lives. Thus for example, authors such as Rieff (1966) argue that psychoanalysis has contributed to the symbolic impoverishment of our culture by ignoring the concepts of communal commitment. For Becker (1975), the same may be said in response to the failure of psychoanalysis to come to grips with the objective reality of the immense evil human beings are capable of; an evil which (as will be elaborated in chapter 8) may be appreciated (along with the lie), as one of the more unfortunate "gifts" of language.

However true these objections, they may also be said to ignore a critical point. The creative elaboration of a metaphor is not first and foremost a process of rational choice. Rather, one may assume that the more radical the innovation embodied by the metaphor, the more literal will be its initial presentation. Given the metaphor of man (as conscious and rational) that prevailed at the time of Freud's writing, the phenomenon of repression was radical in the extreme. Hence, Freud's literal interpretation in terms of a force pushing meaning out of awareness. It is to the limitations of this metaphor that the existentialists and others have objected, but they have not proposed a model of the mind to take its place.

Finally, there is an aspect of this shortcoming that has not required the ripening of the Freudian metaphor to come to light, as it has been apparent from the start, insofar as it was Freud himself who drew it to our attention. Freud's (1895) dream was that psychoanalysis would eventually become a branch of neurology. He was firmly convinced (as are many to this day) that the chemical composition of the brain could someday be made to account for the psychopatholgy he studied in his consulting room. Hence his attempt to elaborate a metaphor of the mind which mirrored in many respects the principles attributed to physical phenomenon in his day. The limitation pointed to by this vision is that while today we have much to say about how the brain functions, there is little likelihood that the correspondence between brain chemistry and distortion could yield answers without considering the role of language in the realization of meaning.

One might today wonder how this obvious fact could have escaped the attention of so brilliant a man. To do so, however, would be to ignore the time it has taken us collectively to appreciate this "obvious" fact. Indeed, only recently has Western philosophical thought taken the "linguistic turn" (Rorty 1967) toward an appreciation of the role language plays in defining our reality. The gestalt psychologist Wolfgang Kohler once surmised that if a fish were to become a scientist, this scientist fish's last discovery would be water, given its ubiquitous and therefore all-too-familiar presence. In psychoanalytic theory, the same might be said of language, which has till now been taken as a manifestation of the self's functioning, rather than as an actual feature of that functioning.

Language (when understood as being more than just a medium for the expression of ideas), constitutes a structure of the mind just as surely as our skeletal system constitutes a structure of the body, yet it is also something we have access to via the verbal report. As a feature of the process whereby we realize meaning, language takes up residence within the human psyche as an indissoluble aspect of the self. The ways in which children use language should therefore cue us into the contribution of language to the structure of the mind. The next section will consider ways in which this might be done.

CAPTURING

We have not (in the history of our thought) evolved many ways of accounting for error. Among the more influential accounts within the realm of psychotherapy, the psychoanalytic theory of *parapraxis* states that error arises in the form of omissions or of substitutions. By this view, a specific action or thought is disrupted by the anxiety that occurs when a repressed (because unacceptable) wish is in danger of becoming conscious. This view bears an affinity with the Hegelian view of error as due to incompleteness and onesidedness. By both accounts, error results from a disruption of the process whereby meaning is normally realized. In this chapter, I have adopted this position, with the *proviso* that the role of language must be considered in this process; and that one needs a sense of how meaning is realized so as to understand how it may be deflected from that realization.

If we have few accounts of how we come to be in error, we have even fewer ways of explaining how language participates in the distortion of meaning. The position taken in this book is adopted from Bateson and Jackson (1964). These authors were the first (to my knowledge) to have offered an explanation of pathological thought based upon the view that nonverbal meaning may be confused with verbal meaning. For Bateson and Jackson, given the transformation of meaning that occurs with language (as was described in chapter 2 of this text), problems arise when the nonverbal meaning that was translated into a verbal meaning is then retranslated into a nonverbal meaning. For example, a person diagnosed as hysterical may take the headache as a conventional excuse for avoiding a task, and turn it into a literal headache. The hysteric, in this instance, has transformed the verbal expression (that is *about* having a headache) into a literal expression which, these authors believe, is a regression to the preverbal analog system of meaning.

The explanation offered by Bateson and Jackson hinges upon the difference between the analogic nature of preverbal meaning, and the digital nature of verbal meaning. In an analog system, similarities are based upon the fact that they share a similar structure, as in the map that preserves the relational features of the terrain it represents. In a digital system, however, one content may stand for another, without one's having to assume that these contents are the same. This permits a word to be *about* a meaning, without being confused with the meaning it is about. In a digital system, the headache can remain a possibility that refers to the realm of excuses, as well as pain. In an analog system, the headache *is* pain, and cannot be about a meaning that is other than what it is.

From the perspective of what has been presented in this book, the Bateson-Jackson theory of distortion requires that a regression to preverbal thought must occur within the context of thought already structured by language. That is, distortion occurs not as a result of regressing to a preverbal mode, but of collapsing the metaphorical mode that emerges with language into a literal meaning that operates like a preverbal meaning. For example, persons suffering from a hysterical conversion symptom will experience pain according to where they verbally *think* it should be, rather than in relation to the locations that conform to the body's organic structure. The verbal meaning literally *becomes* the message (as in analogical thought) since it is the word that determines the location of pain, rather than the pain itself.

One might still ask how the metaphorical function of language contributes to the realization of meaning. Only when one has some means of describing this process might one discuss how the process is interfered with. Fortunately, the view of distortion I am presenting is similar to one that has been described by a number of authors, including the philosopher Ortega y Gasset (1956), the philosopher economist Karl Marx (1932), and the existential psychoanalyst Erich Fromm (1947). While these authors do not implicate the role of language, they provide valuable insights into how meaning is realized. For example, Ortega y Gasset has described the act of reflection as a "radical shift" in which man may "turn, so to speak, his back on the world and take his stand inside himself, attend to his own inwardness or, what is the same thing, concern himself with himself and not with that which is *other*, with things" (1956, 27). The obverse of this process is therefore one in which we turn from this inwardness to that which is other. The otherness of things described by Ortega y Gasset may be understood as the world of the literal that emerges with language, as when a word is taken to *be* what it refers to, rather than an aspect of its meaning.

For Ortega y Gasset, objectifying the world as otherness may also refer to our tendency to treat our fellow man as an object. It is in this sense that Marx and Fromm as well, have described the reifying effects of ideology as a dynamic for alienation. When, for example, we are enjoined (in the name of some ideological belief) to act for the "common good," or for the "glory of the state," the potential meaning of our act may be reduced to being a token of that belief. To act in the name of what one takes to be the common good may be understood in several ways. It may be seen as an act of altruistic sacrifice. But it may also be seen as a way of reducing one's act to the dictates of an ideology; and of treating the person's act, not as an opportunity to realize meaning, but as a token of the ideology.

For Marx, Ortega y Gasset, and Fromm, we (as individuals) discover ourselves in the intentional assertions of our acts. All three authors have related this assumption to the role of ideological belief. When a political system is geared solely to economic expansion, for example, then the individual is no longer treated as having a position of his or her own. From the perspective of this essay, this form of reification cannot be the result of an ideology alone, since it depends upon the literal-metaphorical dimension of meaning introduced by language. If we are to discover ourselves in the intentional assertions of our acts, it will not be because a political ideology grants us permission to do so. Rather, it will be because we have learned that a communication asserts the self's intention when it is *about* meaning. Granted, any loss of this intentionality results in what Marx and later Fromm, describe as *alienation*. This occurs, for example, when an act is reified as a token of an ideology, as when one claims that the ideological end justifies the means. Having assumed such a position, one may no longer suffer the full consequences of one's act as an intentional realization—which is to say, as a purposeful and responsible realization. One's purpose in this instance is preempted by an ideology; and the meaning of one's act is grounded in an ideological presumption, rather than in the responsible pursuit of meaning.

Alienation may therefore be understood as a function of the way language works; i.e., our capacity for symbolic realization may be captured by a belief system or ideology, which is not grounded in individual experience. That language may operate in this fashion was described earlier in terms of Stern's notion of the "linguistic sieve," whereby the general level of the prototypic episode organized by language makes it difficult for children to refer their meaning to a specific experience. What is added here is the idea that this prototypic generality of language may continue to alienate us from our experience, while nonetheless providing us with a (misguided) sense of having something to say.

Stated in the terms of this book, when individuals adopt a belief that is not grounded in personal experience, this form of distortion (to be referred to as "ideological capture") is a function of language's ability to convey meanings and beliefs that are adopted in spite of not having been personally experienced. Ideological capture may therefore be seen as one of the means whereby we are deflected from the self-realizing potential of our acts. Our intent (in ideological capture) is waylaid by a borrowed notion of what we should be about, which effectively bypasses the possibilities of a reflective exploration. Ideological capturing occurs because (with language) the meaning context of a setting need not be grounded in first-hand experience. Thus, for example, an act may be in the name of some ideology or belief that is not responsive to one's individual sense of purpose and responsibility, as in careers which are built solely upon parental expectation. Or one may substitute what is assumed for what is known from experience, as in the pretensions of caste and class. Or one may act upon what one presumes is so, based upon what is said, rather than upon what one knows is so, based upon what is done.

In short, ideological capture depends upon the fact that what we say or believe about ourselves does not always correspond with what we in fact do. For example, a person may believe that he or she is capable of organized, directed activity, and yet depend upon the pressure of a last-minute deadline to accomplish important tasks. Because these functional deficits correspond to a lack of experienced meaning in relation to some verbal belief about the self (as when avoidance precludes an awareness of what is being avoided), they are self-perpetuating. The process is similar to the forms of capturing parents may inflict upon their children. The reproach "you're bad!" when inflicted in a setting in which this appellation is meaningless to the child (which is to say all settings), effects a form of ideological capture by imposing a meaning that cannot be related to the child's actual experience. In the terms of this essay, when verbal meaning induces an experience that has not arisen as a consequence of a purposeful and responsible act, the induced experience operates as an ideological capture. That is, it creates and perpetuates primitive meaning contexts by isolating those contexts from the possible challenge of a freely experienced setting.

A further example. The stricture "don't put your fingers there!" will be adopted by the child, not because it makes sense not to pick one's nose (what could be more natural?), but out of intimidation. Once adopted as a part of those rules which assure acceptance (though hopefully pursued in private), it will (in polite company at least) become a relatively stable prohibition. Eventually, the prohibition will be accepted as a choice one makes. If, however, the stricture has become reified as a part of a primitive belief system of the order of "these are the rules you must follow if you want Mommy to love you"; and this belief system has yet to meet the light of conscious reflection where it might be challenged, then the stricture itself will operate unconsciously, and will therefore be immune to challenge.

What I have described as ideological capture covers much the same ground as the psychoanalytic notion of a super ego. In mainstream psychoanalysis, the superego arises from the resolution of the oedipal conflict. In essence, it entails the individual's willingness to impose upon the self the strictures that are initially imposed by one's parent. The potential harshness of the superego however, is attributed to the need to literally squash any thought of murdering father (or mother) so as to sleep with mother (or father). In this manner, it comes to stand for the unconditional NO! The persistence in later life of superego injunctions is in turn attributed to the fact that they, like the impulses they are instituted to repress, must remain unconscious.

In this text, the harshness of superego strictures is due to their literal nature (given the age at which they are adopted); and to their lack of evolution or conscious awareness, since they are divorced from any experienced sense of being related to the self. In other words, the superego described by the mainstream is (by this view) none other than the manifestation of how, with language, we may establish categories of meaning that are lacking in personally experienced content, and therefore in awareness. Since the content is not there to be challenged, the categories may go on indefinitely imposing their strictures on our lives, until we find a way of making them explicit.

But what of the id impulses, which (for the mainstream analysts) constitute such a problem in our lives? An important feature of mainstream drive theory, is that these impulses carry an affective charge. That is, the infantile impulse to devour the breast, for example, or to incorporate the penis are accompanied (normally) by anxiety. In this text, I will assume as well that anxiety plays a significant role in distorted meaning. But I will attribute this role, not to the contents of libidinal and aggressive impulses per se, but to the disruptive effects of anxiety upon the realization of meaning. That is, the anxiety that arises to disrupt the symbolic realization of meaning is not a function of the content of warded off impulses per se, but of the literalization of their meaning.

When, as a child, I start to fear boogeymen under the bed—having adopted this fear, say, from a sibling or peer—I may not challenge this fear until I have come to accept the boogeyman as a figment of my imagination. Until I have achieved this reflective ability, I will be unable to challenge this fear on my own, and will therefore depend upon the reassurance of a comforting parent, as the fear itself disrupts and replaces the normal context (i.e., precludes the ability to check this fear by peering under the bed). That is, I have no means of relating to the context that is lost, and would have to be available to challenge the erroneous meaning. With the reflective awareness that arises out of a maturing language function, I assume the ability to challenge these primitive beliefs and their attending fears as figments of my imagination.

The situation becomes far more difficult, however, when the affect in question causes a collapse of the very function that permits reflected awareness. This is a phenomenon I will refer to as an *affective* capture. That is, when an intensely felt emotion subverts or captures the meaning context in which it occurs, and thereby aborts the reflective phase of symbolic realization, we are (as in ideological capture) deprived of the full consequences of our act. Burnham (1970) describes an example of this process in a hospitalized patient diagnosed as schizophrenic, which he refers to as a "word capturing." The situation he describes occurred on the hospital ward at Christmas time, when this patient responded to the mention of Santa Claus with the comment, "Sainted claws, hands that have never masturbated" (201). In this example, the conventional significance of Santa Claus is aborted in favor of a highly personalized preoccupation; i.e., the patient's emotional conflict over masturbation and purity which (one may assume) gives significance to the literal translation of *Claus* into *claws*.

The notion that the meaning contexts of our acts may be captured by our emotional preoccupations is hardly new. It was documented early on in Freud's (1951) seminal *Pyschopathology of Everyday Life*. In keeping with Freud's insight into the affective underpinnings of distorted thought (though not with his metapsychological explanation of that thought), the affective capture of turning Santa Claus into "sainted claws" subverts the conventional meaning, and traps the individual in an autistic world or isolated experience. In contrast to ideological capture (which pertains to the verbal realm of *shoulds*), affective capture pertains to the wants, needs, and fears of our affective life. The beliefs and needs of these capturings are different from the beliefs and needs which enter into intentional forms of symbolic realization. As described above, ideologically captured beliefs and affectively captured needs correspond to meanings which have become isolated from this reflective or self-related form of meaning. By this view, a capturing may only occur when the belief or need has become frozen in the reified beliefs or a primitive belief system, and is therefore isolated from the individual's network of reflectively known beliefs.

The distinction I am drawing between these two modes of capturing should not be taken to mean that the one could exist without the other. Both are always to some degree present in pathological thought. The distinction described above is based upon which aspect (the verbal or the affective) predominates. For example, when an act is captured by an unacknowledged compliance with another's belief, the individual sacrifices his or her capacity for self-assertion and integrity. The person is acting in accordance with what Sartre (1956) has described as bad faith, since the meaning of the act does not reflect the individual's integrity; i.e., the individual's ability to be challenged in a manner that promotes discovery and growth. The capture in question is called ideological, insofar as it involves adopting another's belief; but it includes an affective component in the implicit fear of standing on one's own.

In the affective capture of irresponsible acting out, the struggle for responsible control has not achieved a personal significance. That is, the affective component (e.g., the "intolerable" frustration that drives one to excess, or the inner despair of not being able to control that excess) deflects the individual from other aspects of his or her life which might temper the excess; e.g., the awareness of the consequences of one's act, or the capacity to endure pain for the sake of a loved one. And yet, one might not imagine an affectively based acting out that is not also under the aegis of some belief. Thus, for example, impulsive behavior may be grounded in the belief that frustration is lethal to the self; or that immediate gratification is an entitlement; or that the adoption of constraints would constitute a self-betrayal, or would be impossible to live up to. Basic to any capturing (by this view) however, is the fact that the meaning context has remained relatively primitive and isolated from the capacity to realize responsible and purposeful acts. Thus, compliance as a source of security would abort the possibility of self-assertive modes of symbolic realization, while remaining isolated in its lack of explicit awareness; and the acting out of affective preoccupations would constitute a habitual form of release which effectively precludes both the struggle for restraint, and the assumption of responsibility for this mode of behavior.

As noted above, common to both forms of capturing (though for different reasons) is the collapse of the very function that permits reflective awareness. This function, referred to earlier as our *meta* function, corresponds to our ability (introduced by language) to reflectively question the meaning of a meaning. It is in this reflective state of mind that a word is understood as being *about* something; i.e., as being capable of expansion in relation to other meanings, and not as immutably fixed in some independent reality. In terms of the example of the schizophrenic patient cited above, the meta meaning of Santa Claus as metaphorical figure has collapsed into the literal association "Claus-claws," "claws-hands," and "hands-masturbation." Capturing therefore depends upon the fact that language's meta structure may collapse under the weight of literal meaning, as when purity and sex remain trapped in the reified notion that they are mutually exclusive, and must therefore remain in perpetual conflict.

At this point, a possible misinterpretation of what is being claimed should be raised. Our capacity to switch from a reflective to an objectifying state of mind is not taken here to be a source of pathology per se, as it is deemed essential to our functioning. For example, one may switch from the reflective mode of considering the feasibility of alternative courses of action to the active mode of enacting a course of action in an objectified world. To act, one must (by this view) cease to reflect upon alternatives; one must objectify one's reality on the basis of one's expectation. What is critical in pathological thought is not the fact that we may alternate between a reflective and a reified view of reality; rather, it is the fact that we may lose the reflective capacity of the self's meta function in moments of high anxiety, stress, or panic, when it is most needed; or we may be incapable (as was the unfortunate Hamlet) of abandoning reflection when the time for action has arrived. Having discussed why language must be implicated in the distortion of meaning, and how that distortion may be understood, we are now prepared to look at how language participates in the creation of meaning.

7.
LANGUAGE AND THE CREATION OF MEANING

If words are simply the labels we apply to an independent reality, then the creation of meaning would have to be ascribed to the reality words name. If on the other hand reality is something we create, then the words we use would have to somehow participate in this creation. Words could not (in a created reality) work as labels, for the same reason that growing children cannot keep wearing the same clothes. If you are growing, the structures that envelop you must grow as well. This chapter offers a view of how language plays a critical role in the symbolic realization of new meaning. Beyond the reality we create perceptually, the emergence of new meaning is seen as depending upon a characteristic of language which has already been described: the deliteralization of words that occurs with reflection. In our development, for example, we gradually come to understand that words are *about* meaning (rather than *being* meaning), and are therefore capable of expansion in terms of the content they refer to. For this reason, new meaning arises with the maturing of the individual, as he or she comes to dereify the literal representations of childhood.

As was described in chapter 5, the existence of reflection (and the act of introspection it permits) has been questioned of late by philosophers of language, yet these authors in turn have failed to appreciate the role language plays in this process. And while the mainstream psychoanalytic view also neglects the role of language, the explanation to be offered here shares an affinity with their position. For the mainstream, new meaning arises as a result of lifting the repression we impose upon unconscious contents. In this text, new meaning is often a function of liberating primitive meanings from their literal preconceptions. Both models view new meaning in terms of our ability to express verbally, meanings which were previously nonverbal. The mainstream model has difficulty explaining how we discover new meanings that are unrelated to biological impulses; and how our discoveries are often a function of historical and cultural patterns that are independent of our biology. The model proposed here therefore adds an extra dimension to the mainstream psychoanalytic view. That is, it sees the assimilation of cultural and historical patterns in the development of the individual as essential features of the self; and it provides a medium (language) for the assimilation of these features.

The view of symbolic realization I am about to describe is adopted from Mead. It is also implied in the writings of Ortega y Gasset, Merleau-Ponty, and Eugene Gendlin. While it has not been developed in relation to the role of language by these authors, the view they offer as to how new meanings arise presents us with invaluable insights into how the reflective process leads to novel meaning.

HOW WE CREATE NEW MEANING WITH WORDS

The Dialectic of the I *and the* Me

In *An Essay in Esthetics by Way of a Preface*, Ortega y Gasset (1975) makes the wry comment that when Kant urges us to act so as not to use others as means but as ends to our actions, he is saying that we must guard against a tendency to use our fellow man as an object. And yet this tendency might be effectively countered, Ortega y Gasset indicates, since a thing ceases to be a thing when we reverse this process by making the thing an *I myself*. "The I (is) the one thing we not only do not desire to turn, but we cannot turn, into a thing. This is to be taken literally" (132).

While he does not relate man's objectifying tendency to the nature of language as has been done in this text, Ortega y Gasset is describing the capacity we have to use words in both a literal and a metaphorical way. That is, he is contrasting our capacity to experience a person or object as a thing, with our ability to reflect upon that experience as being ABOUT something. When I make the thing an *I myself*, I am reflectively aware that it is *I myself* who had the experience I am reflecting upon. In other words, this act of reflective awareness dereifies the thing by reversing my tendency to attribute my experience to things. By reflectively focusing upon my experience as mine, I reverse the process whereby my experience is attributed to its object, rather than to the body which has it.

According to the dictionary, to reify is to regard something abstract as a material thing. As used here, the term *reify* refers to our capacity to attribute to the thing the experience that is of our body; i.e., as when we presume that meaning in inherent in the object, and not in our experience of the object. In the terms of this essay, we attribute our experience to the object when we literalize the word as being the content it refers to. That is, the word not only stands for, but becomes the content it represents.

Interestingly, the process described by Ortega y Gasset is identical to one described by George Herbert Mead—though what Ortega y Gasset describes as an *I myself,* Mead describes as a *me.* Both authors refer to our immediate, unreflective experience as an *I.* For Mead:

> The *I* is not a *me* and cannot become a *me.* . . . The *I* does not get into the limelight; we talk to ourselves, but we do not see ourselves . . . the *I* of this moment is present in the *me* of the next moment. There again, I cannot turn around quick enough to catch myself. I become a *me* in so far as I remember what I said. (1934, 174)

In this instance, Mead seems to be adopting James's view of reflection as an awareness from memory. While Mead appears at times to agree with James, it is clear that reflection inheres (for Mead) not in memory per se, but as a phase of the dialectical relationship that exists between verbal and nonverbal meaning. In this vein, Mead describes the relationship between the *I* and the *me* as a continuous *reciprocal* process of *mutual transformation.* To picture this process, one might borrow a metaphor from Rapaport (1951). In his description of how the body builds constraints upon our biological impulses, Rapaport compares this process to the reciprocal interaction of a river with the banks that constrain it. When a river deposits sediments, this effect is "felt" by the river, insofar as the banks affect its flow, by slowing it down where the banks are built up. In a similar vein, the nonverbal *I* and the verbal *me* have an ongoing effect upon each other, such that each is continuously responsive to and changed by the other.

The *me* (as symbol) is readily reified as a static fixture. One may therefore miss the fact that the importance of the *me* lies not in what it represents as symbol, but in the process it permits. That is, it is because of the *me*'s relation to the *I* that we may engage in the process of reflective awareness. How might this process be understood? Ortega y Gasset has described this process in terms that are very similar to Mead's: "In order for me to see my pain, I have to interrupt being in pain and become an *I* that looks on. This *I* that observes the other one in pain is now the true *I*, the executant one, the present *I*" (1975, 134).

What Ortega y Gasset refers to as the executant *I*, is what Mead refers to as the *me*; i.e., it is the *I* experienced a moment ago, reflected upon via the symbol. For Ortega y Gasset (as for Mead and for this text), nothing can exist *for us* unless it has been captured symbolically: "The *I* that I seem to have so close at hand in only an image of my *I*. . . . it is a passerby, with face hidden, that crosses my consciousness, giving me no more than a glimpse of a back draped in a Spanish cape" (ibid., 135).

In the terms of this discussion, our symbols operate as empty slots which capture meaning in the same way that a suitcase contains clothes. The symbol can only be an image of the experience it reflects. And yet, however pale this image may be in contrast to the density of immediate experience, one may not, as Mead reminds us, imagine the one without the other: "There would not be an *I* in the sense in which we use that term, if there were not a *me*. There would not be a *me* without a response in the form of an *I*" (1934, 182).

But, one might ask, if the *me* is a symbol of the *I*, why would there not be an *I* in the absence of a *me*? As the body's innate ability to relate meaningfully to its milieu, the *I* predates the *me*. But our meaning is not understood as pertaining to an *I*, until it has been captured by the *me* of language. Only then might these two aspects of the self enter into a mutual process of reciprocal transformation, via the act of reflection.

The act of reflection does not by this view correspond to some inner awareness which splits the event into an observer and an object of observation. Rather, reflection is seen as a process whereby distinct meanings are juxtaposed and contrasted to each other so as to permit a sense of the ways in which they are alike or different. This creative aspect of reflection has been addressed by Gendlin (1962), Merleau-Ponty (1962), and Ortega y Gasset (1975) in ways that are virtually identical—a fact which suggests that this understanding of how we create meaning with language has been brewing in our zeitgeist for some time. In what follows, I will report Ortega y Gasset's description, as it offers what I take to be an incomparable example of the very process described.

THE METAPHOR AS DE-CREATION

Ortega y Gasset (1975) addresses the transformation of meaning in creative expression in terms of the metaphor (as does Gendlin 1962). His example is taken from the Valencian poet López Picó, who describes the cypress as being the "ghost of a dead flame." The process of transformation Ortega y Gasset sees as being released by this metaphor is described as follows:

> "First, we are invited to think of a cypress; next the cypress is removed and we are asked to place the ghost of a flame in the same ideal spot. That is, we are to see the image of a cypress through the image of a flame; we see it as a flame, and vice versa. But each excludes the other; they are mutually opaque. And yet it is a fact that while reading this verse we discover the possibility of a perfect fusion of the two—that is, the one, without ceasing to be what it is, can assume the same place as the other; we have in short, a case of transparency occurring in the emotional place common to both. (ibid., 145)

"Opacity" for Ortega y Gasset is what gives the act of perception its character of separation between the thing known, and the person who knows. "Transparency," as in the transparency of glass, has the opposite effect; it allows us to perceive beyond the surface of the thing known. Poetry permits us to transform the opacity of things into a transparency, by "the transposition of the thing from its real place to its emotional place" (ibid., 145). In this last sentence, "real place" is taken here to be "literal place," and "emotional place" is taken to be the felt meaning described by Gendlin as the nonverbal component of what we know. In other words, the poetic metaphor permits us to do two things. We deliteralize a familiar meaning; and we discover a previously nonverbal content which may now be referred to with words.

The process I have just described is in keeping with what Ortega y Gasset perceives to be the purpose of art, which is "not to tell us about things, but to present them to us in the act of executing themselves" (ibid., 138). That is, the work of art could not be about some process it refers to; it would have to embody the process of creating itself!

Lest this last statement be questioned as going beyond what might be demonstrated by this simple example, I will attempt to show how López Picó's metaphor illustrates this point. In one sense, the expression of a cypress as the "ghost of a dead flame" presents its own self-execution as symbolic realization: the cypress as embodiment of a *dead* flame; i.e., the flame is not only dead metaphorically, but as a concrete example of the transformation it permits. In another sense, the image is made palpable by this burning instant of transformation. In short, both images (the cypress and the flame) embody concrete objects as well as the process whereby images are transformed. Ortega y Gasset's point, however, is that this creative process is not merely one in which images are made palpable, but also one in which the images execute themselves in the sense of killing off their earlier meanings.

To facilitate a grasp of this last point, I will shift to Maurice Merleau-Ponty's (1973) approach to this issue in terms of what he describes as the "silent structure of language" (xiii–xiv). Language, he notes, would have to be responsive to the expressions it permits, or we would soon become limited in our ability to generate new meaning. For language to be responsive to our expressions, these expressions would have to bring about a constant dislocation within the structure of language itself. Hence his view that we use the silent structure of language in the same way that we use our bodies, without thought or explicit awareness of the structure we are bringing into action at any given moment. In contrast to our use of our body however, the meaning structures which support speech are necessarily altered by its expression. That is, it is the very enactment of these structures in our speech which results in a kind of coherent deformation of this silent background to our speech. Our speech acts, it may therefore be said, are the result of a dislocation-transformation of the procedures which enter into the production of speech. Yet what Merleau-Ponty is referring to here could not be the formal structure of speech; i.e., its syntax and grammar, for example, which hardly change at all within the space of several generations. Rather, one must conclude that he is referring to the premises we make in *using* words. That is (reverting now to the terms of this essay), he must be alluding to changes in the implicit content of words, and to the fact that the dereification of words is accompanied by the integration of novel implicit meanings which had been (till then) excluded from verbal meaning.

In chapter 4, this process is described in terms of Jacques Derrida's project to carry us to the limits of language by elaborating strategies of deconstruction. By analyzing the basic assumptions of a position so as to reveal what is left out, Derrida has evolved an influential philosophical and literary form of criticism and questioning which bears directly upon the process of discovery and change being described here. As one of our earlier deconstructionists, Ortega y Gasset presents a similar position when he describes creative expression as always being a "de-creation," as when he states "Art is in essence De-creation" (1975, 147). De-creation, or the reverse of bringing something into existence, adds to Merleau-Ponty's notion of "dislocation" as an active undoing in order to bring something new into being. What is added (in keeping with a principal thesis of this text) is the idea that a loss must occur if room is to be made for new forms of understanding: "to disturb our natural vision of things, so that by virtue of this disturbance, what ordinarily passes unperceived —the emotional value of things—becomes visible" (1975, 148).

If one substitutes Gendlin's "felt meaning" for "emotional value," then Ortega y Gasset is describing the thesis of this essay. To borrow the language of classical psychoanalysis, the thing must be decathected, but not as the Freudian analysts would have it, of libidinal energy; rather, it must be dereified in order to free the "emotional" or "felt meaning" or "amodal content" which is trapped in the objectification of meaning by language. Only then might we tap into the underlying emotional value so as to allow for the emergence of new meaning. Under what conditions may this be said to occur?

Asking for the conditions of creating new meaning is like asking how, in the *I*'s relationship to the *me,* the *me* alters its relationship to the *I.* Mead touches upon this issue briefly (1934), in terms of those situations when the *I* and the *me* are experienced as one. That is, when we are in the grips of a heightened emotional experience, the *me* as symbol is afforded an opportunity to become one with the *I,* as when external threats to the community promote a selfless sense of communal sharing; or (though this is not Mead's example) when in our love for another, the emotional union with the beloved dislocates the conventional *me* from its usual moorings. In these instance, we effect a form of union with another which transcends the consciously set limits of our symbolic *me,* and may in some way alter the *me* that we recover when we "return to our senses."

Merleau-Ponty refers to the same kind of transformation when he describes how we may transcend the reifying limits of the *me* by a "genuine sympathy" (1964, 120); a sympathy which he states "does not presuppose a genuine distinction between self-consciousness and consciousness of the other but rather the absence of a distinction between the self and the other" (146).

But how, it might be asked at this point, could we conceivably transcend (à la Mead) the conventional moorings of the me, or (à la Merleau-Ponty) the distinction between self-consciousness and consciousness of the other? Would such a state not be akin to a psychosis? Perhaps, it might be said, insofar as this state corresponds to our one permissible psychosis; i.e., the state of love. For Merleau-Ponty, "to love is inevitably to enter into an undivided situation with another" (ibid., 154). The experience of love "tears me away from my lone self and creates instead a mixture of myself and the other" (ibid., 155).

These statements by Mead, Merleau-Ponty, and Ortega y Gasset suggest that a common process underlies our symbolic realization, our ability to create, and our capacity to love a fellow being. In all of these instances, meaning is (so to speak) forced momentarily from its nominal or symbolic place to its lived emotional place. In some instances it is the awesomeness of fully encountering another being which throws the *me* out of kilter. In other instances, the challenge to the *me* may arise out of dire necessity, or the sudden insight that comes from abruptly encountering the limits of one's preconceptions. Whatever the occasion, in the transformations of meaning, of creativity and of love the established relationship between a symbol and its felt experience, or of our *me* and our *I* is suddenly undone, and gives way to a novel fusion between experience and its symbol, or between our *I* and our *me*.

Obviously, much remains to be understood regarding this process. We are still at the reified stage of understanding, which is to say that for the moment, we must rely almost entirely upon the creative intuitions that are grasped in the metaphors proposed by these authors. In this vein, Ortega y Gasset describes the emergence of new meaning in terms of the confrontation of disparate images: "Their hard carapaces crack and the internal matter, in a molten state, acquires the softness of plasma, ready to receive a new form and structure" (143).

This striking image reflects an understanding that one repeatedly finds in the writings of authors who address the creative process in poetry. For example, the poet and critic Helen Vendler (1984) describes the poetry of Cezelaw Milosz as giving rise to that "temperature which comes when two words that have never before lived side by side suddenly mingle." This breaking down of "natural compartments," Vendler goes on to say, "is one of the most powerful effects of poetry, which by its concision and free play can represent better than most prose the fluid access of a daring and unhampered mind to its own several regions."

To what should one ascribe Vendler's "temperature"? Clearly, the opposition of just any two words will not do. It must be words which have "never lived side by side." Words which provoke what we feel when we read (as per Vendler) of "Marvell's green thought,' Traherne's 'orient and immortal wheat,' Donne's 'unruly sun,' or Keats' 'sylvan historian'." In other words, the temperature of creative heat is exciting! Apter (1982) ascribes the enhanced arousal of creative work, the "eureka!" of discovery, to an effect that is similar to the one noted by Ortega y Gasset in his response to the metaphor of the cypress as "ghost of a dead flame." Apter ascribes this excitement to the opportunity of experiencing the normally disparate properties of two events in some identity. A toy ship for example, derives magic from the fact that it shares in the identity of a real ship, in spite of also being a plastic or wooden object.

The idea being developed here is similar to Winnicott's (1971) notion of the *transitional object* as vehicle for the child's discovery of symbolic meaning. Winnicott focuses upon that period in the child's growing separation from its mother where the blanket or teddy bear come to stand for and assume the ability to induce the comforting presence of mother. For Winnicott, the child's ability to accept the blanket or teddy bear as both an object and the nurturing experience it stands for, is due to the child's capacity for illusion. That is, the blanket as transitional object offers us one of life's first examples of the symbol's capacity to become the thing it symbolizes.

Winnicott's notion of "illusion" points to a paradox that is basic to how we create meaning. The very aspect of language that promotes the distortion of meaning (i.e., the confusion it permits between the word and its content), is also at the heart of how we create meaning. Our capacity for illusion, as when the child treats the blanket as if it were the absent parent, is in a sense a literalization of the blanket. The blanket as symbol is treated as if it were the thing it refers to (mother's comforting presence). The difference however, is that the blanket performs this function because it is *like* mother's comforting presence (in its warmth, texture, and smell for example). The illusion introduced by our symbols allows us to draw analogies between patterns, and to then treat them as the same (as when one compares the mind to a combustion machine, or language to a filing system).

There are two other quite different approaches to signification which concur with the view of the generation and transformation of meaning proposed by Gendlin, Mead, Merleau-Ponty, Ortega y Gasset, and this essay. For the linguist, it corresponds to what has been described as the most important relation in linguistic structural analysis: the relation of binary opposition. The term *binary oppostion* refers to the fact that in juxtaposing any two items, the observer is forced to explore qualitative similarities and differences so as to derive some meaning from their disjunction. Jacobson and Halle (1956), for example, argue for the principle of binary opposition as basic to any structural analysis. They also suggest that binary oppositions are inherent in language as a basic operation of the mind.

An example might help to clarify this last point. The role of binary opposition may perhaps best be understood in the example of the oxymoron, a form of metaphor defined in Webster's dictionary (1979) as "a figure of speech in which opposite or contradictory ideas or terms are combined (e.g., thunderous silence, love's sweet sorrow)." In other words, the oxymoron presents words which (as per Vendler) have never lived side by side, or at least don't ordinarily do so. If, for example, you were to imagine hearing "love's sweet sorrow" for the first time, you would have an example of the generation of novel meaning. The juxtaposed experiences of love as being both sweet and sorrowful come to convey the added notion that the very sorrow of love is also sweet. Once familiar with the notion conveyed by the metaphor, the experience of love can no longer mean quite what it meant prior to our hearing this expression. By simultaneously presenting us with the rapture and pain of love, the metaphor enriches our understanding; i.e., it juxtaposes these specific states in a manner that did not exist for us before, and thereby generates a new meaning.

One might counter what has just been claimed by saying that if sweet-sorrow is an analogy (as the term metaphor would indicate), then it could not correspond to a novel meaning. That is, it would have to refer us to an experience we've already had. Granted, I would respond, for this is precisely the point; i.e., that experiences I've already cast within the preselective categories of language, when juxtaposed in an unusual or unexpected manner, may dislodge those categories in favor of a new meaning that had not till then been verbalized. It is for this reason (and not merely as a means of organizing and classifying meaning) that binary opposition should be viewed as fundamental to human language and thought.

The other approach to signification alluded to above is found in research work conducted on how people think creatively. Barron (1968) for example reports that creative individuals are unique in their preference for the unbalanced, the asymmetrical, and the incomplete in art and symbolism, as well as their enjoyment in resolving these asymmetries. Other authors have focused upon the use of divergent and convergent thinking in creative thought (e.g., Getzels and Jackson 1962; Hudson 1966)—the notion being that the creative elaboration of meaning requires both the divergence of disparate experiences (as in the juxtaposed images of the metaphor), and the convergence of these disparate qualities, as when binary opposition of disparate meanings promotes a reflective assimilation. That is, the creative process has been found (in these observational studies at least) to entail a willingness to tolerate the ambiguity of disparate contrasts, as well as the incentive to reflectively elaborate the meaning which emerges out of these contrasts; a process which bears a marked similarity to the one presented here as a model for a functional appreciation of symbolic realization.

The main point of this description of how some of our most discerning authors have described the process of creative discovery has been to highlight the role of language in this process. Language may be used to juxtapose experiences in a way that enables us to discover meanings which had been literalized, or had yet to be symbolized. In this manner, an already meaningful response is *deflected, dislocated,* and *decreated* in the following manner:

> *To deflect*—to turn aside or off course—refers to the fact that the juxtaposition must challenge our habitual assumptions. We do not normally think of a cypress as a "dead flame."
>
> *To dislocate*—to displace from normal connections—refers to the fact that the deflection makes room for a new meaning by forcing an experienced comparison of similarities and differences. It is out of this comparison of felt similarities and differences that a new meaning reconciling these difference may arise.
>
> *To decreate*—to undo a prior creative synthesis—refers to the fact that the experienced aspect of meaning must be pried loose from its symbolic mooring, in order to be cast into a broader level of significance. That is, since the newly discovered emotional significance of the cypress as ghost of a dead flame synthesizes previ-

ously disparate meanings, it reintegrates these meanings at a "higher" (less literal) level of meaning. The juxtaposed experiences which assist in displacing the familiar meaning come to establish a sense of common identity which did not exist prior to their being experienced in this way.

In these creative realizations, the self is posed between the familiar and the novel, or between the security of a literal world, and the expansive potential of a metaphorical world. Hence the creative heat of anxiety/delight. To promote this possibility, one must (as in the subjects described by Barron, Getzels, and Jackson, and Hudson) be willing to tolerate the discomfort of ambiguity. In short, one must permit a process that is purposeful, responsible, and uniquely individual. Purposeful in that it accepts the discomfort of incongruity and ambiguity in order to challenge accepted ideas. Responsible in that it assumes responsibility for this process by permitting its purposeful engagement. And uniquely individual in that its outcome hinges on the actual, concretely experienced meanings which are unique to each individual. Having presented a view of the role of language in the creation of meaning, borrowed from the writings of two Americans, a Spaniard, and a Frenchman, I will now examine the psychoanalytic theory of creativity, from within the context in which it emerged; i.e., the interpretive process of psychotherapy.

THE INTERPRETIVE PROCESS IN PSYCHOTHERAPY

In this section, I claim that our understanding of the talking cure inaugurated by Freud has evolved. It has shifted from an earlier emphasis on explaining how contents of the mind become repressed, toward an interest in how we realize meaning. With this shift, however, one also sees less interest in the metapsychology that was initially formulated to explain how and why contents get repressed. Thus, while practitioners of psychotherapy have gained in knowledge and awareness through their work, there is today no commonly accepted theory of meaning to which they might relate their findings. I conclude with clinical material in order to illustrate how the theory of meaning presented in this book may be applied to the evaluation of what goes on in psychotherapeutic work.

Language and Interpretation

From the early mainstream perspective of Otto Fenichel (1941), interpretations are said to promote change in five distinct ways: 1) when the interpretation brings to light a content that had been isolated; 2) when the patient's attention is drawn to an activity formerly viewed as passive (i.e., as not under the aegis of the self's intentionality); 3) when motives that were not in awareness are revealed; 4) when new connections in the associative process are discovered; and 5), when new observations correct former distortions.

Fenichel goes on to say that this description is incomplete, in that it does not account for the patient's *resistance* to the process. From this early perspective, the isolation, dissociation, and repression which Fenichel states are corrected by interpretation, are invariably due to unacceptable biological impulses. The resistance he speaks of is therefore a resistance to the understanding that comes of acknowledging our biological needs.

From the perspective of this essay, Fenichel is describing the various ways in which the content of meaning may be distorted, or kept from awareness. While the reasons he gives for this distortion and repression are questioned by this essay, his description of what one finds may hardly be improved upon. Like Rappaport (chapter 1), Fenichel explains this process in a language (the cathecting and decathecting of libidinal energies) which was (at the time in which he wrote) the height of the creative elaboration of the Freudian metaphor. And while one might today question this metaphor as having missed the role of language in this process, one should still respect the descriptions it gave rise to. Had Fenichel perceived the role of language in promoting meaning, he would certainly have grasped its relevance to the interpretive process, for he was (in this 1941 article) describing interpretation as different ways of *naming* a content that has been isolated, disowned, not seen or distorted, and of accepting that content as belonging to the self. He might also have appreciated resistance as an inherent feature, not of the content of what gets repressed or displaced, but of the way in which meaning is realized. By this view, resistance is inherent to the questioning of reified meanings. We are loath to question meanings once they have become objectified, or to consider what they leave out. It is for this reason that symbolic realization is said in this essay to be purposeful and responsible, in that it must overcome a resistance we all share (in varying degrees) to reflective analysis. The point I would stress in discussing this early mainstream article, is that while it is imbued with the implications of drive theory, it nonetheless implicates language use, and what occurs as a result of that use, in the interpretive process.

Since Fenichel, the mainstream view of the interpretive process has evolved away from the earlier emphasis upon the content of what gets distorted, toward a greater interest in the process of generating meaning. For example, Shapiro (1979) summarizes the position of several authors by describing the interpretive process as one of putting into words "expressions formerly indicated by more cumbersome idiosyncratic vehicles, such as patterned behavior, gestures, and interpersonal and transitional events" (106). The problem has been reframed, in that it is not the content of meaning that interferes with its conscious expression, but the "idiosyncratic vehicle" which structures it. The shift in emphasis from uncovering repressed contents per se, to finding a way of expressing unconscious meanings, is entirely in keeping with the position proposed here. That is, Shapiro's description could as readily pertain to any nonverbal meaning which for whatever reason has yet to be integrated within the structure of language. Shapiro's description is taken here to be symptomatic of a trend, whereby descriptions of the process have moved from the narrower consideration of how biological needs are repressed and distorted, to the broader interest in how meaning itself finds verbal expression. In doing so, however, the practice has dislodged itself from the metapsychology, without having anything to take its place.

Another important aspect of the mainstream position on interpretation is that this "putting into words" is not to be understood as a mere labeling for the patient. Rather, the patient and the therapist are jointly engaged in a process in which the analyst's interpretations attempt to anticipate what the analysand is on the verge of discovering. As described by Lowenstein (1951), the language of interpretation "performs the function of a kind of scaffolding that permits conscious thought to be built inside. [The analyst] lends the words . . . which will meet the patient's thoughts and emotions half way" (465). This metaphor of an "internal scaffolding" was borrowed earlier in this text to describe how, in assimilating a language, the child must build an internal structure that substitutes class inclusion for the intuitive part-whole relationships of nonverbal meaning. That is, Lowenstein is (by this view) describing how the "building" of conscious thought is a function of integrating the unconscious with the structure of language—of providing the words which "meet the patient's thoughts and emotions half way." In other words, the patient and analyst must forge a way of expressing heretofore nonverbalized meanings, so as to build a more conscious representation of his or her world. The next step in this developing view of the interpretive process, would be to question the idea that the analyst already knows what form these expressions should take.

In meeting the patient halfway the analyst must take care not to induce experiences in the patient, or preempt in any way the patient's responsibility for discovering his or her own words. There is therefore a paradox in Lowenstein's view of this process. How could the analyst lend words that are the patient's? A common response to this question is the observation that the therapist meets the patient halfway through empathy. Thus, for example, Heinz Kohut (1971) has referred to the empathic response as the "essence of psychoanalysis" (303). Kohut describes empathy as "our ability to know via vicarious introspection" (306), and does not feel that we should, at this point, attempt a more precise definition. Independently of mainstream analysts, Carl Rogers (1950) has given detailed attention to the process of empathy, which is a cornerstone of his client centered therapy. Rogers describes empathy as "sensing the client's inner world of private personal meaning 'as if' it were the therapist's own." Gendlin (1974) has added to this notion by relating empathy to a manner of listening in which the therapist strives for and responds to experiential concreteness and specificity. That is, the therapist's responses are (as with Lowenstein) meant to focus upon those feelings which are only hinted at by the client, so as to bring them to light in a way that is new but not alien. Rogers and Gendlin differ from the mainstream psychoanalytic position of twenty years ago, in that these feelings need not be limited to sexual or aggressive contents. It may be just as important (and difficult) for a client to acknowledge feelings of intimacy or helplessness, as to express shameful lusts or unacceptable aggressions. What matters in the interpretive work is that it pertain to an event that has been experienced by the client, and not to a presumption on the part of the therapist. Today, one would be hard put to find an analyst who does not acknowledge the importance of a patient's articulating feelings of intimacy or helplessness, or of working toward concreteness and specificity. In other words, the focus has shifted from interpreting contents on the basis of what your theory says must be there, to one of acknowledging the creative process of discovery as basic to the therapeutic process.

This shift should not surprise us, as it conforms to Freud's original view, before he became entranced with the metaphorical elaborations of drive theory. Prior to Freud's adoption of a biological metaphor as a model of the mind, his psychoanalytic theory was a theory of *meaning*. In this early view, Freud related pathogenic states to the "incompatibility between the single idea that is to be repressed, and the dominant mass of ideas constituting the ego" (Breuer and Freud, 1895, 116). Freud abandoned this valuable insight when he turned to a metaphorical energy rather than symbolic meaning to explain repression. Late in life however (1925, 140), Freud shifted back, from a mechanistic hydraulic model, to his original emphasis upon meaning:

> At one time I attached some importance to the view that what was used as a discharge of anxiety was the cathexis which had been drawn in the process of repression.... My present conception of anxiety as a signal given by the ego in order to affect the pleasure-unpleasure agency does away with the necessity of considering the economic factor.

A number of psychoanalytic authors have anticipated the theme of this book by resurrecting Freud's original (and later) emphasis upon meaning. For example, G. S. Klein (1976b) has described the disowned quality of a repressed meaning, not in terms of an unconscious impulse, but (as in the Freud of 1895), as being dissociated from the person's "self concept" (241). That is, Klein brought repression back to Freud's initial concept by relating it to a conflict having to do with the self's identity.

For Klein, conscious identity is a function of our ability to engage actively that which had been passively endured. The notion is akin to the idea that when you drive a car yourself, you retain a better idea of the route taken than if you are passively driven. Active engagement by this view is an essential ingredient of conscious awareness. From the perspective of this essay, Klein's observation would follow from the view described earlier (p. 157) of symbolic realization as purposeful, responsible and uniquely individual. That is, only (as per Marx and Fromm) when an act engages the active intent of the individual may it be said to result in the creation of a self-consciously aware understanding. What I would stress at this point is that for all of these authors a similar process is presumed, if not always acknowledged. In Klein's notion of active reversal; Fenichel's naming of contents which have been isolated, disowned, not seen, or distorted; Shapiro's putting the idiosyncratic into words; Lowenstein's meeting the patient halfway; Kohut's empathy; Rogers's sensing the client's world—all refer to the fact that a meaning has been isolated from conscious awareness. And all indicate (or imply) that this meaning must be named if it is to become accessible to the relations and differentiations of other conscious experiences.

The problem with the positions outlined above, however, is that there is no attempt to describe this process in terms of what we in fact have access to, namely, our language! That is, mainstream, object relations, Rogerian, Adlerian, Jungian, Horneyan, or interpersonal analysts fail to appreciate this transformation in terms of how we realize meaning with words. These various schools have either limited themselves to considering the conditions under which therapy succeeds (e.g., the "unconditional regard" of the Rogerians); or elaborated metaphors of the mind which (as with the mainstream) are no longer taken seriously; or have explained the process in terms of some aspect of our humanity (the need for individuation, the will to power, or will itself), which is presumed as essential to our being. All currently ignore Freud's original insight: that any metapsychology must first and foremost explain how we represent our reality!

For today's mainstream analyst, in view of the growing understanding that has resulted from the practice of psychotherapy, it seems clear that the tenets of drive theory must be questioned. Therapists no longer limit themselves to a search for unacknowledged biological impulses. Yet the need for a metapsychology remains as valid today, as it was when Freud and his followers concerned themselves with the question as to how the mind represents its reality. The fact that drive theory has failed as metapsychology, does not divest us of this responsibility. In the absence of such a theory, psychotherapists lack a basis for challenging the premises that support their practice; their theory is therefore incapable of growth.

A further characteristic of the schools of psychotherapy described above, is that while they share a common assumption about the therapeutic effects of naming disowned or unacknowledged meanings, they differ radically in how they explain why this is effective. In this regard, Levenson (1983) has described how analysts of an "intrapsychic" persuasion (such as those in the mainstream, who view the mind as an entity unto itself), see reality as a jumping-off point for an autonomous fantasy process that is internally driven. The fantasy might be of devouring the preoedipal breast, or of consumating the oedipal wish, or it might pertain to some aspect of the separation-individuation conflict that is presumed as part of the formation of the self. If a person is in need of an orthodox analysis, the assumption is that such a fantasy exists, and must be discovered and worked through. For the interpersonal analyst the patient is said to be disabled not by an anachronistic fantasy system, but by an uncomprehended reality. The meaning gap of concern to the interpersonal analyst is not located between an internally driven fantasy and an external reality, but within the individual's ability to realize his or her reality in a meaningful way.

Why should these two positions be viewed as contradictory? Couldn't one anticipate difficulties stemming from reified fantasies (as are described by mainstream analysts) as well as from a failure to comprehend? The contradiction stems from the fact that each camp seizes upon one piece of the puzzle, which is then promoted as the solution to the entire field. In other words, the issue said by Levenson to separate the mainstream from the interpersonal analyst is a *pseudo* issue. It reflects our failure to reach that common ground of understanding that is the mark (as per Kuhn) of a mature science. That is, it is the failure to appreciate the role of language in the realization of meaning that has fixated us at this Tower of Babel stage in the development of psychotherapeutic theory.

From the perspective of this essay, a psychoanalytic inquiry is aptly referred to as a "talking cure," for without language there would be no inquiry! An understanding of how language functions is therefore critical to the work itself. I will at this point state four principal reasons why language should be viewed as critical to the work, before presenting an example, in relation to which these points might be applied.

First, the very interpretive process described above requires that the individual be capable of shifting from a literal to a metaphorical grasp of meaning. It is for this reason that Winnicott (1965) has described how patients who have not yet learned how to "play" (i.e., who are stuck with a literal grasp of meaning, and may not engage in metaphorical elaboration) require a kind of supportive maintenance until they have learned to do so. *Playing* by this view corresponds to the ability to reflect upon words as being about something, and not the thing itself. In order to appreciate this point however, one must understand how words may function in both a literal, and a metaphorical way; and one must have a sense of how reflection enables one to deliteralize the suppressed content of a particular capture so as to open its meaning to the elaborations of metaphorical thought.

Second, words promote *explorations*. They do so by virtue of the fact that they exist in a network of meaningful relations to other words. They are therefore necessary if one is to explore a meaning in relation to the experiences one seeks to make conscious. Hence the ubiquitous psychoanalytic question which must cross school lines in the frequency with which it is asked: "What comes to mind?" which should read "What *words* come to mind?" Hence also the fact that in explanation as in confrontation, what counts is the analyst's ability to use the appropriate words; i.e., those which will most effectively resonate with the analysand's frame of reference, and dislodge literal meanings from their frozen state of isolation. Freud's method of free association was an explicit acknowledgement of this function of words; i.e., that they constitute a bridge to the unconscious by virtue of the associated meanings they are attached to. What should be added to this understanding, is an awareness of how language is the medium whereby meaning is transformed and therefore realized anew. That is, language not only provides the scaffolding with which we come to classify events; language is also the tool with which we realize meaning.

Third, our clients-patients-analysands might better be seen as suffering, not only from a conflicted oedipal fantasy, or a serious case of mystification, or a need for unconditional acceptance; they should (by this view) also be appreciated as suffering from faulty modes of symbolic realization. An appreciation of this last point may only be attained if it is discovered in relation to the experienced context the client fails to adequately symbolize. That is, much of the work (as has been proposed by Zucker 1967) consists in making certain that the analyst has a detailed grasp of the event the analysand is referring to, so that the way in which the analysand expresses what is meaningful about the event may be evaluated in terms of possible distortions and omissions.

Fourth, words are also the vehicle for the transformations they themselves promote. This point of necessity overlaps with the first point presented, as it follows from the dual function of words—as literal presentations, and as metaphorical elaborations—in presenting reality. That is, as was brought out in chapter 5, the reflective property of words (i.e., the reflection they permit) is taken here to constitute the creative process which a psychoanalytic inquiry taps into. That is, words are not only the vehicle for describing what's gone wrong, they are also *a part* of what's gone wrong; i.e., they must be *dislocated* and *decreated* into a metaphorical form, so as to permit the individual to reflect upon his or her experience, and find a way of representing these previously unconscious contents. The process of "making the unconscious conscious" by this view, requires an appreciation of how language makes this transformation possible.

For this reason, a psychotherapy may be viewed as a context in which the client discovers him or herself as a creator of meaning, since this is what is implied each time a reified capturing of the past is unfrozen. If the work (regardless of theoretical persuasion) may be seen as first and foremost a procedure whereby the person comes to understand and accept him or herself, then it inheres (by this view) in discovering and resolving the affective and ideological captures of the past due to the incursion of language. This view of psychoanalysis (as a procedure for resolving captures) corresponds to what one finds across theoretical schools. It fits in with the selective attention and dissociation described by Sullivan (1953), whereby reified states of the self are disowned, much as in the "splits" described by the object relations theory of Fairbairn (1952) and Kernberg (1975). It concurs with descriptions of the countless primitive fantasies of childhood which become trapped as reified foundations for the self—be it the grandiose or abasing self described by Kohut (1971), the projective and introjective identifications describd by M. Klein (1964) and R. Langs (1976), or the false self described by Winnicott (1965) seen here as an objectified self that has lost its analogical moorings. The notion of capturing also conforms to the reified states of dependence and guilt described by Arieti (1973), to the obsessional states described by Barnett (1966), whereby a reified state is adopted as a characterological style; as well as with the violated "love maps" and the paraphilias (disorders of love) described by Money (1986) which testify to the endurance of reified fantasies when they result from abuse. Rather than elaborate further upon the continuity that exists between the position of this text, and that of earlier authors, I will at this point question the adequacy of psychoanalytic evidence, in order to show how the nature of this evidence is altered by the thesis of this book.

THE NATURE OF PSYCHOANALYTIC EVIDENCE

The process of discovery I describe at the start of this chapter does not merely give us a sense we were lacking as to how meanings change. It also answers some of the questions raised about the nature of psychoanalytic evidence. Having a sense of the process of change permits one to focus more clearly upon what (in any given analytic session) allows for change.

That is, it enables one to pick out the indices of change in an analytic session, by attending to what changes arise in the way a person expresses his or her experience. The importance of this last point (if correct) is that it enables one to answer to criticisms of psychoanalysis as a scientific procedure, that have been leveled in two principal areas.

A first area refers to the weak linkage between the theory and its clinical observations (Edelson 1977; Grunbaum 1984). A similar point is made in the first chapter of this book, in the discussion of how the observations made by analysts are themselves grounded in the assumptions that support their theory. While the same point may be made of any theory, the problem specific to psychoanalysis is that it has so far failed to relate the processes it presumes to some index we could all agree to. The theory therefore strains the credulity of the nonpsychoanalyst who has not adopted the complex web of assumptions which allow one to go (some would say, none too critically) from the observation one makes, to its interpretation.

A second, related point (presented most recently by Colby and Stoller 1988), is that there are no reliable observations in psychoanalytic practice, since there is no method for converting raw information into datal evidence. For example, analysts have failed to come up with rules of observation which would assure that events are reported in a reliable fashion. Since we can never know how the reports presented in psychoanalytic journals are connected to the events themselves, they fail to qualify as acceptable scientific data. As described by Colby: "The zero-to-low fidelity of the clinician's undisciplined observation report, is the central reason why the field is unable to make empirical progress. There has been no accumulation of new facts and no iterative cycles of feedback correction to eliminate mistakes" (Colby and Stoller 30).

A further, related criticism is that it is very difficult to state what observed events are instances of theoretical terms. In observing raw-data videotapes of clinical sessions for example, psychoanalysts do not agree among themselves about what is happening. With regard to laboratory data, while agreement is possible to reach, the experimental procedures have a questionable relevance to the theory. That is, they do not feed back into a modification or improvement of the theory, because they are of necessity restricted to some isolated term. Erdelyi (1985), for example, points out that while experimental psychology has no trouble validating instances of selective information rejection, avoidance of aversive stimuli, and of many psychological processes that occur outside of awareness, "what is in dispute and has not been demonstrated experimentally is the conjoint fact, that is, all the component facts integrated into a higher order fact" (259). As noted by Colby, "The field lacks the preliminary agreed-on data sets essential to getting even a purely natural history phase of inquiry off the ground" (1988, 31).

In this section, I argue that the agreed-upon data sets essential to getting psychoanalysis off the ground as science are not a function of the difficulties we encounter in obtaining the data (though the problems posed by this kind of data are not to be scoffed at!). Rather, it is a function of having failed till now to understand the role of language in how we represent our reality. Lacking this understanding, we have also failed to seize upon the one source of observation which could inform us of how the mind of the individual takes shape; and thereby elaborate a theory of the mind that could elicit consensus among the field's practitioners. To illustrate this possibility, I will describe a clinical case.

In our initial interview, Jim, a writer in his early thirties, presents the complaint of not having fully committed himself interpersonally or professionally. He questions his recent separation from a woman he had lived with for two years—he had grown to depend upon her and she was devoted to him—because he felt incapable of "cementing the bond." In his work as an author, he "fades out" when attempting a sustained focus and has yet to settle upon a distinct style of his own.

Jim describes his childhood as having been marked by his father's periodic decompensations and prolonged states of depression. To cope with this situation and to contain the father's disturbance, Jim's mother enlisted the aid of her three children. A frequent admonition for unwanted behavior was "It'll disturb your father!" While he felt burdened by this imposition, Jim remembers himself as a cooperative boy, and cannot recall ever having quarreled with his mother. The main exception was that as a juvenile, he engaged in petty thievery from stores belonging to the company that employed his father. At the end of the first interview (during which this information was obtained), Jim requests a lower fee than had been quoted and offers, in compensation, to pay me in cash "so you won't have to declare it (to the IRS)."

In order to address the ways in which this interaction sheds light upon possible captures, I must question at this point what might be taken to be the unconscious aspects of Jim's behavior. Based upon this first interview (i.e., the information reported above) I assumed the following:

1. Jim's offer to collude over the fee corresponds to a *mode* of relating; that is, it implies a belief as to the possibilities of involvement that need not be consciously known. Modes (as opposed to the experience they structure) cannot be directly reflected upon but must be inferred. That is, Jim might reflect upon his experience during this first interview, and discover that he felt some anxiety. That he handled this anxiety by attempting to collude with his analyst is (and in fact was) readily dismissed as "no big deal." I therefore assume that the possibilities of involvement implied by this behavior are under the aegis of a capture.
2. Jim's captured belief about involvement is grounded in fear (not to collude threatens father and the family), and in a family myth (the family's basic role is to support father). Jim is aware of these effects upon the family's functioning. He would not however be aware of the extent to which this solution to anxiety affects his relationships with others, as it follows from a capture, not from intentional behavior.
3. Jim's attempt at a collusive trade-off with me (he will cater to what he assumes is my unacknowledged need, if I will cater to his) precludes an awareness that would be a grievous blow to his self esteem; i.e., his dependence upon a mother who sacrifices his welfare to his father's need. His anger, in reporting on the family, is reserved entirely for father. His standing with mother is as yet unquestioned.

My conclusion at this point of the inquiry is that Jim's ability to generate his own position has been captured in two complementary ways. It has been captured ideologically by the family myth that father's pathology must not be challenged but, rather, should be contained at all costs; and it has been affectively captured by the fear that failure to subscribe to this myth will provoke untold harm to the family. I am at this point assuming that Jim's collusive mode of involvement as well as the fear of challenging the collusions he finds himself captured by, were induced in him before he had developed the capacity to question this mode of relating. This in turn would have sidetracked his ability to master the challenges he would have to face if he were to forge a more indivudated stance.

So far, the rational for the inferences I draw must seem fairly obvious. I use information provided by Jim, along with information that arose out of our interaction in the session, to hypothesize an explanation for Jim's presenting problem; i.e., his inability to commit himself to his work or to a relationship. The inferences I make based upon his attempted collusion with me, as well as upon the familial situation created by father's depression, are similar to what I believe many analysts of differing schools would make. The difference between the position proposed here, and that of other schools begins to become obvious in the way these initial inferences are checked against further inferences.

In his second session, Jim reports a dream he recalled a few weeks before calling me for an interview. From the perspective of this essay, dreaming corresponds to a mode of realizing meaning in the absence of the self-referential sense of agency and purposefulness that is a part of conscious, waking thought. For this reason, our dream images are to a degree liberated from the sequential logic of language, and express the analogical mode of preverbal thought. Dreaming is therefore seen here as a mode that is ideally suited to expressing those reified meanings that have become trapped in our development, and impede the growth of the self. That is, dreaming is *not* seen as a function of our need to dissimulate or defend against unconscious content. Rather, the "irrational" nature of dream content is because in sleep, we realize meaning in the absence of the purposeful reflection of being awake.

For these reasons, one may assume that dreaming will express two kinds of content. We may in our dreaming express understandings that transcend the bonds of what can be grasped verbally—hence the frequently noted revelatory character of dreams (Jung 1967; Fromm 1951). In a dream state, we are also in a position to relate to captured meanings that are isolated from the conscious elaboration of verbal thought. That is, since these isolated and therefore preconscious meanings generate gaps in our understanding, they are the source of ongoing, unresolved conflicts, and will therefore appear as the residue of our daily concerns. As in the affective capture expressed by the schizophrenic patient cited above of Santa Claus into "Sainted Claws," the dream medium lends itself to those concretely realized analogs that express the individual's unresolved preoccupations. In the analogical mode of dreaming, the medium is the message, and symbols are free to operate with the impact of the analogical gesture which directly induces the meaning intended.

In his dream, Jim has left his belongings in a convent for safekeeping. When he returns to collect them, he learns that they have been "ripped off" (i.e., stolen) by two "junkie" (i.e., drug-addicted) nuns who are under the protection of a mother superior. In describing this dream, Jim relates the two nuns to his two sisters, and to the fact that he resented them. He assumed that they enjoyed a closer, more intimate relationship to his mother than he did. This was the extent of what came to his mind about this dream.

The oxymoron "junkie nuns" is an admirable example of the creative work of dreams. It not only conveys the perils of dependence in analogical form—don't invest your emotions or they'll be ripped off; it also opposes the basic terms of Jim's conflict: his inability to come to terms with a profound sense of betrayal and loss. That is, the profane world of indulgence and theft cannot be reconciled with the sacred world of caring and devotion. As a child, Jim's reified notion of good and evil must have been severely tested by the irrational behavior of his father, as well as by the acquiescence toward this behavior by his mother.

When notions such as good and evil lose their moorings in their preverbal base; i.e., when a *good* is not grasped as relative to a *bad,* but becomes reified as a state, then a split-off good may be imposed in a manner that operates as a captured meaning, in that it prevents the individual from developing a sense of responsible participation in the elaboration of the good. Good and bad will then operate in the form of an unattainable idea, and/or a goading sense of worthlessness. Further splits of this nature are suggested in terms of irreconcilable opposites such as male-female (the convent's sisterhood is exclusive of men); superior-inferior (mother superior is ineffectual in relation to the junkie nuns); and caring-anger (what is cared for is ripped off).

Because the familial devotion was defiled by collusion, there cannot be a secure sense of dependence. In his involvement with those he would naturally have depended upon, Jim feels excluded and ripped off; that is, he is grounded in a belief that brings to every endeavor an ambivalence forbidding complete engagement. Finally, Jim's dream suggests that a grandiose expectation—his affiliation with a mother superior—blocks him from the working through of his conflict. He is entitled, it would seem, to a better deal, even though he did not get one.

The dream (by this view) reinforces the assumptions made from the initial interview, that Jim's collusive mode of relating expresses the unconscious conflicts (capturings) which occurred in his early family life; and that the resulting splits (good-bad, male-female, superior-inferior) have precluded a fuller realization of (and hence a coming to grips with) his sense of betrayal at the hands of his mother (which is deflected to his sisters).

Granted, one may not point to the dream as an independent source of information, and then claim that it validates the inferences drawn from the initial interview. The data is clearly contaminated by the fact that the same interpretive assumptions are applied to both. What may be said, however, is that the initial interview and the dream permit one to organize this information in relation to what is presumed to be critical to Jim's functioning; i.e., where, in his development, did he succumb to the literalizing effects of language? That is, where did the potential distortion of ideological and affective capture (described in chapter 3) isolate areas of potential growth from the ongoing development of his self? So far, the inferences being made are inescapably circular. They depend entirely upon the assumptions that support them. However, there is a way in which the inferences an analyst makes from clinical observations escape circularity.

In any analysis, the analysand will at some point express a sense of having clarified, or newly seen, or suddenly resolved some point of confusion, or discovered some facet of the self not seen before. Whether this is in response to an interpretation by the analyst, or as a result of the analysand's own reflective exploration, these responses are an inevitable feature of any analysis with a suitable analysand. From the perspective of this essay, these statements of increased awareness should correspond to a deliteralization of meaning, when compared to previous statements pertaining to the same topic. Deliteralized meanings are evident, for example, when the words used are clearly *about* meaning, and are not confused with the content they refer to. Other indices of deliteralization include the discovery of an aspect of the self that had previously been attributed to others, but not owned as a self aspect; the sudden discovery of a connection between two aspects which had been kept separate; the conscious discovery of a mode of relating that was implicit, but not consciously known; the ability to explore previously unchallenged fears; and the discovery of beliefs that have little basis in fact.

The reader will have noted the similarity of these examples of dereified meaning to the five ways in which, according to Fenichel, psychoanalytic interpretations change behavior. The difference however, is that the explanations used here do not refer to a content, but to the ways in which language is used. This position therefore eschews the impossible task of demonstrating the existence of unconscious motives and defenses, and focuses entirely upon the way meaning is expressed. Comparing expressions according to clearly defined indices of literal versus metaphorical meaning, would enable one to avoid those areas described earlier as not permitting reliable evidence. First, the process presumed is linked to an index that all could agree to—the degree of literalness of the language used, compared to previous statements. Second, the observations to be made are subject to consensual agreement as the data is readily recorded and analyzed. The process permits what Colby describes as the "iterative cycles of feedback correction to eliminate mistakes." Third, it is readily possible to indicate what observable events are instances of the theoretical terms, as they pertain to language use. Finally, the process offers agreed upon data sets that Colby has described as essential to the "natural history phase of inquiry."

An example from a session of Jim's analysis will attempt to clarify these points. Jim's troubled relationship with his father was related by him to the fact that in his early years (seven to twelve) he had been relegated by mother as caretaker to his father, during father's bouts of depression. This excessive responsibility, and the spectacle of father in such a dejected, helpless state had prompted contempt. Normally, the contempt children may feel in relation to another's weakness is gradually deliteralized, as the child comes to discover that he or she has weaknesses as well. However, if contempt is felt for the very person one needs to hold up as an ideal, it becomes very difficult to temper one's contempt with an awareness of one's weakness, as one cannot (in this instance) afford to be weak! Jim has therefore continued to literalize his contempt for the helplessness of others, as will be brought out in the material which follows. That is, he saw weakness as *being* the person, rather than as an aspect of the person. This in turn blocked the potential differentiation of contempt in relation to feeling (and understanding) the other's frame of reference. For this reason, Jim continued to respond to the dependency needs of a lover with contempt, and to have difficulty resolving the normal ambivalence of a deepening involvement. The following therapy exchange occurred at a point where Jim is expressing concern over the fact that his initially fond feelings for Jane (whom he has been seeing for over a year) are turning to contempt. Jim has just been asked by the analyst (A) to describe a setting in which he experienced contempt for Jane:

> Jim: "I had invited Jane to a dinner party I was giving for friends. Jane asked if she could bring something, and I told her that wasn't necessary, to just bring herself. She showed up with some fresh fruit, and I felt angry even though I knew there was no reason to feel that way."

A: "Could you say more about the anger you felt?"
Jim: "I hadn't asked her to bring it. I didn't want to owe her for it."
A: "That she could make some kind of claim on you?"
Jim: "Yes! Like I would somehow owe her for it. Like she was reminding me of a debt."
A: "Similar to how you feel about the relationship?"
Jim: "Something like that (pauses reflectively, then suddenly starts up with excitement), it's the old guilt trip isn't it! Like I'll always have to take care of her."
A: "Feels like a real burden."
Jim: "Exactly!"
A: "Like if you don't hate her, you'll have to take care of her?"
Jim: "Those two positions again . . . Where's the middle ground?"
A: "What comes to mind?"
Jim: (long pause) "Flashed back to a hiking trip I took years ago with a friend. We had paused to rest and this gangling adolescent—couldn't have been more than sixteen—comes up asking for a smoke. I yelled *NO!* There was so much anger in that *NO* I startled my friend. I *hated* that kid's gangling awkwardness, his pleading, his helplessness . . . That's me isn't it. That's what I'm hating in Jane."

Jim's sudden realization enabled him to examine his contempt for Jane in relation to his own feelings of helplessness; feelings which his challenge had evoked in Jane, and which he felt repelled by for want of having resolved them in himself. The capture in this instance is of Jim's sense of helplessness which has been isolated from his conscious identity, and was therefore unavailable as a means of understanding another's vulnerability. Appeals for assistance from another are experienced as a burden and are rejected with contempt, to the point where even a friendly gesture (Jane's bringing fresh fruit to his party) is felt to be intrusive.

One might question the degree to which this example validates the thesis of this text. Jim's realization that his ambivalence toward Jane was grounded in his contempt for her weakness could have been due to some other process. Based upon the example, one would more readily claim that the very act of talking about how he feels brought Jim to a closer awareness of what his feelings mean. A way must therefore be found to explain how merely talking could have such an insightful effect.

In this example the analyst helps Jim to dereify areas of blocked awareness in a variety of ways:

— By focusing Jim's attention upon a specific setting in which contempt for Jane arose, so that the setting might be used to re-evoke and reflectively clarify the nature of this experience.
— By helping Jim to focus upon and stay with what he felt.
— By reflecting back a particular content so that Jim might expand upon the experience ("That she could make some kind of claim on you?").
— By relating the understanding Jim is elaborating in reflective awareness to a related context ("Similar to how you feel in the relationship?").
— By reframing a discovery in relation to a theme that has been uncovered in the work so as to broaden the scope of what has been reflectively elaborated ("If you don't hate her, you'll have to take care of her.").

It should be noted that, just as the indices of literal versus metaphorical language use are specified and observable, each of these functions performed by the analyst is subject to observation as well (e.g., Rice and Greenberg 1984). Agreement may be arrived at among observers as to what constitutes an act of focusing Jim's attention; or of helping him stay with what he felt; or of reflecting back a content, or of relating one meaning context to another. Once agreement of this kind has been reached, it becomes possible to determine whether or not interventions of the type described above lead to the kind of discovery reported by Jim. In other words, the explanation proposed in this book as to how we discover new meaning, permits one to assert what *should* take place in a successful analysis, and in a way that may be observed and challenged.

By this view, a psychotherapeutic inquiry relies upon the therapist's ability to support reflection on the part of the patient. The interpretive process may therefore support the reflective awareness that comes of contrasting and comparing different meanings. To fulfill this function, the therapist proceeds along two dimensions: a vertical dimension whereby blocked or disowned areas of meaning are identified; and a lateral dimension whereby the identified meanings are then elaborated in relation to other meanings. In the sample provided from Jim's analysis, the vertical challenge is initiated by Jim himself who notes that he had no reason for feeling angry at Jane. He then goes on to clarify the suppressed content

—that it pertains to feeling angry *and* guilty—which is reflected back by the analyst as a sense of feeling burdened. The analyst then relates the contempt to *hatred* over feeling burdened. This triggers the memory of the gangling adolescent which enables Jim to uncover how his own helpless feelings had been blocked by the contempt.

In other words, each intervention described above attempts to promote a lateral form of reciprocal differentiation (i.e., of the patient's experiences in relation to each other). Jim's anger at Jane first has to be summoned in relation to the setting where he experienced contempt, so that it might evoke and be differentiated in relation to his guilt ("I didn't want to owe her for it."). Jim's guilt in turn must be differentiated in relation to his discovery of feeling burdened ("I'll have to forever take care of her."). Only when he has acknowledged and separated out the irrational anger from the guilt could Jim come to the realization that his responsibility-resentment toward Jane masked his own feelings of helplessness and inadequacy.

Once they emerge, these new meanings will be poorly differentiated and tenuously related to the more familiar aspects of the self. They must be "brought up." In the example of Jim described above, Jim's guilt-contempt had remained relatively primitive in its lack of differentiation. Hence his inability to own feelings of helplessness or to feel compassion for his partner. To accept his own helplessness, and to empathize with his partner, Jim needed to discover that it was possible to identify with his partner (as had not been possible with his father) without having to assume her pain as personal burden.

To bring up these newly discovered self aspects—the ability to feel helpless, and to empathize without feeling burdened—Jim had to rely upon the reflective procedures that were promoted by his psychotherapy. In this manner, feelings of helplessness were found to underlie a host of reified states, such as his jealousy of a colleague, his possessiveness of a friend, and so on. For example, he would at times express a sense of withdrawal. We would then search for the setting in which the withdrawal occurred; e.g., a work setting in which he suddenly felt self-conscious, or an exchange with a friend which caused him to "close off." The withdrawal could then be analyzed in terms of the event which occasioned it. In this manner, Jim came to discover a number of unsuspected areas of literal meaning, as in the self-recrimination he experienced in failing to achieve an illusory and poorly defined ideal in his work; or the threat of betrayal in deepening involvements. The ability to relate a state of withdrawal to the setting which prompts it is of significant value in a psychotherapy, since it enables the patient to recover the context normally lost to awareness. For example, the unacknowledged belief that his work must match some illusory ideal was met again and again within the settings of Jim's writing. Confronting this belief enabled Jim to give more consideration to what he could in fact expect of himself, and to learn how to master the withdrawn-depressed states normally prompted by his writing. In our work together, Jim came to appreciate the act of reflection as a critical source of discovery. As a result, he was able to recover much of the relational texture of meaning lost to the incursion of language.

8.
THE LITERAL/METAPHORICAL DIMENSION OF THE SELF

THE SELF AS METAPHOR

Unless the role of language is shown to make a critical difference in our view of personality development, the thesis of this text will not be meaningful to practitioners in the field. Those of a psychoanalytic persuasion, for example, will wonder how one could have a personality theory without invoking biological needs, or the inevitable conflict that arises between the biological and the social. Or how one could imagine a personality without the family drama of the oedipus triangle?

From the perspective of this book, personality development depends upon the adoption of a language in two critical ways. First, in literalizing our reality, language provides us with a self-conscious identity we could not otherwise have. Because of language, we may think *about* the self as a distinct entity that is independent of the settings in which it participates. The named self is not just something one can point to. It has a reified sense of having value and entitlements. Gradually, the verbal self is held responsible for what we do; i.e., is seen as worthy of praise and blame. The self's reified sense of worth and need for acceptance generates a special kind of vulnerability in people. We are *hurt* by the rejection, disdain, and contempt cf others. We *thrive* upon the acceptance and love of our caretakers. At times, we indulge in an exaggerated sense of our own importance, or plummet to the despairing futility of a sense of utter worthlessness. We may become demanding, clinging, resentful, and relentlessly possessive. We may attribute qualities to others which they scarcely possess, or fail to notice the importance of a loved one until they are absent, or gone. All of these qualities—the sense of our value and entitlements, of our responsibilities, of our need for acceptance and love; our vulnerability to psychic pain, grandiosity, and depression; our demanding possessiveness and overvaluation of the other; our failure to note the other's emotional importance to us—all depend (in some measure) upon having a language with which to define the self. That is, they all depend upon our ability (having defined the self with words) to literalize the self as a thing, and to then (for example) feel the need to belong as being a function of reified tokens of acceptance. If children may be mortified by a verbal rebuke, it is because hearing "you're bad!" stands for a literal loss of acceptance and worth.

In what follows, this identification of the self (with language) as a literal thing (i.e., that can be possessed or rejected by others, praised or blamed, and feels entitled to recognition) is referred to as the self's *narcissistic core*. It is referred to as a core, because it is assumed to be the basis for all that follows. By way of analogy, in the Stanley Kubric film *2001, A Space Odyssey*, a computer named Hal has to be unplugged because it has taken control of the spaceship it is supposed to service. Once unplugged, Hal progresses through a series of language stages which the computer had mastered on its way to acquiring an identity of its own. At the very last stage, which corresponds to the stage it had to first establish to build its identity, Hal recites the children's verse "Mary had a little lamb" in a halting childlike tone. In a similar vein, the narcissistic core is seen here as the first stage in the child's socialization. This is not to say that in the absence of language, we would fail to become socialized. Our capacity to bond with a caretaker, to establish dependent ties, and to form into groups are (as with our animal brethren) built into our biological make-up. Only with language, however, do we literalize these features as parts of the self's conscious definition; i.e., as something the individual may believe *about* the self. Other animals do not question their belonging, or feel responsible for their failures; i.e., they lack a self-conscious self to which to attribute these aspects. Nor do they literalize these qualities as being capable of possession or loss.

Were this all that the adoption of language does, we would scarcely have survived as a species. The narcissistic core is seen here to be narcissistic in the traditional sense; i.e., it accounts for those qualities that can make our children quite unbearable, in their moments of demanding self-centeredness. The literalization of our reality is not just something we all have to live through on our way to adulthood. It is also a prescription for enmity and strife. Literalized realities give birth to border wars and genocide. They are essential to the pretentious grandiosity and greed that lead individuals and groups to strive for ascendance and control over their neighbors. Narcissism also plays a part in the emergence of passion, and of creative discovery. The point being that our survival as a species must (by this view) be attributed to the fact that narcissism alone does not make a person. Language also brings to our development a quality that counters the narcissistic trend described above. As noted in chapter 7, language also introduces the ability to reverse the literal meanings it causes. That is, the holding function of language allows us to deliteralize meaning in the act of reflection.

The narcissistic core does not, in other words, disappear. It remains as a core feature of the personality, but gradually learns to co-exist with the reflective self, in a way that allows each of us to acknowledge and work through the inevitable distortions which come of having adopted a language. That is, the person is understood in terms of how she or he realizes meaning; and of how the self is at all times a function of the ways in which individuals define themselves in terms of their beliefs (which does not imply that there need be only one set of beliefs, or that these beliefs are consciously known). The self is therefore seen as a (normally implicit) system of beliefs that emerges with the assimilation of a language, concerning who we believe we are, and what we believe we need in order to be who we are. These beliefs in turn are best understood (by this view) in terms of the degree to which they have evolved out of the original matrix of the narcissistic core; i.e., the degree to which they are *literal* or *metaphorical*.

The Freudian approach to personality is described as psychodynamic. It conceives of each person as existing within an ongoing development, grounded in biological need. The fuel for this dynamic comes from the conflicts that arise as the individual attempts to integrate opposing biological needs, as well as the social demands of our cultural milieu. In this text, the emphasis shifts from biology to meaning. The conflicts relating to biological need and societal demand are understood in relation to the way in which we *represent* that need or demand. The questions one would ask of a person's development would still pertain to how well they have managed to integrate their personal needs with societal demands, but this would not be the most basic question to ask. More basic still would be the question of how well a person has realized the metaphorical dimension of the self. Physical needs and demands could not (short of being reified) have a direct impact on the self, insofar as the self is not a physical entity. Needs and demands may only impact upon the self as a system of representations. It is the vicissitudes of these representations, i.e., the degree to which they affect the self's functioning as meanings, that will be considered in this section.

When Whitehead speaks of the "souls of men" as the "gift of language to mankind," how is one to understand the meaning of "soul"? Many today would likely agree with Gilbert Ryle's view of the notion of a soul as a "category mistake"; i.e., as manifesting our mistaken tendency to grant independent status to some "ghost in the machine." For Ryle, to speak of a soul is to literalize the content of the mind in terms of some inappropriate category. Yet, if the notion of a soul might be taken literally, it might also (as metaphor) be said to address aspects of human functioning which should somehow find acknowledgment in our understanding.

The problem, however, is that if you try to include what's important in your account, you invite a good deal of ambiguity. For example, while (by Whitehead's [1938] account) "body and soul are inescapable elements of our being, each with the full reality of our immediate self . . ." he goes on to state that "neither body nor soul possess the sharp observational definition which at first sight we attribute to them." Thus, while a "claim to an enduring self-identity is our self-assertive personal identity" (161), we have as yet failed to ground these terms in a way that might promote consensual agreement. Yet this absence of observational definition should not (Whitehead goes on to say) cause us to ignore the "complex data from which philosophical speculation has to account for in a system rendering the whole understandable" (ibid., 162).

As an example of the kind of factors which need to be considered in any responsible account of our nature, Whitehead offers the following "remarkable characteristic"; that while in one sense the "world (we experience) is in the soul," one may also claim that "the soul itself is one of the components within the world." This observation is then used by Whitehead to support what he refers to as the "doctrine of mutual immanence," whereby "each happening is a factor in the nature of every other happening." This doctrine sounds very much like the holism (described in chapter 2 of this book) proposed more recently by Putnam and Quine. Whitehead, however, contributes his distinctly personal flavor to this concept, as might be grasped in the following quote—which may bring to mind the writings of the mystic Nicholas of Cusa, and the visionary Jean Jacques Rousseau; writings which had the prescience and temerity to point to new horizons in our definition of man:

> We are in the world and the world is in us. Our immediate occasion is in the society of occasions forming the soul, and our soul is in our present occasion. The body is ours, and we are an activity within our body. This fact of observation, vague but imperative, is the foundation of the connexity of the world, and of the transmission of its types of order. (ibid., 165)

For Whitehead, "Philosophy is akin to poetry," in that both seek "to maintain an active novelty of fundamental ideas illuminating the social system" (ibid., 174). In keeping with this aim, and with Whitehead's view that "the soul is the gift from language to mankind" firmly in mind, I will now presume to interpret this proposition in terms of the discussion of language provided by this essay. From the perspective of this text, Whitehead's soul may be understood as the metaphor of the self permitted by language. More specifically, the self as metaphor arises as a function of the literal and metaphorical aspects of meaning introduced by language. This dual (literal and metaphorical) aspect of the self not only accounts for the "remarkable characteristic" alluded to by Whitehead (that the world is in the soul, i.e., metaphorically, while the soul is in the world, i.e., literally); it also accounts for the "immanent", and by implication the created reality we must continuously realize, in terms of the ongoing synthesis we forge between the nonverbal and the verbal. More to the point of this essay, it is the metaphorical dimension of man and womankind that Freud and his followers omitted in their biological metaphor of the mind. Freud missed this dimension, insofar as he was led (in his metapsychology) to collapse the metaphorical into the literal; i.e. to portray representations as if they were physical things.

Following Whitehead, one needs to account for the "complex data" that has yet to be taken account of in our academic perspectives on the mind. What better candidate than a metaphor of the self that explains the self as a metaphor? The fact that metaphors collapse, as when the metaphorical turns literal, or expand, as when the discovery of novel relations opens and deepens our grasp of meaning, conforms to at least some of the human complexity we should seek to account for. The notion of the self as metaphor also answers to the existence of psychic *pain,* in terms of the anxiety that comes of not being able to make sense of one's world, or the depression (as internal collapse) that comes of having lost any hope of doing so. In sum, the self as metaphor offers as ultimate concern, *not* the homeostatic regulation of the self proposed by mainstream psychoanalysis, but the self's ability to generate meaning.

The notion of the self as metaphor also answers to the responsibility of each individual (within the fairly narrow limits of reflection) to generate meaning in a way that respects the physical and social constraints of our being; i.e., to shun the lie, and to face the pain of unresolved conflict. That is, only in facing the conflicts that inevitably arise when the literal reality of our childhood confronts the realities of adult responsibilities, might we discover the seeds of our renewal. In a similar vein, the metaphor of the self as a process of symbolic realization answers to the extremes we are capable of as human beings. The ideological zealot who leaves a trail of carnage and destruction in his or her wake, for example, has reified the constraints of meaning as a province of personal choice and privilege. A similar presumption is at the heart of the systematized delusion of the paranoid personality, who has sacrificed objective reality to the reified delusions of self-reference. What should be emphasized (as will be done in detail shortly) is that our potential for these conditions must not be viewed as isolated aberrations, but as aspects of the human condition we acquire in receiving the Trojan gift of language. The obverse of these reified presumptions is found in the equally human quality of humility; i.e., the ability to embrace these constraints as our principle source of renewal, discovery, and growth.

Finally, the self as metaphor contributes to our understanding of pathology and creativity. It is to the self as a system of self-definition that one must look, if one is to appreciate the vicissitudes that arise in negotiating the literal way station we adopt with language. The self as metaphor is grounded in the literal prototypes of our narcissistic core, yet extends beyond itself via its metaphorical dimension, to whatever heights the current zeitgeist permits. As metaphor, this notion should be pursued to its ultimate implications (as the mainstream analysts have had the courage to do with their metaphor); i.e., one should show (literally!) how we come by it, how we might lose it, and how it functions. The elaboration which follows will therefore address four questions which are ignored by the Freudian metaphor (in its neglect of the metaphorical dimension of the self). How does the individual develop a narcissistic core? How do sociocultural patterns become integrated within the self? What is motivation (when not reified as a biological need)? And, what is a conscience (when not reified as an agency of the mind)?

THE NARCISSISTIC CORE AS LITERAL DEFINITION OF THE SELF

In discussing the issue of distortion in chapter 3, mainstream theory was criticized on the grounds that it fails to consider the role of language in the distortion of meaning; and because its biological metaphor neglects important dimensions of our human condition. A more telling criticism of mainstream psychoanalysis, however, is that if the position I have outlined here is correct, the mainstream has seriously misled us as to the basic nature of the human personality. I will use the term *personality* to refer to a person's characteristic way of being—behaviorally, cognitively, and emotionally—which presumably develops out of the integration of one's biological endowment with the socialization of one's cultural milieu.

For the mainstream, the foundation upon which the personality arises is instinctual. That is, while the so-called narcissism of the individual emerges in the course of development in relation to what Winnicott described as a "good enough environment" (i.e., a loving mother), the foundations of the self are presumed to be instinctual in nature, even though its forms of expression, and the degree to which it survives, are a function of experience. From the perspective of this essay, the narcissistic core of the individual could not be instinctual, for the simple reason that it could not arise without language! That is, those features assumed to be at the core of what it means to have a self—the ability to care about one's self, to hope in the future, to feel entitled to love and acceptance, to fear rejection—none of these core issues that are described by mainstream psychoanalysts as being grounded in instinctual narcissism, could exist without language.

The reason I make this claim about the self's narcissistic core pertains to Mead's thesis about language. For Mead (and for this text), a person does not have a reflexive identity until it arises with language. That is, a person may not preverbally think of him or herself as being a certain way, or as expecting things from others, or as having value or entitlements, or as being rejectable under certain circumstances. This is emphatically *not* to say that preverbal children don't have expectations and fears. Rather, it is to say that they don't think of themselves as having expectations and fears, because without language, they cannot think about themselves! Therefore, all of those needs ascribed to infants under the rubric of narcissism—the need to feel valued, to have worth, to receive love—cannot really exist as a basis for behavior in the reflexive sense (as being a belief one has *about* the self) until language establishes a reflexive self.

Does the definition of narcissism proposed here conform with the mainstream psychoanalytic definition? Freud used the term *narcissism* to refer to an investment of libido in (i.e., the cathexis of) aspects of the self as opposed to external objects. For Freud, an individual who became fixated at this stage of development was considered to be inappropriate for an analysis, as he or she would not be capable of establishing a transference with the analyst; i.e., the libido that should be available for the projection of early involvements onto the analyst, is presumed to be tied up in the self.

But what can it mean to invest the self with libido? Is this not a reified attempt on the part of the mainstream analyst to explain a development in the self that has to do with meaning rather than physical energy? When one looks to how the term is used by mainstream analysts today, the notion of narcissism as "libido invested in the self" is clearly seen to be a metaphor; i.e., it offers an analogy of energy distributions in order to explain how the self becomes reflexive. In their use of this term, however, the mainstream analysts are clearly referring to a person's self regard; i.e., to his or her belief about his or her self-worth. This meaning is brought out in the use of terms such as *narcissistic object choice,* where a loved one is chosen because of his or her similarity to one's self. To make such a choice, one must first have the belief that being like one's self is of value. The term *narcissistic hurt,* used to describe a blow to one's self esteem, only makes sense if the blow relates to one's *belief* about how one *should* be treated. The notion of *narcissistic supplies,* which refers to the amount of feedback one is receiving as to one's worth, only makes sense if one has a belief that one's value depends upon other people's approval. In each of these instances, a reflective sense of self is necessary, since each has to do with the kind of self one takes oneself (or wishes oneself) to be.

A point in need of clarification is that, given the assumption that a belief about the self requires language, one must distinguish between *self beliefs,* and *self modes.* Let us assume that a child brought up in a family that values self-reliance (conceived of here as a behavior mode), will adopt this mode, and will feel accepted as a result. The same could be said of a child whose family values a dependent mode of relating. In neither case need the mode be consciously known (though it may become so with language). These behavior modes will relate to how one feels about one's self, insofar as they can be more or less successful, but they cannot, in their nonverbal form, be sources of implicitly or consciously *valuing* the self; i.e., they may not yet (preverbally) be related to the objective self of language which gives us some*thing* to value.

By this view, we (as narcissists) do not suffer from an arrested state of instinctual development. Rather, we develop beliefs about the self that are not grounded in behavior modes which we can feel responsible for. For example, a person who believes he is self-reliant, when his preferred and most developed mode is in fact geared to dependent manipulation, is not only operating on a false belief. Because the mode he uses has no bearing upon the belief he has, he lacks any means of correcting this misconception about himself. The deficit is not in the development of what the mainstream refer to as an "ego instinct" for self-preservation. Rather, it is in the lack of a relationship between characteristic behavior modes, and the person's *beliefs* about him or herself.

As described in chapter 6, one's beliefs about reality and the self may be captured. That is, they may become frozen at an early stage in their development, because they lack a functional ground, or because they have been trapped by a strong emotion. When for example, a sense of value may only be felt if one is being supported and praised by another, no amount of self-preserving behavior will feel as good as praise or support. With the adoption of a language, we may therefore develop beliefs which have little bearing upon who we "really are," though we gradually *become* those beliefs. That is, the beliefs children adopt are based, not upon what a child is told about the self, but upon the literal understanding the child must suffer through in integrating language with what is known nonverbally.

For example, the commonly encountered belief that "If Mommy loves you, you're good; if Mommy doesn't love you, you're bad!" sounds like a fairly direct transcription of what the child is being told by a caretaker. What may be missed in this assumption however, is the literal nature of this definition. That is, the definition accords with the way language works for children, in that the child's very identity is taken to result from mother's love. In a similar vein, the notion that "When things go bad, I must be bad!" or "Because I'm good, I deserve what I want!" are also literalized responses in which the child confuses the definitions of language with who and what he really is.

One conclusion which may be drawn from this discussion is that a pervasive misunderstanding exists among mainstream psychoanalysts concerning the genesis of the infant's reflective sense of self, insofar as they have attributed functions to the preverbal infant that could only arise with language. For example, psychoanalytic authors presume (as did Piaget) that the human infant initially lacks a sense of differentiation from the mother, and therefore exists in a state of symbiosis, or undifferentiated dependence. As noted in the Appendix such a state has been ruled out by our most recent infant observations (Stern 1985). An infant who is functionally related to its milieu from the start could not be vulnerable to this kind of confusion. The assumption, however, continues to prevail among the mainstream, and the task of their theory then becomes one of explaining how a narcissistic self could emerge out of this symbiotic state.

Margaret Mahler was one of the more prominent proponents of this initial symbiotic phase in which the infant is said to confuse its own boundaries with those of its mother. As described by Mahler, Pine and Bergmann (1975), "The essential feature of symbiosis is hallucinatory or delusional somatopsychic omnipotent fusion with the representation of the mother and, in particular, the delusion of a common boundary between the physically separate individuals" (45). The problem with this assumption is that for the infant to fuse its boundaries with those of its mother, it would have to have achieved a sense of itself as existing independently of its mother. Otherwise, the infant could not distinguish reflectively between itself, and the not self delineated by its boundaries. That is, the infant would have to develop a reflective sense of being different from mother, in order to then confuse itself with mother. Only when the infant has developed a reflective sense of self might it confuse its boundaries with those of mother. And only with language will the infant have a capacity for this kind of confusion. The argument here is identical to the one developed in chapter 1, in response to Piaget's notion of egocentrism (which is similar to Mahler's notion of symbiosis). Both authors (by this view) are attributing abilities to the preverbal child that could only arise with language.

In a slightly different vein, Fairbairn (1952), has promoted the notion that infants internalize and then split off bad aspects of the self. For Fairbairn, this internalizing and splitting is the infant's only means of coping with destructive experiences. The strategy is akin to that of a nation which systematically annexes troublesome neighbors so as to subdue them. The problem with this intrapsychic annexation, however, is that this defense results in the accumulation of "bad internal objects" which must then in some way be exorcised:

> It is to the realm of these bad objects . . . that the ultimate origin of all psychopathological developments is to be traced, for it may be said of all psychoneurosis and psychotic patients that, if a True Mass is being celebrated in the chancel, a Black Mass is being celebrated in the crypt. It becomes evident, accordingly, that the psychotherapist is the true successor to the exorcist, and that he is concerned, not only with the "forgiveness of sins," but also with the "casting out of devils. (70)

Pattison (1984) quotes this passage as an example of how (in the object relations theory inaugurated by Fairbairn) the problem of evil is reduced to a therapeutic problem, not a moral issue; i.e., human values are persistently defined as health values. What I would underscore is the fact that although the process of splitting and internalization proposed by Fairbairn is said to occur in the preverbal child, it in fact would require the presence of language to occur as he describes. For an object (e.g., a primitive representation of a parent) to exist internally, it would have to exist independently of the setting of its occurrence as a separate entity. That is, it would have to take up residence in the child, where it may (under its various guises) frustrate, humiliate, or sadistically abuse the self whenever the self exhibits the kind of behavior that evoked these reactions in the real parent. In this manner, the judgments he or she must suffer are attributable to the internal bad objects. But these judgements are nonetheless reflections upon the self, and could not occur without language.

Winnicott (1965) has described how the "good enough mother" must foster the illusion that the preverbal infant is creating a world over which it has full control. This illusion of control is considered to be a prerequisite for the emergence of the narcissistic self. For the infant to experience what Winnicott describes as an "illusion of omnipotence," the infant would have to be capable of distorting its self-concept. This in turn would not be possible without a self-concept subject to distortion, which could only arise with language. Winnicott and his colleagues (I believe) have consistently confused the notion of a *sense* of self (which is taken here as inherent to our functioning) and the reflective sense of self that arises with language. Given our current grasp of infant functioning described in Stern (1985), the infant is indeed creating a world, so that the infant's realization is hardly illusory. Only with the reflective ability that arises with language, however, might the individual start to have illusions about its world.

Kohut (1971) holds that the infant discovers a self through the reflection or empathic mirroring of the adult. A grandiose self is born of mirroring, and an idealized self is born of the infant's merger with an idealized parent image. Together, these poles of the self establish a dynamic between self-directed and other-directed sources of value. Just what occurs in the course of these processes of mirroring and merging is never specified. These terms may therefore be described as the reified limits of Kohut's discourse, as they presume what they would explain, and constitute the ground for all that follows. The point being that, as with Winnicott, Kohut posits grandiosity as necessary to the emergence of the self. From the perspective of this essay, this is correct in one sense, in that the reified self born of language is grandiose as a function of its literal grasp of reality. That is, grandiosity and idealization relate to the reification introduced by language, when it is placed in the service of over-investing value in someone who represents what one would like to be; or when one finds reasons to invest that value in the self. To attribute an exaggerated importance to the self or to others, one must objectify the self as having an independent, specifiable identity. Language (as has been frequently noted in this text) is necessary for this objectification of the self to occur.

Before moving on, one might ask what becomes of the narcissistic core introduced by language? Does it remain like a protected pit at the core of the personality? Are there provisions for its evolution and growth? What is assumed in this text is in keeping with what a mainstream analyst would probably say concerning the optimal conditions for the self's development. In a climate of acceptance, understanding and support, these primitive beliefs may come to be challenged, and to evolve into more adaptive expectations. Under other conditions, however, they may go underground, so to speak, and continue dictating the shape of the person's reality, well into his or her maturity, without undergoing change.

THE EFFECT OF SOCIOCULTURAL PATTERNS ON INDIVIDUAL DEVELOPMENT

Dare (1983) notes that one must acknowledge a change in the concerns of psychoanalytic authors (in the United States and England) with the advent of self and object relations theorists of the 1950s and sixties. Today, the focus may clearly be seen as having shifted from the conflicts of biological need, to the infants' pressure to remain close to a caretaker, and to enact specific relational needs. Among the English-speaking mainstream at least, the thrust of interest is more toward an appreciation of the human qualities of attachment and dependence, and less toward the impingements of biological drives. While this shift may well be "the outcome of one hundred years of psychotherapeutic practice," as Dare claims, it has not, as yet, resulted in a significant shift in the theoretical underpinnings which support the practice. That is, there continues to be no provision (in the theory) for how social patterns and cultural influences contribute to the structure of the mind, other than the antiquated (and today largely ignored) drive theory.

With the important innovations of ego psychology in the 1950s and sixties the mainstream perspective shifted toward more of a concern for how individuals come to integrate the biological with the social. This concern is shared by this essay. Both positions view the biological self's integrity as being guaranteed, so to speak, by its biological inheritance, since that inheritance insures our ecological fit to our milieu. However, the demands of our social milieu (for the mainstream), and the incursion of language (for this essay) skew this adaptation in distinctly different ways, depending upon which position you adopt. For the mainstream, the demands of our social milieu require that we defend against (and learn to compensate for) the imperatives of instinctual drive. In the individual's development toward what Mahler describes as "separation-individuation," the individual must either creatively integrate instinctual impulses with societal demands, or succumb to them as limitations.

Notice that in this last description I have not alluded to how frustration transforms biological lust into creative energy, or how the defensive strategies of displacement and sublimation enable the child to redirect biological needs into cultural concerns. Most of the mainstream of today no longer use these energy terms. In applying Mahler's notion of "separation-individuation," for example, you don't need to invoke the mind's structure, as the meaning you wish to convey is more readily grasped in terms of a description of the child's behavior. If you were to ask one of today's mainstream analysts how the ability to compensate for social restrictions arises, the response you would get would be in terms of what he or she presumes are the optimal conditions for raising a child; it will not (in my experience at least) be in terms of how the child represents his or her reality, or how these events are reflected by the structure of the mind. While this development has had a laudatory effect upon the way mainstream authors write (it now sounds more like they are writing about people!), this has been at the expense of examining the basis for what one claims. There is no longer any attempt to explain how the social becomes an intrapsychic part of the self, beyond specifying the conditions thought to promote this integration. The omission is a serious one, as it suggests an approach which is more characteristic of religious belief than of scientific interest.

From the perspective of this essay, language is the medium whereby sociocultural patterns are adopted by the child. By this view, adopting a language is tantamount to adopting an entire sociohistorical perspective on how human beings communicate. The implicit assumptions which underlie our ability to use language (i.e., to impose definitions on our reality) constitute a perspective on how we communicate that distills millions of years of practical use. Thus, once a language is adopted, one has a view of human communication that transcends individual characteristics. The prototypical meanings we establish with language are therefore shared by all who speak the language. In addition, language greatly facilitates the task of education, insofar as the categories of language are readily captured for the purposes of indoctrinating the child.

The question might still be asked, why don't more of our toddlers rebel against this imposition? Granted, childhood autism may in some instances be a refusal to accept language. However, the possibility that some children refuse language out of defiance is difficult to document, and therefore rarely raised as an explanation. Nonetheless, the fact that children usually adopt language does not explain *why* they do so. Explanations which invoke imitation, or conditioning, or other forms of social reinforcement are justly criticized by the mainstream as superficial. They neglect the profound nature of the change taking place. Since these changes could not occur without sacrificing to some extent, the deeper needs of our biological nature, why do toddlers so readily assent to such an imposition?

From the perspective of this essay, the mainstream analysts are quite correct in questioning the child's willingness to eventually constrain aggressive or sexual behavior; or to accept the ethic of toilet training; or to refrain from overt manifestations of selfishness and greed; or to willingly succumb to the unrelenting pressure to conform. Something more must be involved than the pleasures of imitation or reinforcement. There must be some compelling reason to curtail one's functioning in ways that are not always compensated for. But the reason need not by this view be due to what is frequently invoked by the mainstream: our fear of biological impulses. In their development, children do not simply curtail these impulses; they do so in the course of adopting a cultural frame of reference. One should therefore look to this frame of reference (it would seem), and not simply to the impulses it comes to constrain, in order to understand why our toddlers routinely make this sacrifice. From the perspective being developed here concerning the metaphorical dimension of the self, the reason one must look to for this transformation of the individual, is the *literal self* of childhood.

The childhood self (as noted above) takes itself literally, in that it *is* what one can *say* it is. This literal self is unstable; it readily collapses (i.e., loses its metaphorical dimension which takes a while to become established in any reliable way). It is therefore vastly dependent upon others for the reassurance it needs to negotiate these falls, and to regain its shape (as it does when it may feel a part of things). One might be tempted to say (following Winnicott) that it is the illusory base upon which the childhood self rests its integrity that constitutes its vulnerability. Since the child initially lacks the reflective ability to resolve its anxieties and fears, he or she is often dependent upon the acceptance and support of a caretaker to maintain a viable sense of self. Any sense of being a viable concern *must* be illusory, insofar as the child lacks most of the abilities it would need to survive on its own. Yet, were one to make this assumption, one would be committing the same error attributed to the mainstream. That is, if the self is a *representation,* then the self's vulnerability may not be understood in relation to the circumstances of its development per se; it may only be understood in relation to how these circumstances *are perceived, representationally,* by the child!

The child's literal beliefs about the self must be appreciated (by this view) as a kind of ideological capture. That is, a child who accedes to the parental imposition of language has no way of knowing what is really in store, until it is too late to do anything about it! Children adopt these broadly general notions about the self because, having fallen for the seductive appeal of language, they suddenly have no choice. Nor are children in a position to realize that these definitions of the self have less to do with who they genuinely are, than with quasi magical beliefs about the self that result from the literalization of meaning with language. For example, at the stage of early language assimilation, any threat to a child's literal need for acceptance strikes terror in the heart of that child. Could this explain the child's willingness to conform, at the expense of more basic needs? A need to conform in order to gain acceptance could not be the only reason for the sacrifices described above. A cared-for child is not always operating under this dire threat. Rather, the main reason the child adopts the constraints of society, by this view, is that he or she comes to believe that they are in fact the kind of person they are portrayed as by their caretakers. This in effect, is the notion proposed by Cooley, Veblen, and Sullivan, that the self reflects the appraisal of others. What is added to this notion here, is that children do not reflect, so much as reify these appraisals, in the form of a literal template. Templates are used in woodwork to test the accuracy of a form against a metal prototype. The child's template of the self is similar, in that it establishes a basis for what matters. Hence, the explanation that it is because of the metaphorical nature of the self as representation that children come to so literally believe that they are what they are told they are, and thereby come to sacrifice much of their biological nature to conformity. As noted earlier, this process (fortunately!) does not quite succeed, insofar as much of who we are continues unconsciously as the nonverbal part of our being. We are therefore protected (for a while at least) by the bifurcation language introduces into the self, until that day comes when the self's integrity in adulthood starts to require a more coherent sense of integration.

One may not deny the paramount role parents play in the pressure to conform. The child who cannot adopt the solutions provided by his or her culture will be relegated to the marginal position of the outcast, or to the institutional world society has set aside for the deviant and the misfit. A child's inability to adopt these solutions must surely strike terror in the heart of the parent if not the child! Thus, everything conspires to have children adopt the conventional perspectives of our social milieu. Not only is it built into the language we use to define ourselves; it is an inevitable result of the child's literal approach to what he or she is told. Granted, many of our children are quick to learn defiance, and to rebel against the pressures to conform. But the defiance and rebellion of this stage are just as literal in what they presume, and may not be divorced from the conformity they challenge. The only counter to this adaptation (short of the rebellious acting-out just described) is to challenge these beliefs in the act of reflection; a possibility that only arises during what Piaget refers to as the stage of "formal operations," in adolescence. Prior to that time, the limits set by a parent are an essential feature of the child's growth. In sum, one might not by this view appreciate the process of socialization, without grasping how language literalizes the self. Only when we question the beliefs we define ourselves by—when we start having a conscience—do we begin to establish the ability to counter the otherwise irresistible forces that impose conformity on our lives.

WHAT IS A MOTIVE?

Where would the mainstream analyst be without the notion of a motive? The *raison d'être* of psychoanalysis, it would seem, is that it alerts us to unconscious motives. Why else would we want to be analyzed, but to discover what these hidden motives are, so that they might be dealt with more rationally? In this text however, the mainstream explanation of what a motive is, is taken to be a reified explanation of our behavior. That is, the mainstream notion of a motive objectifies the self and its object as independent entities acting on, rather than in relation to, each other. Motives are treated like physical things impacting on other physical things. To claim that a sexual impulse (as motive) *causes* one's behavior, for example, is to neglect the conditions under which an act is realized; i.e., conditions which include how that impulse is *interpreted* by the person who has it.

This last point is nicely illustrated by Dretske (1988), in his example of why beliefs and motives must exist within a network of meanings:

> A spy, working alone in the field, may have a certain information-gathering function. But as *more* spies are deployed, and their information gathering activities start to overlap and become interdependent, the responsibilities of each may change.
>
> This so-called holistic character of belief has been much discussed and debated in recent philosophy. The present view of belief ... not only implies that beliefs *have* this holistic character, it reveals *why* they have it. As beliefs become integrated into more tightly structured cognitive systems, their indicator functions become more interdependent. (150)

From this perspective of this book a particular act and its motive may not be understood apart from the conditions that prompt our behavior. These conditions in turn must be understood in terms of the beliefs that inform our "indicator functions," by helping us to identify what will satisfy a particular need. Furthermore, motives, by this view, do not exist in the abstract. Wanting and needing are always related to some *thing* one wants and needs. Values as well, must be attached to what is valued, be it an object, an accolade, or a wish to act with integrity. One may not therefore presume to know a person's motive, without carefully considering the context in which it arises. Nor might a motive be considered in the absence of the meaning it has for the individual who has it. By this view, while not all motives are conscious (i.e., available to reflective awareness), all are related to the way in which the individual who has them defines him or herself. The reason for claiming this last point, is that a motive (for this essay) constitutes a belief about the self and its possibilities. The fact that these beliefs are mostly unconscious is a discovery that is basic to the entire psychoanalytic enterprise. What must be reintroduced to this discovery is Freud's original notion that what we repress is an idea. That is, we need to recover Freud's first insight that motives express *beliefs* we have *about* ourselves. A person who is motivated by a desire for sex, or money, or power, is expressing the *belief* that attaining these goals will be gratifying; i.e., it will provide pleasure, or it will enhance the self. Less conscious motives would be the beliefs that one must please one's parent figures at all cost, that one is entitled to praise and acknowledgement, or that to get what you want, you have to be *good*. The point being that these motives are without exception related to what these desires mean to us, not to biological energy. Were this not so, an individual's motives need not be characterized in terms of the conflicts, denials, splits, or confabulations with which he or she defines him or herself, as may clearly be seen in any description of a psychoanalysis. Nowhere else in our lives do the basic problems of the self enter so clearly into what we do, than in the expression of our motives.

The biological contribution to what is to become a motive is in one regard like any other event impinging upon our sense receptors. As information, it awakens the mind's ability to frame information within a context that is meaningful for the self. In the case of motives however, the information pertains to what the individual believes the self is entitled to, wants, or should avoid. To contribute to a motive, therefore, a biological need must be interpreted from the context of what is referred to here as the individual's narcissistic core. For example when an individual's sexuality starts to mature, some adolescents may completely ignore the changes taking place to the point of delaying their appearance. For the mainstream analyst, this demonstrates how biological urges are capable of being repressed. From the perspective of this essay, however, this repression must in turn be related to the definitions available for identifying these changes within the body. When not acknowledged, they are presumably too discordant with the self's prevailing definitions to be accepted within the main body of reflexively known beliefs. The meaning pertaining to these changes is therefore captured under the aegis of repulsion, fear, or self-righteous denial, and cannot be integrated with what is known about the self at a more conscious level.

For most people however, the hormonal imperative of our needs breaks into conscious awareness as desire. What must be understood about motives, for this text, is the degree to which the individual's definition of that need has remained literal. Hence the need to consider motives within the literal-metaphorical dimension of the self. I will attempt to illustrate this point. A mature man discovers in the course of his analysis that he harbors a belief about himself he had not till then been aware of. He believes (against all evidence) that he is a reckless and untrustworthy person. This label had been attributed to him often enough by a father who had no sense (beyond his own inflated expectations) of what could be appropriately expected of his son. Because the humiliation of father's disapproval could not be defended against, the label stuck as a capture. In response to this chronic source of humiliation, the patient had painstakingly established over the years an unrelenting approach to making decisions. Every aspect of the decision to be made had to be examined endlessly, in minute detail, and from every conceivable angle, before even the most insignificant of choices could be made.

At the time he started his analysis, however, this patient's ability to arrive at a balanced view had enabled him to ease up on the obsessiveness that had attended any decision making. In this development, he had benefited in an unexpected way. He had evolved considerable skill in his ability to reflect upon issues, and to arrive at a well-balanced position. Having chosen (not surprisingly) the law as a profession, he also benefited from this harnessing of his reflective ability to the mastery of legal reasoning. But in making decisions that could have serious consequences, he continued to feel compelled to check out every conceivable angle, rather than trust in his (by now) well-validated judgement. One might (as mainstream analyst) explain this compulsion in terms of his not having resolved the inherent ambivalence between an aggressive need to assert the self and the passive dependent longings for acceptance and support. The motive, in this case, is the patient's attempt to resolve a conflict without having addressed its source; namely, his inability to reconcile a wish to aggressively destroy his abusive father, with his continued need for father's support. And yet, (and here is my principle point), this conflict had, at its more basic level been resolved, or he could not have demonstrated the reflective skill I have described. That is, father's support was in fact no longer needed, as the patient had arrived at an ability to handle his affairs on his own. The fear that prompted his obsessive behavior was irrational, in that it could not be a function of really *needing* father's support. The motive in this instance must therefore be ascribed, not to an unresolved oedipus conflict (which had in fact been resolved), but to the continued literalization of the process of decision making, due to an unresolved affective capture.

Motives, by this view, must always be appreciated in relation to the way in which the self is defined, and to the possibility that these self definitions may be captured. Since a reflective sense of self is seen in this text as necessary to having a metaphorical grasp of one's self, then a collapse of this meta function is viewed as a collapse of the self. Hence the notion that the patient described above continued to succumb to the pressure of decision making with a collapse of his reflective self. This state of collapse is said to occur when a challenge to the self's ability to cope literalizes one's reality in a way that inspires fear or panic. The state I am referring to is commonly known as one in which one feels "jarred," "thrown-off-balance," "out of kilter," or "off-center." For example, a child may have maintained a particular sense of being "bad" that has not been assimilated to what is consciously acknowledged about the self, but is evoked in situations where he or she is accused of having a "bad smell." In an immature personality, these situations may trigger an acute state of tension or panic, causing the self to shrink uncontrollably to a literal perspective that cannot itself be questioned. Under these conditions, the unassimilated context remains isolated and immune to change for as long as it may not be challenged.

In a similar vein, an unstable self or a self weakened by chronic stress, fear, or fatigue is more prone to literalize situations which are mere possibilities, as when the suspicion of disease triggers the panic of its presumed certainty. Or, when a challenge to my self-esteem occasions a self-conscious preoccupation (Do I have the ability? Will I be found wanting?), I may succumb to the doubt obsessively as delineating a literal state, and fail to question the doubt itself as a question *about* my reality. Or when in questioning my adequacy in comparison to the accomplishments of others, I may reduce myself to the literal dimensions of an extrinsic standard, and fail to consider what I know about myself from a more personal frame of reference. What is lost in these instances is a sense of the self as being a metaphor about one's self.

One would think that if the self is a metaphor (i.e., a schema that establishes basic assumptions about the self, and that helps to organize one's reality), then it should not be vulnerable to the collapses described above, since (as metaphor) it should transcend the settings in which it is challenged. However, a metaphor by this view, is not merely a way of seeing; it is the reality itself! That is, the self as metaphor may not always transcend the settings in which it must work, if (for whatever reason) it doesn't work, because it constitutes the reality of our survival. The self by this view does not merely organize our reality, is *is* our reality, insofar as *self* and *reality* form (in health) an undissolvable whole. Furthermore, the beliefs that support this self-metaphor are not subject to our conscious control. We may fabricate our appearance, and to some degree the impression we make upon others. We may not, however, fabricate the approach we take to creating our reality, any more than we might consciously intend *any* creative discovery. When we do so, it is under the aegis of an ideological capture, and compromises our integrity. The best we can do (by this view) is uncover and confront the reified beliefs of childhood, so as to gradually wean them from their literal moorings, and open them to renewal and growth.

The term metaphor is therefore used in this text to describe the self, not because the self is considered analogous to something else. Rather, it refers to the metaphorical process as creative realization; i.e., to the self's ability to transcend the literal definitions of the narcissistic core in its development, in the act of reflective awareness. The term *metaphor* is therefore an allusion to the self's meta function introduced by language. It is this meta function that generates the self's metaphorical dimension. And it is this metaphorical dimension that may collapse into a literal perspective, under conditions of pressure or stress. In considering a person's motives, therefore, one must determine if one is dealing with a desire that stems from a particular self definition (e.g., it will enhance me to be admired); from a need to resolve conflicting self definitions (e.g., if

I am admired, I will no longer have to prove myself, as I really wish to be taken care of); or from a loss of the self's meta function due to stress, as when a compulsive need to please is substituted for a genuine wish for recognition.

CONSCIENCE AND THE SELF

If, following Whitehead, the time has come for our theories of the self to address the complexities of what it means to be a human being, then we could hardly (in this account) ignore the fact that people are said to have a conscience. Freud appears to have taken this fact into account by instituting a special agency—the superego—for keeping unacceptable contents out of awareness. Today, this view of morality as keeping various kinds of instinctual impulses in check may appear naive; a classic case of how, in the development of revolutionary ideas, their reified beginnings inevitably attempt to account for far more than could be their due. That is, the notion of a superego obscures the degree to which our morality is embedded in the *symbolic* elaborations of each particular civilization. It is in ignoring the symbolic context of human morality that psychoanalytic theory may be said to have been most negligent of our human condition.

In a recent assessment of psychoanalysis and the concept of evil, for example, Pattison (1984) concludes that "the psychoanalytic tradition per se does not provide an adequate theoretical or empirical base for the root concepts of morality, in which good and evil are embedded" (61). Evil for Freud was what the superego was instituted to fight against, which tended to vary as he developed his theory. Wallace (1981) has noted that while Freud was ambiguous about the exact nature of evil, he tended overall to view it as that part of human instinct that needs to be channeled and controlled by the "good" instincts. In this regard, Pattison points out, what was considered "good" or "bad" varied in Freud's writings. "In 1915, the egoist instincts were good and social instincts were bad. In 1920 and 1921, the aggressive drive was bad and libidinal drive was good. In 1930, uninhibited sensuality was bad and aim-inhibited libido was good" (ibid., 65).

Few today would (I believe) challenge Pattison's principal point. The concept of morality is philosophical, not behavioral. You will not discover what is of value in human beings by merely observing them. The value you attribute to the way in which people behave is a function of the premises you bring to your definitions. Furthermore, in order to understand what it means to have a conscience, or to grasp the nature of good and evil as moral issues, it would seem clear today that these must be understood in terms of the symbolic elaborations (the legal, educational, political, and religious traditions) of each culture. But in doing so, one must also grasp how the self establishes its narcissistic core; for it is in relation to this core that the value of what one is, as well as what one does, comes to assume a social frame of reference.

The narcissistic core by this view is the reified definition of the self we elaborate in terms of literal notions of place, belonging, and entitlement. *My* house, *my* mommy, and *my* toy are for the child the literal beliefs that contribute to the fledgling self identity born of language. In becoming objectified by language, the self also assumes the capacity to reflect; i.e., the self not only attributes value to itself, it questions these characteristics in itself. Thus, language (as per Whitehead) not only gives mankind a soul, it gives individuals a conscience as well! Only with language do we begin to develop those distinctly human qualities (the conscience and the lie) that distinguish us as human beings.

Once the child has words with which to describe the self, these words (as beliefs about the self) become what the child takes itself to be. Once they take root, these narcissistic beliefs may not be relinquished (short of shattering the self), but must gradually be weaned from their reified state. The "illusion of omnipotence" proposed by the mainstream analyst as an inherent feature of the preverbal child, conforms to the fact that in initially defining a self, the child mistakenly attributes to the self capacities which it depends upon its caretaker for. By this view, the child does not *need* to feel omnipotent (as Winnicott, for example, claims), so much as presume that he or she possesses the adaptive skills parents put at the child's disposal because language permits this presumption. When such a presumption is challenged, it is undermining *not* because the child needs to feel omniscient, but because (by this view) these features are vaguely assumed (thanks to our linguistic sieve) to be a part of the self.

A mature self does not result from questioning the self. When an individual questions the basic foundations of the self (Am I a viable entity?), he or she is in fact undermining the ability to be productively critical by focusing on the self's acceptability rather than upon what is needed for a particular task. If criticism is in order, it should be directed (reflectively) to what one does, rather than (objectifyingly) to what one is. From the perspective of this essay, this self-undermining inclination results from having had the illusions of the self shattered prematurely. A good deal of maturity must already be established if one is to benefit from questioning the beliefs that support the self, or suffer through the rigors of a psychoanalytic character analysis. To be weaned of its literal self-centeredness, the self must be subjected to an ongoing tension between self-interest and the legitimate demands of others; or between individual need and the pleasure of communal sharing; or between self-realization and a respect for the accomplishments of others. In other words, to develop a conscience, the self must be part of a group which holds its individual members to certain standards of integrity.

Because of language (which introduces the lie), one might (in this development) systematically neglect one pole of this dialectic in favor of the other. The mechanism for this kind of distortion was described earlier in terms of ideologic and affective capture. By the former, we ascribe to ourselves attributes we may not possess, as when the child attributes value to itself on the basis of what is said (by way of approval, for example), rather than what is done; or in terms of what one wishes to believe about the self. By the latter, actions which result in disapproval, for example, may be disowned, since the fear and anxiety generated by parental rebuke come to capture the meaning context, and dissociate it from the self. From these distortions are born the many boundary problems encountered by psychotherapists; i.e., those difficulties people have in determining where they leave off, and where the other begins. In this vein, feelings of guilt ascribe responsibilities to the self which don't belong, while genuine responsibilities remain unseen. Or one might doubt abilities one in fact has, and insist upon the unnecessary support of another, while at the same time ascribing to oneself abilities one scarcely possesses. The feeling of self-worth we survive by is hardly a gauge of true value, as it may be paramount in the buffoon and tragically lacking in the accomplished virtuoso. Once my integrity has been skewed in this manner, I will have built into my *self* as a metaphor a systematic distortion that feeds upon itself. Evil may be understood in part as one of the abusive effects (toward the self or the other) that this distortion may have. Indeed, it need not be limited to those monstrous acts of greed, selfishness, and manipulation that are among the more obvious manifestations of self-interest gone amok. An overemphasis upon the disinterested pole of the self's dialectic might generate just as much destruction by those who place efficiency above human feelings and values.

Given the view of the role language plays in the emergence of the human being, the existence of evil may not be seen as an aberration, or as a developmental failure. Rather, its potential is an essential component of our humanity, as it arises out of the very elements that constitute the self. The reality of evil has become painfully obvious with our gains in technology, which have enhanced both its scope, and our ability to record and communicate its presence. This reality should not detract us from its more prosaic manifestations, as in the individual who refuses to relinquish the dependent ties of childhood, or in the literal morality of the Boy Scout for example; or the "well-intentioned" concern of the intrusive mother. It may also be discerned in the complacency of the dreamer who never tests the waters, or in the reassurance junkie who demands unrelenting support, or in those "good" people whose integrity is grounded in compliance. The point being that there is ample opportunity in elaborating a metaphor of the self, for this process to be placed in the service of lies, conceits and self-interests, given the illusory base we all start with.

In short, morality could not be a function of our mental health, as some mainstream analysts have claimed (as discussed in Pattison 1984), for the simple reason that a moral perspective must be taught. It is not therefore any less healthy to be amoral, than it is to be uneducated. The morally perverse individual may (by this perspective) have a perfectly healthy (i.e., functional) self. Having a conscience by this view does not unfold maturationally on its own, but must be inculcated in the child, along with many other abilities we mistakenly take to be a function of maturation alone (Kay 1982). The values adopted by a person are as readily geared to the selfish or murderous designs of a particular group, as to the human responsibilities of equality, reciprocity, and a respect for the other. The myth we owe to Rousseau's romantic notion of the "noble savage" who must be salvaged from the impingements of a corrupt society has been vulgarized today in terms of the popular psychoanalytic notion of a "true self"; i.e., the core self who in all his or her pristine purity, awaits to be born via the administration of the psychoanalyst as midwife. Granting that a psychoanalysis may enable one to contact the "child within," that child must still be "brought up." The constraints that give shape to a moral being are not something the child might discover on its own. Once we have been socialized, the particular decisions we make are grounded in higher-order moral principles (Feather 1975; Rokeach 1968). They depend upon the historical, collective development and maintenance of a cultural metaphor as crucible for the development of the individual. We may not (by this view) dispense with such a framework, any more than we might continue to ignore how such a framework promotes the development of responsible individuals.

I conclude this chapter with notes on issues which also pertain to the metaphorical dimension of the self, and must therefore be alluded to in this preliminary account of the effects of language upon individual development. These include a note on the preverbal development of the self, on the relationship of the self to biology, and on diagnostic categories for the self.

A NOTE ON PREVERBAL DEVELOPMENTS OF THE SELF

The ideas proposed in this chapter raise the question of whether or not pathological meanings exist prior to the assimilation of a language. The assumption made in this text is that the inherent unfolding of a child's development, supported by "good enough" parenting, may in some ways be blocked or stunted by a failure of what Winnicott (1958) has referred to as a "facilitating environment"; but that the child requires language to actually distort (in the sense of misrepresenting) its reality. Stated differently, you do not (in rearing the preverbal child), alter the child's mind. Rather, you provide the child with the structure it needs to adapt to a social world. With the added level of meaning introduced by language, however, you do alter the structure of the mind; i.e., you introduce a capacity for literal meaning and for reflective awareness which profoundly changes the child's relationship to its reality, and which now includes the possibility of distorting (misrepresenting) that reality.

Children are often rebuked and humiliated over issues that they are unable to comprehend. If these rebukes occur repeatedly within a given setting, the child's context is in danger of being captured by the parental rebuke. In this vein, Stern (1985, 222), has described a mother who responded to the expectable maladroitness of her one-year-old boy with a "depressive signal." When something was knocked over, or a toy was disarranged, the mother would express "long expirations, falling intonations, slightly collapsing postures, furrowing the brows, tilting and drooping the head, and 'Oh, Johnnys' that could be interpreted as 'Look what you've done to your mother again' . . ." As a result, Johnny's exhuberant exploratory activity was habitually dampened in the contexts of maternal care. From the perspective of this essay however, a blocking of Johnny's exhuberance in this setting need not preclude its emergence in a more accepting milieu. There is as yet no reason to assume that this deleterious effect might not be reversed given the opportunity to experience a more open acceptance from others. Prior to the objectification of the self with language, Johnny's experience (short of physically harmful deprivation or abuse) remains functionally grounded. His experience is not yet in danger of being reified as not belonging to the self. Johnny does not yet *have a self*, in the sense taken here of a reflective representation that is *about* him. With the objectification of the self that occurs with language, however, Johnny's dampened experience will become frozen as a reified belief as to who Johnny is, since the possibility of correction is precluded by the capture. The context of exploration will have been captured by the built-in sense of being unworthy, once Johnny's identity can be reified with words.

Other areas vulnerable to being captured in this fashion include any deficits in development which, with the advent of language, might then be reified as permanent liabilities of the self. Thus, for example, the child's sense of agency, in the sense of being a purposeful participant in events, or the child's capacity for intersubjective sharing, may be seriously thwarted, as has been described in Stern (1985). In these preludes to affective and ideological capturing, the functional integrity of the child is initially blocked by a parent who misinterprets, overloads, or simply fails to respond to the infant's attempts at involvement. The development of the area in question is then stunted and the infant may still be lacking a sense of interpersonal agency or purposeful involvement when he or she begins to reify an identity with words. The failure of an intersubjective sense of sharing, for example, would result in either a self-perpetuating isolation or an extreme form of dependence. The individual who is frozen in isolation is similar to the person who has perpetuated an abject state of dependence, in that both have (by his view) reified a fear of the very contexts that could correct his or her inability to trust. The child comes to substitute for its own growth a dependence upon (or a withdrawal from) those supports which make up for his or her insufficiency. Language has thereby frozen a condition which, given the exposure to more responsive settings might have changed, by precluding the child's subsequent ability to own the experience (of wanting succor or of feeling abandoned) as a feature of the self.

Aside from the phenomenon of capturing permitted by language, there are other features of language functioning which contribute to pathognomic developments in the child, that could not (by this view) occur preverbally. During the transformation of the individual that occurs with language, he or she (it is assumed) is at considerable risk. As the child starts to use words, the meaning contexts which come to be defined by language are vulnerable to being captured by events which evoke a strong reaction, such as excitement, anger, anguish, or fear. In chapter 4, I described how, in assimilating a language, the child literalizes meaning by assuming that the words used to refer to situations and events *are* those situations and events. One might well imagine the danger that could follow from this initial confusion. Words that are what they express assume a magical power for, as well as in relation to, the child.

This last point will not be news to a parent! Swear words for example, which are known to offend a parent, may come to be used as lethal weapons by the school-age child, or may occasion serious guilt or anxiety at the mere thought of their existence. In a similar vein, words which ascribe qualities to a child (as in "you're bad," or "hateful" or even "lovable") may be taken quite literally as *being* the child (though defiance is available early on to fend off these attributions). Finally, the meaning of an event may become focused upon a single, nameable feature that would otherwise have been embedded in the omnidimensional perspective of nonverbal meaning. For example, a child who in play is rejected by his or her peers will experience a passing sense of humiliation. If that humiliation is attached to a verbal insult ("He's weird!" "She smells!"), it may more effectively lodge in the child's consciousness as a continued source of humiliation which is not easily dispelled. This may be understood in part because of the child's literal interpretation of words (the rhyme "sticks and stones will break my bones, but names will never hurt me," is wishful thinking for the young child); and in part because of the referential function assumed by words, which tends to divorce their meaning from the setting in which they occur, and thereby assume a life of their own.

For these reasons, symbolized fears—fears which take on a name—may at first be very difficult to assuage. The child's fear of the boogeyman under the bed for example, may not be allayed by implicating the child's imagination until quite late in his or her development. The child cannot at this stage appreciate him or herself as a creator of meaning. The faulty attribution of meaning (i.e., of danger to the fictitious boogeyman) cannot be challenged. The normal contexts or expectations regarding these settings have been disrupted by an emotional reaction that is intense, discontinuous, and immune to challenge. That is, these reactions will either have to dissipate with time, or await the maturing perspective which enables the child to question fear as a function of his or her way of seeing things.

A NOTE ON BIOLOGICAL ASPECTS OF THE SELF

The fact that the biological aspects of the body may not be used to explain motives does not preclude questions as to the relationship of these aspects to the self. The areas of interest would include familiar ones such as the effect of our chemistry upon our mood; and less familiar areas such as the effect of the physiology of the brain upon our use of language. For example, Miller (1986) reports that there is evidence to suggest that the biological substrate for the left hemisphere of the brain (said to mediate language) matures later in life than does the substrate for the right hemisphere (said to mediate nonverbal, emotional modes of understanding). By Miller's account, the cerebral commisures (which relate the two hemispheres of the brain) are themselves insufficiently developed at the time of language acquisition, so that the child may initially have difficulty integrating feelings and emotions with words. As described by Joseph (1982), because of the (presumed) absence of information exchange between the two hemispheres,

> learning and associated emotional responding may later be completely unaccessible to the language centers of the brain, even when extensive interhemispheric transfer is possible. In this regard, the curious asymmetrical arrangement of function and maturation may well predispose the developing organism to later come upon situations in which it finds itself responding emotionally, nervously, anxiously or "neurotically" without linguistic knowledge, or without even the possibility of linguistic understanding as to the cause, purpose, eliciting stimulus or origin of its behaviour. (24)

Miller, in concurring with this view, describes how individuals with functional commissurotomy (lack of integration between the cerebral hemispheres) may be at a disadvantage for achieving self-insight, and more prone to channelling expression in the form of somatic symptoms. In short, the very introduction of language as a functional feature of the child introduces a potential for confusion or mystification, which has to do with an organically-based impediment to the realization of meaning.

This line of inquiry could have a bearing upon individual differences. It is presented here as an example of how (by this view) the body's physiology enters into the organization of the self.

A NOTE ON DIAGNOSTIC CATEGORIES FOR THE SELF

Finally, while I will not here attempt a systematic treatment of how the notion of a metaphorical self pertains to our traditional diagnostic categories of psychopathology, I will present two examples of how the notion of literal and metaphorical meaning is helpful in addressing these phenomena. Arieti (1973) has described a type of psychotic depression as a "claiming depression," in which the message is: "Help me; pity me. It is in your power to relieve me. If I suffer it is because you don't relieve me of my suffering. If I sustain a loss, it is because you did not give me and still don't give me what I need" (128).

According to Arieti, the prepsychotic picture of a claiming depression is one in which security was maintained, not by one's own effort, but by receiving support, praise, and admiration from others. In normal development (for Arieti), we gradually internalize the interpersonal in the form of an intrapsychic ability to regulate our self-esteem and to come to terms with our responsibilities. That is, having been encouraged to exert control in an interpersonal setting, this control becomes adopted as a feature of the self. The person suffering from a claiming depression, having been deprived of this encouragement, is seen as being unable to transform an important part of the interpersonal into the intrapsychic, and as therefore not able to obtain autonomous gratification.

In the terms of this essay, the medium of the transformation alluded to by Arieti is language. The person vulnerable to a claiming depression is said here to have literalized a state of dependency in a way that comes to preclude the experience of being capable of independent control. By this view, the infant's capacity for purposeful striving is thwarted. That is, the infant's preverbal sense of agency may be stunted in its development, when it is captured by an overly controlling parent, or forced into extreme patterns by a depressed parent. The emergence of an objectified sense of self with language will then reify this state of affairs—the infant's inability to strive on its own behalf—as a believed feature of the child that perpetuates its own dependence. The literalness of this belief (and of the demands placed upon others) thwarts the potential expansion of the self as metaphorical projection in the very areas that would have to be assayed, in order to contact this potential in the self.

In addition to the claiming depression described above, Arieti also refers to a "self blaming" depression, where a profound feeling of guilt results from a sense of not having lived up to what Arieti refers to as the "dominant other" would expect. In other words, whereas the "claiming" position suffers from a loss of support and reassurance, the "self blaming" position suffers from a sense of having failed the expectations of another. From the perspective of this book, the incursion of language has in this instance obscured the relational foundations of the self, and distorted the lines of individual responsibility. The notions of "good" and "bad" have been literalized as either-or propositions which depend, not upon what one does, but upon what a parent *says* about what one does. Once the self's value has been literalized in this fashion, the ascription of self-worth is placed completely in the hands of the "dominant other." The self's capture, in this instance, has placed it under the aegis of another's value system, and in a manner that precludes developing a value system of one's own.

Addressing a different area of pathology, Barnett (1966, 1973), has related obsessional neurosis to a particular dynamic that is thought to occur between the infant and its caretaker. That is, once parental control and infant submission became a basis for interpersonal intimacy (i.e., once submission to parental control becomes a condition for receiving love and recognition), then the infant's enforced dependence upon the parent becomes a basis for the denial of those needs. As described by Barnett, control in the obsessive is "basically organized around the obsessional's extreme dependency problems and their denial, serving to maintain innocence and avoid the shame and humiliation that would be inevitable if these aspects of the self-system were comprehended" (1973, 189).

Stated differently, the child must disown its need to feel loved and accepted, because acknowledging such a need would bring with it a sense of the humiliation of having had to submit to a parent in such an abject way. At issue (from the perspective of this essay) is the fact that to disown a feeling or expectation (e.g., need for love), the child must have access to a language. A need per se (by this view) could not be disowned; only the reflective awareness of that need that arises with words. Furthermore, in a nonverbal mode need and control are mutually defining. Excessive control on the part of a parent could stunt the development of initiative in the infant, but could not of itself result in the kind of split or disowning described by Barnett. The literal meanings introduced by language however are well-suited to the rigid objectifications that are maintained in obsessional neurosis in order to deny dependence or need. That is, language enables us to split off the controlling part of our behavior from its (preverbally) related dependence, and to treat control and dependence as separate (reified) states. Thus, if the obsessional described by Barnett must deny his or her dependence, it is because control-dependence have been literalized as being mutually exclusive. Hence the unacceptability of dependence, for it appears (in this literal guise) to entail a total loss of control.

In short, the pathological states described by Arieti and Barnett point (I believe) to be a very specific failure; namely, the failure to integrate the verbal with the nonverbal, under conditions where there has been a preverbal thwarting of the infant's development. This failure (it is claimed here) cripples the child's ability to regulate dependency needs as well as its own sense of self-esteem. In so doing, it exposes the child to a self-perpetuating sense of helpless need, or to the self-condemnatory obsessional judgements of a verbal self; i.e., a self that has lost its experiential moorings in analogical relatedness.

In chapter 7, the notion was suggested that in a psychoanalysis the analysand discovers him or herself as a creator of meaning, for this is what is implied each time a reified capturing of the past is reversed. If an analysis is first and foremost a setting in which the individual comes to understand and accept him or herself, then it must be added that lost aspects of the self must be wrested from the capturings of the past so as to participate more fully in the reflective realizations of the present. Thus a critical aspect of analytic work by this view inheres in discovering and resolving the affective and ideological captures of the past due to the incursion of language at a stage when the child is particularly vulnerable to its pathological effects.

This aspect of the work (resolving captures) corresponds to areas that have long been of concern to psychoanalysts. In contrast to the Freudian metaphor however, these developments may be understood, not in terms of a fictitious process of cathected energies, but of the observable vicissitudes of each individual as he or she assimilates language as an actual component of the self.

9.
LANGUAGE AND THE SOCIAL ORDER

DEREIFICATION AS A HISTORICAL PROCESS

Today, the attempt to describe *any* historical process is subject to deep suspicion. In Europe, Lyotard (1984) has dismissed the classic philosophies of history as our last embodiments of an "illusion of order." In the United States, Rorty (1985) describes the grand schemes of our philosophical discourses as having lost touch with the concrete realities of our existence. For Rorty, we have imposed concerns which are irrelevant to our actual condition; i.e., we have tended to scratch where it doesn't itch. The philosophy of history has been but a means of inventing an order that does not truly exist. Might the thesis of this book be extended to the social order without inviting the same accusations? In this chapter, I will argue that this has already been done in the work of Jürgen Habermas (1987, 1985, 1984, 1971).

One way of applying the thesis of this book to social organization is to assume that social systems progress toward an increasing clarification of the meaning systems that mediate a society's representations of reality. Just as individual development progresses (in health) toward an ongoing deliteralization of the reality we represent with language, so should the organized groups of society. In fact, the notion that social meaning undergoes this kind of differentiation is not new. It is basic to Max Weber's notion of "rationalization," though his view differs from the one proposed in this book and by Habermas in a critical way.

For Weber (1864–1920), the scientific advances of the nineteenth and twentieth centuries have freed us from the illusions and deceptions of the past, but at a cost. We have "desacrilized" our natural and our social worlds. In differentiating the political, the economic and the legal realms of meaning so that they might be dealt with on their own terms, we have paved the way for the modern industrial state, and the administrative organizations of early capitalism; but we have done so at the cost of "disillusion." The metaphysical and religious systems which were supplanted by the nineteenth century ethos of scientific objectivity are not in fact systems of irrational belief; they are meaning structures which secure our place in the universe. If rationality (in its Weberian sense) is viewed as the ability to chose the most efficient means for realizing a particular goal, then the rationality of a society would be tied to its administrative efficiency. That is, it must ultimately depend upon the degree to which order and planning are imposed upon the affairs of the governed. For this rationalizing process to occur, however, there must be a change in the society's methods of social action. The traditional norms and values that have been basic to communal forms of action must give way to the more impersonal norms dictated by market strategies, governmental policies, and the like. As described by Wellmer (1985):

> Once the cognitive structures of a disenchanted consciousness are institutionalized as secularized systems of cultural discourse and social interaction, a process of rationalization—now in the specifically Weberian sense—is set into motion which tends to undermine the social basis for the existence of autonomous and rational individuals. For this reason there is a profoundly pessimistic philosophy of history implicit in Weber's theory of modern rationalization. Humanity's becoming rational—i.e., reason's coming of age (which after all, is humanity's task and destiny)—by an internal logic triggers historical processes which tend to depersonalize social relationships, to dessicate symbolic communication, and to subject human life to the impersonal logic of rationalized, anonymous administrative systems—historical processes, in short, which tend to make human life mechanized, unfree, and meaningless. (43)

Today it seems clear that we need not abide by this pessimistic view of humanity's destiny, any more than we need subscribe to the utopian visions that arose in its wake. Having focused exclusively upon the analytical reason of science, Weber had in effect reified reason as a self-contained faculty. The presumption that this aspect of reason alone determines what is to be viewed as objective is never questioned. For example, there is no consideration for the possibility that the values which support social relationships and communication may themselves follow a course similar to the differentiation of our institutions. That is, they as well, may become more clearly grounded in the ability each of us has to clarify the assumptions that support our belief. It is not possible therefore, to envisage (from Weber's perspective) a point that is made by Habermas: that in a democratic society, the validity claims which support the rights of an individual are communally forged; and that it is this participatory mode which establishes a sense of objectivity as well as a basis for involvement and responsibility.

We are today more than ever in need of understanding the effects of the technological discoveries and political developments of our age upon the individual's quality of communal life. Without a surer grasp of the social conditions which promote an individual sense of purpose and responsibility in Western society, for example, we are in danger of evolving into a society which fails to inculcate these qualities in its individual members. Rather than retreat to the drastic pluralism of a Rorty, or the aestheticism of a Lyotard, Habermas has responded to these concerns by building upon the tradition of the grand philosophical narrative. That is, he has constructed an evolutionary theory of social organization which may be seen as grounded in our growing awareness of how language contributes to the communal creation of a reality.

The most obvious problem faced by a theory of social organization is in deciding just what the subject of such a theory should be. If it is the individual member, how does one reconcile individual consciousness with the social processes one would study? Can the social process as system be studied without regard for the fact that it originates in individual people? And are we not then in danger of reifying those processes (as being *in* the person, or *in* the system) as described above? As Mead would say, what we need are the correct lines of cleavage. That is, we need a way of showing how systems interact with people, so as to define what pertains to each, and how they contribute to each other.

Habermas's solution to this difficulty is to establish as subject of his theory the dialectical relationship that exists between the "life world" of the individual, and the cultural systems which structure that world. Though borrowed from Heidegger, the notion of a life world as used by Habermas differs from the former's meaning, in that it is not tied to an individual consciousness. In this regard, it has a distinct advantage; i.e., it avoids having to describe individuals in terms of subject-object relations. Nor need one postulate some prime mover such as the biological imperatives of love and hate. What matters is not *why* life worlds interact with cultural systems. What matters is *how* they interact, and the communal structures that support that interaction.

This is not to say that the network of involvements of the life world do not serve a purpose. The purpose however is not the fulfillment of some instinctual or power need. Rather it has to do with meaning itself. More specifically, it has to do with the modes of communal involvement which support the realization of meaning. Paramount among these is the ability, shared by the speakers of a common language, to coordinate their actions in terms of cultural norms of agreement and consent. The life world is therefore a network which supports and complements an activity that is basic to our being; i.e., what Habermas refers to as "communicative action." In other words, the focus of Habermas's theory is the domain of everyday life, concerned as it is with social integration and communal involvement. His emphasis however is not upon communication as a mode for expressing some ulterior purpose or need. Rather, it is upon communication itself as action mode; and upon the ways in which people use communication to establish "validity claims."

This last statement may appear to the reader as unexceptional, yet it represents a radical departure from what we are used to. Normally we have felt compelled (in our explanations) to start with a notion of what is to count as valid. When we subscribe to the pronouncements of a prime mover, or to biological imperatives, or to economic determinants and the like, it is in order to invest our theory with the authority of proclaiming what is to count as valid *prior* to the event. For Habermas, this kind of presumption misses a critical point; i.e., that when we argue, or seek to convince another of the value of our claim, we do so on the basis of procedures which are not merely a function of our belief, but of the structure of the discourse we use to arrive at agreement. Thus the process Habermas is addressing is the dialogic nature of the discourse itself, and the ways in which it permits us to arrive at a consensus as a basis for belief. In true deconstructive fashion, Habermas has turned our normal assumptions upside down. It is not because of the eternal class struggle or the pursuit of power that we proceed as we do; rather, it is because in proceeding, we forge beliefs and justifications in our dialogues. Because of our wish to justify our behavior, we may then do so on the basis of a "class struggle" or "power needs." Granted, we may not discover the dialogic nature of our validity claims by listening to discussants attempting to impose some self-serving reification upon their partner! Rather, it

LANGUAGE AND THE SOCIAL ORDER

is discovered when two individuals genuinely attempt to persuade each other of the correctness of their position. We would not (states Habermas) have convictions with which to contradict each other, unless we believed that they could be decided on the basis of good reasons.

> Convictions can contradict one another only when those who are concerned with problems define them in a similar way, believe them to need resolution, and want to decide issues on the basis of good reasons . . . As long as we take part and do not merely look over our own shoulders as historians and ethnographers, we maintain precisely the distinctions . . . between valid and socially accepted views, between good arguments and those which are merely successful for a certain audience at a certain time. (1985, 194)

The question then becomes, what constitutes a valid view or a good argument? In communicative action, one often seeks to motivate another's behavior. If a speaker can rationally motivate a listener (without resorting to force, intimidation, or manipulation) it is because he or she may provide reasons that stand up to scrutiny and seem valid. "Only those speech acts with which a speaker connects a criticizable validity claim can move a hearer to accept an offer independently of external forces" (ibid., 305). The validity claims we use to support the truth of what we say can be accepted and rejected only via a critical debate that examines their reasons and grounds. How is this done?

Habermas singles out two principal ways in which we come to forge a consensus. First, in our dialogues we participate in an ongoing differentiation of meaning, along the lines of Weber's "rationalization," but without the impoverished life space of Weber's views. This process may be appreciated, for example, in the gradual distinction that is drawn between the "external" relations of objects, and the "internal" relations of ideas; or between language and the world, or names and the named. In short, a process which corresponds to what is referred to in this book as the deliteralization of meaning. Second, as a result of this ongoing differentiation, we come to separate out distinct spheres of value which had been combined. That is, we establish distinct validity dimensions which include propositional truth, normative rightness, and subjective truthfulness or authenticity. Corresponding roughly to the areas of science, law, and art, these spheres of validity are also basic to the kinds of assumptions one makes in accepting the validity of another's argument.

In order to illustrate the kinds of claims we may make to validate (or reject) a request, Habermas provides an example of a professor who has asked a seminar student to fetch him a glass of water. The student might question this request on the basis of its normative rightness ("Don't treat me like an employee"), its subjective truthfulness ("You want to embarrass me in front of the other students"), or the actual feasibility of the request ("The fountain is so far, I wouldn't be back in time to hear the seminar"). Accepting the conditions that are implicit in a request involves believing that the speaker is asking for something appropriate in terms of norms and feasibility; and that the speaker is being sincere. The fact that not all speech acts involved in communal action make a propositional claim is dealt with by the observation that speech acts inevitably presuppose the existence of a state of affairs, which may then be evaluated according to this criteria.

One might still wonder about the basis for a community's decision as to what is valid. How is such an agreement reached? Following Kuhn (1970), the acceptance of a new idea in science is a function of the degree to which workers in a particular field are willing to believe in its programmatic promise; i.e., that it will lead to more interesting discoveries than had been previously possible. This might be interpreted to mean that new ideas are accepted because they work better than the ones they replace. Yet this could not be an explanation, as the idea must first be adopted, before its effectiveness may be known. A second question pertaining to the objectivity of communally set standards, is that if the objectivity is to be decided on the basis of what works, how is this to be distinguished from political or self-serving concerns which also bear upon 'what works'? Finally, we have many areas of disagreement where there appear to be no way of arriving at agreement as to which position is most valid. How may Habermas's argument apply to these areas?

A source of discord in today's Western societies will serve as example. We have in this century witnessed a dramatic change of attitude regarding sexual behavior, compared to the Victorian ethic of the last century. Some, however, continue to adhere to the more traditional point of view. Should one point of view be accepted as more valid than the other? If so, by what standard? According to one view of sexuality, sexual excitement is perceived to be something children are not capable of tolerating responsibly. Curtailing sexual expression is therefore encouraged as a means of channeling that excitement toward socially acceptable activities, and of protecting the child from the addictive potential of sexual arousal, given the child's immaturity.

Another approach to sexual excitement is to see its addictive potential as a function of its having been so severely curtailed in childhood. The injunctions and warnings used to prohibit its expression make it difficult for children to appreciate sexual activity as a normal biological function. The responsible expression of sexual desire would therefore depend upon the young person's ability to assume responsibility for this behavior by first understanding what it means. An informed guidance geared to having the individual learn about his or her bodily functions, as well as about the nature of desire, is advocated, rather than coersion based upon authority.

From a "conservative" perspective, the difference between the two views described above is ascribed to a breakdown (in the second attitude) of traditional values. From a "progressive" standpoint, the second attitude represents an evolution toward more individuated responsibility; i.e., individuals are encouraged to take personal responsibility for their behavior, rather than adhere to an authority. From a "modernistic" perspective (in Habermas's sense), both perspectives are correct, and describe different aspects of a differentiation of the patterns that enter into the expression of sexual desire. That is, rather than being seen only as a biological need that must be controlled, sexuality is also appreciated as a symbolic meaning. Meanings operate on the basis of understanding, not merely constraint. One's position regarding sexual behavior is permitted to evolve in the direction of differentiating aspects of meaning which had been confounded in the earlier, more literal, view; but this is possible only when one has acknowledged the value of the earlier view, so as to see beyond it.

The point I am attempting to convey is that this evolving attitude toward sexual behavior is not the result of an empirical study of which approach best prepares children for a responsible attitude toward sex. Rather, it has arisen out of the inevitable differentiation of our concepts as they become less literal; a process which is a prelude to the kinds of empirical inquiries described above. Nor might the validity of the later "modernistic" point of view be ascribed to its normative rightness, since it must first arise, before being accepted as normatively right. In short, it is the discovery process itself that is a basis (among other considerations) for the validity of a particular point of view. That is, the normative rightness of a proposition emerges out of the ongoing deliteralization of our approach to events.

Stated differently, one may assume that when a community adopts a new set of norms, it is with the expectation that these norms will help to resolve problems in a coherent and responsible way. That so many historical examples contradict this last point must be ascribed to the fact that those who seize power readily pervert that power to selfish needs. When a government genuinely serves the governed, however, one must assume some agreement as to what is deemed "coherent" and "responsible." Under these conditions, norms would arise creatively out of a differentiation of the literal assumptions of the past. To be accepted, these norms must be perceived by a community as offering a better grasp of reality. Conversely, the group's ability to adjust to this reality will depend upon its ability to recognize and use this feature of the development of meaning. The objectivity involved is not therefore one which depends upon discovering universally valid standards, but one in which the participants allow for an open investigation so as to arrive at a jointly forged understanding. In each instance, we *create* our reality in the reflective realization of meaning that arises out of challenging our literal views.

While this last point appears to challenge Habermas's position on the existence of universally valid standards, I believe it is in keeping with his description of how we come to revise the reasons we have for accepting the claims of another; i.e., our reasons can always be expanded into arguments which we understand only when we recapitulate them in the light of some standard. "In short, the interpretive reconstruction of reasons makes it necessary that for us to place 'their' standards in relations to 'ours,' so that in the case of contradiction we either revise our preconceptions or relativize 'their' standards of rationality against 'ours'" (1985, 204). Habermas is here (I believe) describing the reflective process of symbolic realization as it is understood in this book. It is the basic process of those "non-reified everyday communicative practice(s)" which correspond to an "undistorted intersubjectivity" (ibid., 210). In other words, the life world would simply be a repository of semiotic systems, were it not for the fact that it must also be in the business of *creating* systems. It could not be limited to a sense of established or imposed ways of doing things. The life world must in some way include an ability to discover solutions, and to question the ones that already exist. For this to occur, one must have the ability to reflect upon what occurs insofar as reflection is taken in this text to be basic to creative discovery. I conclude this chapter with a discussion of how this view of the basis for the validity of what we know pertains to the integrity of our knowledge.

WHAT DETERMINES THE VALIDITY OF WHAT WE KNOW?

One might question one of the definitions of validity to be found in Webster's dictionary (1979) ("being supported by objective truth") by asking how one arrives at objective truth. From the perspective of Jean Piaget, objective truth involves the ability to clearly differentiate the "external" from the "internal." As described in chapter 1, however, Piaget's notion of objectivity may be questioned as he failed to consider the role of language in determining what we view as objective.

Applying the Piagetain perspective to the realm of morality, Lawrence Kohlberg (1978) traces the moral judgment of the child in terms of developmental stages which parallel the cognitive stages described by Piaget. From the perspective of this book, Kohlberg's stages in the development of moral judgment may be seen as stages in the deliteralization of moral precepts. That is, moral judgments may be seen as proceeding from the literal perspective of the preconventional level (where the physical consequences of an act determine its goodness or badness) to the conventional level (where law and authority are the ultimate arbiters) to the separation of moral and legal rules, and the recognition of ethical principles.

In order to deliteralize one's perspective, one must have developed a reflective sense of how language works. That is, if language is the medium whereby we distort our reality, then an honest use of language will depend upon our ability to challenge the distortions which arise from language's function. This is not to say that individuals must learn how language works in a technical sense. Rather, one must overcome the childish belief in the reality of the word; i.e., that if you can say something, it must mean that it's true. In this vein, (following Habermas), an honest use of language implies the reflective ability to question the reasons one has for what one says. To deliteralize meaning (i.e., to stop confusing the file with its content), one must appreciate how a belief is relevant to a point of view. Only when we begin to differentiate and to question the premises that support our beliefs might we be said (from the perspective of this book) to be acting in a way that is valid, or that has integrity.

For example, the child who returns a stolen toy because "Mommy will be angry" is still lacking in integrity. The child who does so because he or she can feel what it is like to have something stolen, has discovered integrity. For the first child, the premise that informs his behavior is adopted from mother, and may not be challenged until he discovers that he can have beliefs of his own. For the second child, caring about another's feelings has become a premise for moral behavior because it is grounded in what he knows about himself. The first child has little reason to question his behavior, as it is prescribed by a parental capture. The second child has discovered that he is a creator of meaning, and has begun the process of clarifying the meaning of what he does by reflecting upon the reasons for his behavior. As noted by Habermas (1984), only when one is clear about one's validity claims might they be challenged and debated in relation to the claims of others.

In keeping with this last point, in order to deepen one's understanding of one's premises, they must be challenged. The importance of such a challenge has been described by Burke (1957) in his note "On Dialectic" when he says:

> In conformity with Mead, as I understand him, I take democracy to be a device for institutionalizing the dialectic process, by setting up a political structure that gives full opportunity for the use of competition to a cooperative end. Allow full scope to the dialectic process, and you establish a scene in which the protagonist of a thesis has maximum opportunity to modify his thesis, and so mature it, in the light of the antagonist's rejoinders. (ibid., 328)

From the perspective of this book, only when (as per Burke) you allow full scope to the debate so as to modify and mature your thesis, might you deliteralize your beliefs; i.e., discover the premises that support those beliefs, so as to deepen your understanding of the basis for your beliefs.

A further aspect of the integrity of what one says is that one must be accountable. While being clear on the nature of one's validity claims is a form of accountability, this requirement also follows from the way language objectifies our terms as unquestioned truths. Accountability would therefore require that the reason one has for a particular belief be clearly related to the premise that supports that belief. If one says "I find poverty acceptable, because every one has an equal opportunity to succeed in this country," then one's belief as to equal opportunity must (by this view of accountability) be subject to challenge; i.e., if reasons are found to question this premise, the position it supports (poverty is acceptable) should be capable of being questioned as well.

These points follow from the notion that our symbolic reality is subject to being challenged, not in relation to a world it reflects but in relation to the reality we create. The literal reality we create as children must be continuously challenged by the contradictions that arise as a result of these literal beliefs. Clarity by this view evolves slowly out of the continued work of challenging the reified beliefs of our culture and of our childhood.

In this section, the notion of integrity that follows from the understanding of language developed in this book will be used to examine how the theories we elaborate in the pursuit of understanding may be lacking in integrity. More specifically, this section examines how the terms of a theory may be sanctioned in their reified state (i.e., taken as beyond question) because they have been severed from their premises, and may not therefore be questioned. In the example which follows of the Frankfurt school's appropriation of Freud's drive theory, the reification of Freud's terms follows from what appears to be an uncritical capturing of these terms without regard for the premises from which they originally arose.

The Frankfurt school, whose most prominent members include Horkheimer (1968), Adorno (1966), and Marcuse (1968), has endeavored to integrate Weber's sociological perspective within a Marxist-Hegelian framework. In the course of this endeavor, these authors have also embraced Freud. The basic premises of their position (also known as critical theory), are therefore derived from authors (Hegel, Marx, Weber and Freud) one would not ordinarily think of placing together. The questions raised here will be, Can such a collection of disparate viewpoints be integrated in a way that respects the basic premises of each? Or is the result of this attempted integration lacking in integrity, as that term is defined in this book?

At first glance, the Frankfurt school authors have clearly altered the positions they adopt, but it is not clear to what degree they depart from what is basic to each position. Weber, it will be recalled, left us a profoundly pessimistic view of progress, insofar as any progress (for Weber) would inevitably lead to an erosion of our sense of individual initiative and relatedness. The members of the Frankfurt school adopted this "negative dialectic" while introducing a shift in the meaning of its terms. What Weber took to be rational is now to be viewed as irrational. Rationalization, for Weber, had to do with the organizational efficiency of modernization, not with any justification of norms or values. In a disenchanted or desacralized world, there could be no such justification. For the Frankfurt philosophers, however, this development is attributed, not to the inevitable disenchantment of modernization, but to the reification of social relationships brought on by the early development of capitalism.

According to Marx, a liberated society would someday arise out of the contradictions of capitalist/class society, since the latter could not work. Contrary to this prediction, the Frankfurt school philosophers have maintained that since individuals (in a capitalist society) are presumably subsumed under the capitalist production process, the only possible outcome is a closed system that works at the expense of the individual. A liberated society could only emerge with the dissolution of the negative dialectic (i.e., the overthrow of capitalism). The ideas of freedom, justice, and happiness are therefore seen as having been violated by capitalist society. Reason (in its unperverted form) must be sought in a community where the needs of the individual are in harmony with those of the group. Indeed, a principal thesis of Adorno and Horkheimer's (1982) *Dialectic of Enlightenment* is that only if conceptual thinking is turned against itself and its own reifying tendencies can there be any possibility of keeping this hoped-for (unperverted) rationality alive.

The link that connects these alterations of Weber and Marx may be seen in the notion of reification. As used by neo-Marxists (e.g. Lukacs), the concept of reification differs from the definition provided in this text, as it is not related (by these authors) to the way in which language works. Rather, it is seen as the effect of ideologies which promote alienation, false consciousness, and commodity fetishism by, for example, placing the needs of production above the needs of the individual. From this background, reification came to be joined with Weber's rationalization as a central category in the critique of capitalism—the need to reduce man to a means by making him or her a token of capitalist production. What was needed to further buttress this concern for an integral society, was a rationale for "unperverted" reason. That is, one needed a sense of what man's reason would be like, unfettered by the preverting constraints of capitalist society. This is how Freud came to be one of the four pillars of the so-called critical theory of the Frankfurt school.

Freud's concern with the instinctual ground of human culture led him to oppose the primary process of instinctual need, to the secondary elaboration of rational thought. As noted in chapter 8, however, while psychoanalytic thought sees culture as a force that constricts individual freedom, Freud was by no means clear or consistent on this point. Pattison (1984) has pointed out that in his drive theory, Freud tended to pit the instincts, not against societal constraints, but against other instincts. Thus, in 1915, the egoist instincts were pitted against the social instincts. In 1920 and 1921, it was the aggressive drive against the libidinal drive. In 1930, it was unconstrained libido versus aim inhibited libido.

Marcuse (1968) appropriated the "culture as evil" view as central to the dilemma of the individual in capitalist society. While this view clearly owes more to Rousseau's "noble savage" (perverted by the social lie) than to the Freudian unconscious as caldron of unacceptable impulses, Marcuse claimed to have adopted this notion from Freud. For Marcuse, hedonism and the integrity of pleasure are the biological birthright of the individual, but are sacrificed to the reality principle imposed by the collective. Because a society is inherently unfree, the individual's claim to happiness will only become possible with the abolition of class society. There is no small irony in this neo-Marxist appropriation of Freud. A true child of the enlightenment, Freud valued rationality above all else, and was something of an elitist, as in his ideal for self-control expressed in his famous aphorism, "Where id was, there shall ego be." One might therefore imagine Freud's own astonishment at being embraced as a true revolutionary by the Frankfurt school!

In critical theory, the "biological Freud" was taken as the truly revolutionary Freud. Drive theory, which sought to trace development through the vicissitudes of conflicting instincts, became the embodiment of an unresolvable conflict between the biologically determined individual and the inimical constraints of class-structured society. But why (one might ask) appropriate Freud for this task, if his view of instincts is oblivious to class structure, and offers no provision for including such a notion? As noted above, it is not only Freud who has been altered in this manner. Weber finds a place in this integration because his "rationalization" has been redefined as "irrational"; and Marx, because the evolution he anticipated from capitalism to communism has been altered as well; *evolution* must now be *revolution*. What you have, then, is not a deconstruction in the sense of a reversal of terms which allows you to better appreciate their presuppositions. Rather, you have an alteration of terms that *changes* their presuppositions, without really clarifying what they are.

From the perspective of this book, the problem with this kind of appropriation is that it fails to appreciate the integrity of the dialectical process. That is, it fails to take in the fact that if you wish to modify your thesis so as to mature it, you have to be accountable for your terms.

Freud's "instinct" as appropriated by Marcuse, is no longer the instinct envisaged by Freud. And given Marcuse's scheme, it is hard to be clear about what it has become, so that it might be challenged. In a similar vein, certain psychoanalysts went through a period during which they attempted to appropriate Piaget to drive theory (Wolff 1960). What was missed in this misguided venture was the fact that the presuppositions of Freudian theory as to the nature of reality, of learning, of distortion, are at considerable variance with those of Piaget's cognitive psychology. To assimilate the one to the other without addressing how one is to reconcile these contradictions suggests a failure to appreciate the nature of theories, and of how they work. It is akin (to pick an extreme example) to cutting off the head of a giraffe, placing it on the headless neck of an elephant, and expecting the graft to take without further concern over the contradictions one has generated.

Having appropriated Freud, the adherents to the Frankfurt school proceed to wage war with his descendents. Forced to emigrate to the United States, Hartmann, Rapaport and others also introduced a revision in Freudian theory (described in chapter 1) which became known as "ego psychology." This ego psychology was criticized (by the critical theory proponents of "id psychology") as a backsliding from the revolutionary potential of psychoanalysis. As noted in Whitebook (1985), the émigré psychoanalysts who founded ego psychology are seen from the perspective of critical theory as having betrayed Freud for the sake of making him respectable for American capitalism. Hartmann, Rapaport, and the other ego psychologists had turned psychoanalysis into an "ameliorist and conformist science" (ibid., 142).

Having divorced Freudian theory from its theoretical ground, the Frankfurt school could only debate these issues on ideological grounds; i.e., by referring to political systems rather than the premises that support the theory. The potentially fruitful dialogue between the id and ego psychoanalysts became a pointless argument. There could be no hope of questioning the basis for what was being claimed.

A possible counter to my argument is that it fails to appreciate the metaphorical nature of our theories. As competing metaphors, the id and ego approaches to psychoanalysis cannot be compared on the basis of rational validity claims. Rather, they must be promoted as metaphorical systems, much as one might promote a political candidate; i.e., in terms of which one best suits the needs of a particular situation. Yet the adherents to these views have in fact argued as if validity claims were relevant to their arguments.

For example, in his review of the controversy between the id psychologists who champion the "biological Freud," and the ego psychologists who emphasize developmental adaptation, Whitebook (1985) supports the stance of critical theory. That is, he proclaims the inherent disharmony between human rationality and human instincts. His argument may therefore serve as an example of how this stance is justified. While Whitebook claims to find error in both positions (i.e., in the absolute disharmony between reason and the instincts proposed by Adorno and Marcuse, as well as in the ego psychologist's emphasis upon the adaptive nature of man's development) he also refers to the ego psychoanalyst's eagerness to embrace a more adaptive view as failing to capture "the sense of an 'inner foreign territory' which is a hallmark of Freudian thought" (ibid., 157). For Whitebook, "the dialectic of harmony and disharmony between human rationality and its instinctual substratum" (ibid., 157) is a core notion of psychoanalytic thought. Whitebook is therefore appealing to a validity claim to support his thesis. The validity of one's approach to psychoanalysis is to be decided on the basis of what Freud said!

What the ego psychologists had in fact done was to endow the ego with autonomous functions such as perception and memory. The earlier view asserted that these functions arise out of the id, in response to frustration. As noted in chapter 1, perception and memory have to be included as infant capabilities, as they are necessary to a psychoanalytic portrayal of the infant's relationship to its milieu. The id psychologist is therefore in the self-contradicting position of claiming that perception and memory are differentiated out of the id, but in a manner that requires the infant to already be capable of perception and memory. Should such a contradiction be maintained in the name of preserving core notions? Or should one question the core notion in view of the contradiction? Should the ego psychologist be slighted for not following the word of Freud? Or might one admire their willingness (as per Burke) to "modify his thesis, and so mature it"?

In defending the integrity of Freud's position, Whitebook champions a discontinuity between the rational and the instinctual (or for this book, between the verbal and the nonverbal), without regard for the implications of this position. Is the "categorical distinction between the linguistic and the nonlinguistic" a function of some theoretical fiat? Or might it (whether true or not to Freud's position) be argued in relation to observational evidence? In this text I have presented a view of the basic continuity of the linguistic and the nonlinguistic (the first being seen as parasitic to the second) that leans upon two lines of evidence: observational evidence of infant functioning (described in the Appendix); and evidence as to the way in which language functions. I have also argued that without making this assumption, there is no current way of explaining how language participates in the creation of meaning.

Whitebook's account makes no such attempt, and is therefore seen here as failing in the requirement that a theoretician be accountable for the arguments that support his or her basic terms. Unless one literalizes one's statements on the nature of the Freudian instincts as referring to *real* instincts, one would expect some clarification as to the current reasons for hewing to this view, other than the fact that "Freud said so." If the integrity of one's quest lies in the degree to which one's terms may transform themselves in the ongoing dereification of their meaning, then the position Whitebook takes in this article is lacking in integrity. The oppositions he draws—inner nature/society, linguistic/nonlinguistic, rational/irrational—are presented as unbridgeable dichotomies, not as opportunities to further differentiate each term in relation to its opposite. The terms of his discourse have been reified as dogma; i.e., they are presumptions as to the *real* nature of human beings, as promulgated by Freud. In short, Whitebook has literalized Freud's stance as a position that may not be questioned.

10.
PSYCHOANALYTIC FAILURES IN INTEGRITY

Given the view of language proposed by this book, there are no unquestioned truths. Our points of view will always be relative to a particular time and place, to the process of dereifying our concepts, and to the culture in which our discoveries emerge. The term *objectivity* is therefore used in this text to refer, not to an extrinsic world, but to the quality with which one pursues knowledge. Might such a position imply that anything goes? Or that we cannot hope to ever decide how one position is more valid than another?

Far from being eliminated, the notion of validity proposed here is ascribed to one's willingness to challenge the assumptions and beliefs that support what one has to say. A point of view is valid to the degree that it has integrity; i.e., that it is capable of growth, and that it enables you to see beyond the premises that support that point of view. A point of view is questionable when those who use it objectify the premises that support it. Questionable points of view are positions which have become dogmatized due to a failure (on the part of those who hold to a set of beliefs) to question those beliefs.

The literary critic Kenneth Burke sees the human opponent as the intermediary between error and reality. "Silence the human opponent" states Burke, "and you are brought flat against the unanswerable opponent, the nature of brute reality itself" (1957, 328). Without this opportunity for correction, "you are hurled without protection against the unanswerable opponent, the opponent that, not speaking, cannot be quashed by the quietus" (ibid.). Without the human opponent, we are deprived of the opportunity to challenge (and to deepen) our grasp of the premises that support our beliefs; i.e. we are deprived of integrity. In what follows, I offer two examples of approaches to psychoanalytic work (one on its practice, one on its theory) which purport to be objective, but which (from the perspective of this text) are lacking in integrity.

THE MAINSTREAM APPROACH TO PSYCHOANALYTIC INQUIRY

According to the thesis proposed in this book, distorted meaning may only be appreciated in relation to the particular setting that a person has attempted to (or failed to) adequately symbolize. The actual content of this failure may not be presumed out of context, as it will always pertain to a particular time, place, and cultural setting, as well as to the uniquely individual frame of reference of each individual's experience and stage of development. Our generalizations may therefore only apply to the process whereby meanings are realized, not to what the content of these realizations should be. In what follows, I will therefore question the idea that one may predict the content of a person's mind, regardless of the settings in which that content emerges. I will counter that the assumptions we make about what goes on in another person's mind must be verified. This verification involves checking the way in which a particular setting is symbolized, against what one might surmise about that setting. (I owe my appreciation of the significance of this last point, however imperfectly stated, to Dr. Herbert Zucker) To bring out the significance of this last point, I will start with a clinical example.

The example I will discuss is taken from Langs (1976, 15–112), and is the case presentation of a student being supervised by Langs. As will occur in any psychiatric training institution, the patient being presented had been transferred to a new therapist-in-training because her previous therapist had completed his training and had therefore left the institution. At the start of the patient's session with her new therapist (the student presenting the case), the patient asks why she has been scheduled to be seen twice a week. While she had wanted two sessions the previous year, she had seen her earlier therapist once a week because of his scheduling problems. Now, without having been consulted, she has been scheduled for two sessions a week with her new therapist. The patient now feels that she has improved to the extent that one session would suffice. On being asked by the student therapist to "explore it a little further," the patient states that because it takes her an hour to travel to the hospital, the entire morning is taken up by the therapy session. Since she has a job and is going to school, the extra session would deprive her of a day's work and of time to herself. She adds that she had been unable to work or go to school at the start of the previous year, so that her ability to now do so is a sign of how she was able to benefit from the earlier (once-a-week) therapy. The question of the number of sessions is not further addressed by the student therapist, and is subsequently dropped by the patient.

The patient goes on to relate that she feels confused by her situation with the boyfriend with whom she had been living. She has moved back to live with her mother, and "things seem to be going very well." When the therapist asks her what she would like to continue working on in her therapy, she responds that although she does have problems, it is "just so hard to repeat; it's very boring. I've already talked about it, and don't the records say it all?" The therapist responds that it sounds as though she feels frustrated at having to start over with another person, covering old ground. The patient agrees, and goes on to tell how she broke up with an old boyfriend, Bill, and moved in with a new boyfriend, Albert. She states that she still likes Bill, but doesn't see him because she doesn't want to be unfaithful to Albert. She then repeats that she left Albert to go live with her mother. The therapist asks how that came about. She says, she "just decided;" she doesn't know why. She told her boyfriend she had "something to tell him" and then felt she "had to tell him . . . I told him, and he just said OK, and so I moved out."

On the basis of this material alone, Langs assumes that the basic issue for this patient is the premature termination by the previous therapist (Dr. X). Langs suggests that the patient had made an "introjective identification" with the destructive part of Dr. X, which reinforced her own destructiveness and hence led to her departure from her boyfriend. It is then held that this unconscious fantasy, stimulated by the patient's unconscious identification with Dr. X, is the motive for her wish to reduce the frequency of the sessions. Langs reports the following as an example of what he would have said to this patient at this point:

> It seems to me that you're very hurt and really very angry about what happened. You feel that you were used, and that Dr. X used and then discarded you. You know you're telling me that this is no way to be. You're saying that therapists should be loyal as you are. But most of all you seem to have been very deeply hurt once, and you want to protect yourself from

being hurt like that in your therapy with me. And I think this is another reason why you don't want to commit yourself to a more intense relationship with me, and are trying to protect yourself from it right off. (ibid., 53)

At issue is the fact that the material Langs has analyzed may be understood differently, and that one should therefore be concerned with validating the interpretations one makes. For Langs, at the heart of all psychopathology is a process which he assumes exists for both the analyst and the patient. The process is referred to as an "identification," and may take either a projective or an introjective form. The term *identification* is a misnomer, as it does not refer to the patient's attempt to identify with someone. Rather, it corresponds to the patient's "effort to put his own contents into someone else" (1976, 26). The patient does this "in order to manage these inner contents externally and to possibly benefit from the efforts at management taken by others" (ibid., 26). Introjection involves taking in someone else's content. The assumption is that when a part of the self cannot be assimilated to the rest of the personality, the person projects this unintegrated part into someone else. This is done with the expectation that the recipient of this projection will then help the person doing the projection to integrate this wayward part of the self.

Intuitively, one may appreciate the value of Langs' perspective in terms of facilitating the therapeutic task of uncovering blocked or distorted areas of meaning. The problem is that there is no provision for checking these findings against alternative possibilities. The main reason for this problem is that no attempt is made to specify the medium whereby these projections and introjections take place. How does a person project an identification into another person? How do inner disturbances become "safely worked over" by being "placed" in another person? With words? Or with feelings? Or extrasensorily? We are not told. Langs is of the generation of psychoanalysts who eschew drive theory as an explanation of how we represent reality, without having anything to put in its place. He therefore has no way of relating the projections and introjections he describes to the actual events we might observe. From the perspective of this book, he has no way of verifying what he claims. As will be brought out shortly, Langs cannot check the way in which language is used against the settings it refers to, because there is no provision in his theory for the role language plays in the realization of meaning.

If it is not possible to explain how people project and introject, what is it that one works with in an analysis? According to Langs, the analyst works with "derivatives." Derivatives are more or less disguised expressions of the unconscious projections and introjections one wishes to identify. In the example described above, a patient must be listened to, not in terms of the overt content of what is said, but in terms of how this content pertains to the projections and introjections one may attribute to that patient. For this reason, it is possible to assume that when the patient talks about her boyfriend, she is really talking about the therapist who abandoned her. In other words, the only observations that might be used to check one's assumptions (what the patient says and does), are explained on the basis of those very assumptions. Thus, an important source of validation (the actual events referred to by a patient) is denied the therapist, since everything the patient says must be interpreted as a possible derivative of unconscious processes. There is nothing in the material one might refer to as a check against the assumptions one makes!

Based upon the case described above, might one challenge the assumptions Langs makes in view of what was actually said? Langs claims that the previous therapist is perceived by the patient as a "negative introject," yet the only evidence we have in this regard is that the patient feels positively toward her previous therapist, as he helped her return to work and to school. Langs views this patient's stated sense of improvement—virtually the only statement she makes with any conviction—solely as the enactment of a fantasy. He would undoubtedly defend these interpretations by claiming that these motives are unconscious, so that one may not go by what the patient says. But what about those aspects of her behavior that are not consistent with Langs's assumptions? For example, Langs makes no mention of the fact that after her short-lived attempt to influence the course of her therapy, she withdraws to the passive stance of one who experiences little control over her life. Might one view her willingness to tolerate the refusal (on the part of those who would "treat" her) to seriously consider what she says *in its own right*, as a symptom of what ails her? And if this is the case, shouldn't it be borne out in terms of what actually transpires between the patient and her therapist, or her boyfriends?

One could claim in response that whether this patient is driven by unconscious fantasies or is mystified by a poorly comprehended reality, the outcome might be understood from either perspective to the patient's benefit. Nonetheless, there are critical differences in terms of the areas to be focused upon, the procedures assumed to be helpful for the patient, and perhaps most importantly, one's concern for *the integrity of the process;*

i.e., for the kinds of evidence required to validate the therapist's assumptions.

Let us assume that Langs is correct in his interpretations and that this patient was indeed suffering from a sense of having been abandoned by her therapist. Was she *correct* in feeling so abandoned, as Langs implies? Should her therapist (once he completed his training) have stayed on in order to continue her treatment? Or might one wish to help her understand that his departure should not be taken as a rejection? Presumably, the first therapist is seen as acting destructively because the patient is in no position to appreciate his position; i.e., the fact that the very training system she is benefiting from in her treatment is the result of society's need to train psychiatrists and psychologists so that they might move out into the community. Yet the patient is never questioned on this point; she is never once asked how she interprets her therapist's departure!

In other words, Langs's assumption is based, not upon what a particular patient might or might not be capable of understanding, but upon what his theory attributes to her understanding. Because Langs's theory permits him to presume the content of the patient's thoughts, he is led to ignore the possibility that this patient may have some choice over how she interprets her situation. That is, he ignores how she interprets the therapist's departure in the light of the hospital's training procedures. Since Langs assumes that the patient (in the example cited above) introjected the negative projection of her previous therapist regardless of what actually transpired, there is no opportunity to question the inappropriateness of her feeling abandoned, or the actual basis she might have had for feeling abused by her therapist.

In sum, when Langs claims that the patient has incorporated the therapist's negative identification because he did in fact abandon her, he is ignoring the fact that the therapist's departure was a normal feature of the hospital routine which Langs must be in accord with, or he would hardly be supervising in such a setting (i.e., that abandons its patients). In view of the fact that he presents no other evidence (at the point this interpretation is made) to justify this interpretation, one must conclude that he *has* to presume a negative identification, because that's all his theory allows him to presume. That the patient could genuinely have liked and appreciated her first therapist, or that she could feel helpless in the face of a bureaucracy that fails to consult her on her treatment, or that she needs to develop a clearer sense as to why she leaves her boyfriends;

none of this could matter in a Langian analysis, as it fails to fit into the procrustean bed of Langs's projective identification hypothesis.

The problems ascribed to Langs's position are applicable to the mainstream psychoanalytic approach to analytic work as well. This should not surprise us, insofar as Freud's psychoanalytic metatheory is just as solipsistic; i.e., it includes no provision for how our environment becomes an aspect of psychic meaning. As a result, the basic biological metaphor of the mind may not be questioned in a way that might challenge its presuppositions. Langs's view of identification is wholly in keeping with the traditional psychoanalytic view; i.e., that a projection occurs when a person attributes aspects of his or her own inner conflict to another person, in an effort to solve this conflict. The other (as object of this projection) is irrelevant to the process, which depends entirely upon an internal process of conflict resolution. Notice that as with Langs, nothing is said here of the medium involved, beyond the metaphor of energy distributions and cathecting mechanisms described in chapter 1. In other words, no attempt is made to specify how perception, cognition, and language operate in this process. As a result of this failure, there is nothing to debate! No arguable reasons can be given as to what we might observe to substantiate these assumptions. From the perspective of this essay, the theory is therefore lacking in integrity.

When Melanie Klein and her followers began to require terms which could account for the participation of other people in a person's development, the notion of identification was adapted to this task by being reified as a literal occurrence. As described by Bion (1957), the interest generated by Klein's work in the "containing" functions performed by the mother in early development, led to a need to represent both the contents that are projectively identified, and the container for them. This new metaphor opened up a vast and meaningful area of discovery, as it focused our attention upon the ways in which a mother's behavior shapes the development of her child. Granted, to literalize this relationship in terms of a container and a contained is an obvious reification. Yet having at last noted the importance of external events, this new focus might have encouraged psychoanalytic theorizers to question how the interpersonal becomes an aspect of intrapsychic meaning. Unfortunately, the underpinning for this novel approach remained the same biological metaphor of cathecting energies.

From the perspective of this book, introjections and projections require an ability that could only occur with language. That is, these processes require that the infant be capable of attributing to him or herself aspects that belong to another; and to attribute to others, aspects that belong to the self. Only with language might one establish an independent self, so as to then attribute aspects to that self, or attribute aspects of that self to others. Prior to assimilating a language, the infant could not distort its reality via projections and introjections, as has been presumed by Langs and psychoanalytic theory.

Finally, because the theoretical terms of mainstream psychoanalysis may not be challenged, mainline practitioners not only lack a means of questioning their terms; they are deprived of the opportunity to validate the interpretations they make. They are (from the perspective of this book) engaged in a form of inquiry that is lacking in integrity.

A DEBATE BETWEEN TWO KINDS OF PSYCHOANALYSTS

In this section, I will briefly describe the history of the journal *Contemporary Psychoanalysis*. This will be offered as background for a theoretical debate which appeared in this journal. I will argue that in promoting the kind of debate I am about to describe, the current editors of this journal are perpetuating a state of affairs that has existed since the importation of psychoanalysis to the United States in the 1930s; i.e., the failure to understand the relationship of a theory to its premises, which (it is claimed here) is critical to the integrity of our knowledge.

When the trustees of the William Alanson White Institute founded the journal *Psychiatry* in the 1930s, they formed a holding corporation for endowment monies incorporated by the Washington-Baltimore Psychoanalytic Institute. The trustees of the White Institute (who also edited its journal) included the psychiatrists Lucile Dooley, Ernest Hadley, and Harry Stack Sullivan. Dooley and Hadley were of a mainstream persuasion (Dooley had even trained in Vienna), and would resign in the 1940s as the journal's orientation (under Sullivan's direction) became suspect in the eyes of the American Psychoanalytic Association.

According to Perry (1982), Sullivan was, from its beginnings, the dominant member of this triumverate. He was also something of a maverick in this fledgling community of psychoanalysts, in that while he took an abiding interest in philosophy, sociology, and anthropology, he took far less interest in the tenets of psychoanalytic drive theory. The intellectual climate was not accepting of this kind of questioning, however. Psychoanalysis was in its reified belief stage, where to question was to be against.

As psychoanalysis was not (in the 1930s) in good repute among psychiatrists in the U.S., the journal's interest in psychoanalysis was played down. Later, Dooley and Hadley would (in Perry's words) "define themselves as psychoanalysts, but this was after politics with words had become a big and dangerous game in psychoanalytic/psychiatric circles . . ." (ibid., 363). What was potentially a period of discovery and growth was to a considerable degree curtailed by a growing climate of petty rivalries, and the jockeying for position which arises when political power is substituted for scholarly concern. The catalyst for these unfortunate developments was the arrival in the U.S. of the émigré psychoanalysts. John A. P. Millet (1962) has described the "entrenched hierarchical culture" the psychoanalyst émigrés brought with them into exile:

> As more and more of the refugee analysts became qualified as members of local societies and joined the faculties of the training centers the influence of their authoritarian approach to training became more and more apparent. Regulations as to qualification for training analysts, minimum duration of training analyses, frequency of analytic sessions, number and frequency of supervisory sessions, etc., became more numerous, more exacting, and spread over more areas of the training process. . . . The accolade of knighthood in the order of traditional conceptualists had already been given to a handful of American leaders either in Vienna or in Berlin. Their acceptance of the authority vested in Freud and handed down through the International Association was sustained, fortified, and crystalized through reunion with the exiled colleagues. (131–32)

Born in Germany and trained in social psychology, Erich Fromm also emigrated to the United States in the early 1930s. His perspective, however, differed markedly from those of his mainstream colleagues. He was steeped in the writings of Karl Marx, and had an intimate knowledge of the philosophical and ethical heritage of Western culture. Fromm therefore brought a perspective to psychoanalytic thought that transcended the narrow limits of the parochial psychoanalytic societies of Vienna and Middle Europe. His treatment at the hands of his mainstream peers offers a good example of the kind of dogmatism that prevailed among psychoanalytic circles at that time. As described by Perry:

> By the late 1930s, Erich Fromm had become the red flag for rallying opposing political forces in the American Psychoanalytic Association; he

continued in that role for over a decade—in fact probably until he withdrew to Mexico in the 1950s. The attacks on him were illustrative of the irrationalities that appear whenever a group of people try to discredit a person or persons who are in the way of its particular goals for power or prestige. Thus one of the criticisms of Fromm cited by various people was that he was not a physician; but no such criticism was made of Erikson, who lacked both medical and undergraduate degrees. (1982, 380)

As an example of the kinds of attacks Fromm endured, Perry describes the reaction of Karl Menninger to a paper by Fromm entitled "The Social Philosophy of 'Will Therapy,'" published by *Psychiatry* in 1939. Menninger's chief complaint was that "Fromm talks about *other* than Freud's ideas—chiefly Adler's and Horney's I'd guess" (in Perry 1982, 381). While Fromm does not mention these authors in his article (the ideas of which are his own), the notion is clear that *any* thoughts which diverge from Freud's, or dare appeal to "revisionist" ideas, should not be permitted publication. Menninger is even loath to admit to having read these revisionists!

What could not (at this literal stage of development) be appreciated, is that the importance of Freud's ideas should be approached in terms of uncovering and debating the premises of his belief. Of those who participated in the establishment of psychoanalysis on the East Coast of the United States (as described in Perry and Millet), Sullivan appears to be alone in having understood this point. This is how he expressed it in his response to Menninger: "I think that we have to consider the type of discussion which is needed here to be definitely in the field of philosophy. It is *a questioning of the character of premises and their meaning . . . I think that the serious formulation of basic concepts and the tracing of their implications ought to be done . . .*" (ibid., 382, my emphasis).

Sullivan had anticipated by forty years the philosophy of science debate inaugurated in the 1970s by Kuhn and Feyerabend among others. If he was alone in having understood the importance of questioning the "character of premises and their meaning," it was because this task could not be entertained, if the only validation to be sought was in conforming with the dictates of Freud. Nor could this point be understood by those revisionists whose sole intent was to prove that Freud was wrong. For the original followers of Freud, the issue seemed clear. If you disparage drive theory, deny the phenomenon of transference neurosis, eschew the couch and the association method as sole analytic technique, and question the primacy of the oedipal conflict, why call yourself a psychoanalyst? And yet today, those who continue to hold to the tenets of drive theory refer to themselves as "mainstream" psychoanalysts, suggesting that the term *psychoanalyst* has assumed a broader significance, and need no longer be limited to a particular school.

Meanwhile, the debate as to who was to be considered a psychoanalyst in these early years was turning ever more nasty. In 1941, the New York Psychoanalytic Society voted to disqualify Horney as an instructor and training analyst, charging her (shades of Socrates!) with "disturbing the students." Horney in turn founded the Association for the Advancement of Psychoanalysis, with Fromm and Sullivan as honorary members. By 1943, a new schism developed. Fromm's privileges as training analyst in the new association were withdrawn under Horney's leadership, presumably because she felt that Fromm as lay analyst would jeopardize the relationship of the new association with the New York Medical College. Rumor has it that an affair between Fromm and Horney had turned sour. Whatever the case, according to Perry, "it was, in essence, a red herring, for there were ways in which his privileges could have been protected" (ibid., 387).

Resigning his honorary post with the association, Sullivan noted in the May issue of *Psychiatry:* "These influences [personal and professional insecurity] have combined with the profit-and-prestige motives to make the road to success in professional practice much easier for the gifted and fortunate young psychiatrist to travel in company with his colleagues than [along] the path of critic and innovator" (Perry 1982, 388).

When (in 1946) the New York branch of the Washington-Baltimore Psychoanalytic Institute became separately incorporated as the William Alanson White Institute of Psychiatry, so that benefits to G.I. students could be made available, it also started its own journal *Contemporary Psychoanalysis*. At that time the American Psychoanalytic Association renewed its attack, threatening the students of the New York School with permanent discrediting if they did not immediately sever all course work and analytic training with the disfavored (revisionist!) teachers. This threat was in fact a violation of the antitrust laws and was shortly withdrawn. As noted by Perry, however, "the national association over a period of years would continue to exert a constricting effect on both schools, and some of the intellectual freedom to develop a science of the interplay of human emotions would be impaired after Sullivan's death" (ibid., 391). If psychoanalysis is today in such disarray, could it be for any other reason? The practitioners of psychotherapy (by whatever name!) have been more intent upon proving themselves the sole proponents of what is "true" than upon advancing the state of their knowledge.

When Sullivan died of a meningeal hemorrhage on a trip to Europe, his request (transmitted to his adopted son) for a Catholic burial was unknown to administrators at the White Institute, who had his body cremated. Considerable effort was expended in getting the church to tolerate this unacceptable disposition of Sullivan's remains. Borrowing Patrick Mullahy's response to this situation, had Sullivan known of the shenanigans that would follow in his wake, he would have "turned over in his urn."

One interpretation of the history I have just described, is that the right to call oneself a "psychoanalyst" had become a token of political intrigue and power manipulations. Richard Rorty (1982) paints a sad picture of "philosophy in America today" by summoning an image proposed by Andy Warhol. "The best hope for an American philosopher is Andy Warhol's promise that we shall *all* be superstars, for approximately fifteen minutes apiece" (216). Rorty goes on to relate this outcome to the current climate of discourse: "The kind of name-dropping, rapid shifting of context, and unwillingness to stay for an answer which this culture encourages runs counter to everything that a professionalized academic discipline stands for" (ibid., 654). This "unwillingness to stay for an answer" is our contemporary version of Burke's silencing of one's opponent.

In what follows, I describe the exegesis of a psychoanalyst's text by a colleague, which appeared in *Contemporary Psychoanalysis* (henceforth referred to as *CP*). In an article entitled *Of Mystery and Motive: A Review of "The Ambiguity of Change,"* Greenberg (1987) ostensibly reviews Levenson's 1983 text in order to make the following point. A theory of personality development requires the notion of motives (derived from biological need) as exists for example in the current development of Freudian theory by some psychoanalysts in the United States. Whereas Levenson's theory appears to eschew such a requirement, motives and needs are nonetheless to be found in his text implicitly, as necessary assumptions one must make in order to follow what Levenson says. Greenberg then goes on to spell out the nefarious implications he derives from Levenson's neglect. I will argue that because Greenberg ignores the premises that support Levenson's interpersonal stance, he is simply reducing Levenson's position to his own, without regard for the true nature of Levenson's theory. I conclude that Greenberg and the current editors of *CP* fail to appreciate the relationship of a theory to its premises, and the role premises play in our theoretical debates.

For Freudian psychology, you must assume that people have instinctual needs, and that it is the conflict of these needs with each other that is at the heart of our difficulties in living. For Levenson (who aligns himself philosophically with American pragmatism) when you presume to know a person's need in advance, you are imposing your belief system upon that person. Instinctual needs are therefore not taken to be a prime mover as in Freudian psychology. Greenberg's argument (that Levenson nonetheless implies instinctual need) hinges on the following question: On what basis can psychoanalysis be said to work if it is not on the basis of discovering and clarifying repressed and conflicted instinctual needs?

For Levenson, psychoanalysis is defined by its rules of inquiry, not by its goals or its content. By way of analogy, if you wish to play tennis, what matters is not who you are, or why you want to play, but do you know the rules? In a similar vein, a psychoanalysis may be seen as a procedure undertaken by two participants, which enables them to discover meaning. But (states Greenberg), if psychoanalysis is defined by its rules of inquiry, why does it work? If (as per Levenson), the method involves "The elaboration and enrichment of implicate and explicate order in the patient's life" (1983, 55), then you have to make some assumptions as to the nature of man as needing order and as capable of disorder. If man needs order, then need for order becomes a version of instinct.

Greenberg's point is an excellent example of trying to force the premises of one kind of metaphor (Levenson's pragmatism) into the paradigm of another kind of metaphor (Freudian metapsychology). From the perspective of a Freudian paradigm, man must be described as needing order. For the pragmatist, meaning and order are inherent to the ecological system man is a part of, and may not therefore be implicated as needs. That is, they are a function of the built-in structures that enable us to construct meaning, and are not subject to the variability of Freudian need.

For Freud and his mainstream followers, the mind (as a system for the reduction of tension) determines its contents on the basis of instinctually selected objects which satisfy needs. Since these contents are biological givens, and are therefore known in advance, the need for these contents must exist before the fact as well. It is therefore not legitimate to equate

Levenson's order with Freud's instinct. Not only do they belong to entirely different domains of meaning, they imply a very different understanding of how meaning is realized.

Having reduced Levenson's "order" to his own "motivation," Greenberg may then question Levenson's second proposition, which is said to account for order. Order for Levenson results from the fact that human beings have an innate ability to structure experience. Why (Greenberg then asks) should people vary in the way they structure experience? For Levenson, the neurotic lacks the skill to figure out "What's going on around here." To reverse the effects of mystification (as in a psychoanalysis) one must free up the inherent, meaning-creating function of the mind. The elaboration, elucidation and enrichment of our reality is largely a function of putting this order into words (which Levenson refers to as "semiotic competence"); that is, words that might then be reflected upon and contribute to the expansion of meaning.

According to Greenberg, however, Levenson sees the person's problems as a function of a lack of the skills needed to make sense of reality. This must mean (for Greenberg), that (when not mystified) the child's development consists in acquiring skills as to how to relate to reality. In Greenberg's words, this entails "a vision of the child as a relatively passive recorder of what is done to him" (1987, 698). If mystification is the disease, and semiotic competence the cure, then one must assume that mystification thwarts one's adaptation to an otherwise objective reality. The child's development must therefore be in the service of adapting to an objective reality, and semiotic competence results from learning to see that reality clearly.

The problem, of course, is that these assumptions work only within a frame of reference which, according to mainstream psychoanalysis, splits reality into a reality that is independent of our perception, and our representation of that reality. Only if you presume a reality that is independent of our perception, could you then declare that the child's development consists in assimilating such a reality. Pragmatism on the other hand believes that reality is (to borrow Mead's term) an "emergent." That is, it arises out of the synthesis of what we bring to our environment, with what we find. What is objective about our reality cannot therefore be a function of some pre-existing reality we assimilate; it must be a function of how we *create* our reality.

Having ignored these premises of Levenson's theory, Greenberg goes on to state an interpretation of Levensons' approach which, if true, would be quite damaging to Levenson's reputation. Not only does Levenson overvalue the possibility of objectivity in interpersonal relations; he also ignores the role of distortion in our development. For Greenberg it is the interplay between what we need with what is actually there that accounts for the formation of our uniquely individual perspectives. In a psychoanalysis, for example, the work is not a matter of correcting wrong impressions or of altering expectations, but of enabling individuals to use what they have in a more satisfying way. It is because a patient's transference distortion may be explored playfully and creatively that the patient benefits, not because his or her distortions are corrected. Thus (by Greenberg's account) Levenson uses psychoanalysis not to help patients use their experience creatively, but to correct their lack of objectivity. He has (states Greenberg) "bound himself to language and to the reality it represents, considerably vitiating his clinical vision" (ibid., 703). Because he fails to account for motivation and instinct in his scheme, he is said by Greenberg to ignore "the richness and variety of human experience" as well as "its ultimate ineffable quality" (ibid., 703).

To recapitulate Greenberg's argument, Levenson (in his theory) has: 1. Denied the role of instinct in human development. To compensate for this gap, he has substituted objective order, which he does not call an instinct, but which Greenberg assures us is in fact an instinct. 2. This has caused Levenson to overemphasize the rational side of man (his or her *need* for order) and to deny the positive role of distortion in creativity. As a result, he has "vitiated his clinical vision" and denied to our experience its "ultimate ineffable quality."

In his critique of Levenson, Greenberg points to an area that does indeed constitute a gap in Levenson's theory; namely, how to account for distortion. This does not mean that Greenberg is free to fill this gap any which way he pleases. As we have seen, to presume an objective reality as existing independently of the child goes against the basic premises of Levenson's pragmatism. But what about *Greenberg's* explanation of distortion? A principal problem with Greenberg's thesis is that he goes from instincts—as a biological source of needs in people—to distortion—as in the faulty reasoning or unrealistic assumptions that we discover in our thought—without telling us how we get from one to the other. The process whereby instincts cause distorted thinking is obviously critical to his thesis. If, for example, it could be shown that our instincts (as needs) have nothing to do with the way we distort meaning, then not only would his criticism of Levenson's stance be meaningless, but he would himself have to address this gap in his theory.

My point in presenting this critique of Greenberg's exegesis is to underscore the meaninglessness of comparing theoretical viewpoints when the premises they are derived from are ignored. Levenson's failure to explain distortion leaves a gap that Greenberg fills with his own assumptions about motives. Yet Greenberg's presentation itself lacks an explanation of distortion. He appears to take if for granted that we all know what he means by "instinct" and "distortion" since he never bothers to define or to explain his use of these terms. I might here in turn add my voice to this meaningless dialogue by responding to Greenberg's omission with my own assumptions about distortion. As far as I can tell, the only way to avoid this travesty of a reasoned debate, is to define and to then discuss the premises that support what one has to say.

For example, just as one must look to pragmatism for a description of the premises that support Levenson's position, so with Greenberg one may look to authors (e.g., Hartmann, Rapaport) who have developed the Freudian metapsychology in terms of *its* premises. As was described in chapter 1 of this book, much of what Rapaport ascribes to preverbal development is in fact dependent upon the assimilation of a language. Hence the conclusion in this first chapter that Rapaport's account of how we come to represent reality makes perfect sense if we assume that his energy metaphor is in fact describing the way in which language structures meaning. That is, Rapaport's and Freud's energy model was a highly prescient intuition of the way in which language captures the organism's inherent (conflict-free) meaning system.

Having addressed the assumptions that support mainstream theory in the United States (in chapter 1 of this text) I may then question these assumptions on the basis of the evidence presented in this book. For example, given the view of meaning argued in this text, the earlier psychoanalysts may be said to have *reified* the notion of instincts as being something that exists *inside* the person, and that *pushes* for specific contents. They could not therefore see our biological inheritance in terms of an innate system for creating meaning. Today, unless one is prepared to ignore the results of the past twenty years of infant observation, one must acknowledge that what is instinctual about our nature is *not* that we are programmed to seek certain objects, but that we are programmed to *create meaning*. If (as per Greenberg) creativity arises out of resolving the conflicts between the unconscious and the conscious, one might more productively view this conflict, not in the reified terms of predetermined contents of the mind, but in terms of a conflict between the two distinct systems of communication that arise as a result of assimilating a language.

I have argued that in his article, Greenberg has attempted to force Levenson's perspective into the procrustean bed of Freudian metapsychology, as seen in his failure to appreciate the pragmatic view of reality as a basic premise of Levenson's stance. As a result, his comparison of theoretical viewpoints yields no new insights. We are merely told that the U.S. Freudians are correct, and that the interpersonalists are wrong for not thinking like U.S. Freudians! However, if we genuinely compare the premises of these two approaches in the light of the recent discoveries regarding infant functioning, then we are left with a new definition of the problems to be addressed; that is, to the possibility of a common ground that nonetheless respects the differences of each point of view. Greenberg's challenge to Levenson was a mainstream challenge to interpersonal theory, and demanded a response that could encompass the premises of both points of view. While these are clearly Byzantine entanglements in a very small pond, I have described them in the hope of providing some insight into why the warring factions of this beleaguered discipline have as yet failed to arrive at a commonly accepted paradigm. These problems I have argued, have to do with a failure of integrity (as defined in this text), rather then with the nature of the data per se. In the words of Kenneth Burke, "in so far as you spawn [your meanings] and maintain them by organizational efficiency without the opportunity of correction, you are hurled without protection against the unanswerable opponent, the opponent that, not speaking, cannot be quashed by the quietus" (1957, 328).

AFTERWORD

Language, it has been argued in this book, is an essential ingredient in our elaboration of both a *literal* and a *metaphorical* reality. We require a literal reality, for it is the world in which the members of a particular culture find the common agreement necessary to organize themselves politically, to engage in commerce, or to conduct scientific research. But we also require a metaphorical reality, for without it our literal world would become stagnant, and would fail to keep up with developments which seem to be occurring (culturally) at ever greater speed. Without a metaphorical reality there would be no literature and no art. We would all be trapped within the reified limits of an immutable and unchangeable world. Without a literal reality on the other hand, there would be no basis upon which to create our metaphors. Both in turn (the literal and the metaphorical) require language to exist. Indeed, it is within the structure of language that the literal and the metaphorical co-exist (in health) in a continuous process of reciprocal transformation.

If we need language to create a literal world of facts, to what do these facts, in turn, refer? Does not the very notion of a fact imply a world you can see and touch; i.e., that is *independent* of what one makes of it? This text builds upon observational evidence that our preverbal ability to discern analogies is a biological given. That is, we are inexorably linked to our environment from the start of life. The idea that we exist in a reality that is independent of how we experience or perceive is an illusion, which, I have argued, is born of the assimilation of language. That is, language permits us to objectify a world of facts, which is then taken to be an immutable world; i.e., a world that exists independently of how we perceive it. The notion of an immutable reality is therefore a fiction, which like all fictions, requires a language to invent.

Assuming for the moment that there is truth to this argument, how is one to understand our willingness to believe such an illusion? Should one ascribe it (as has Hilary Putnam 1981) to a wish to align ourselves at all costs with some illusion of permanence? Or might we understand this reaction in terms of difficulties as yet poorly understood, which arise in our functioning as the result of assimilating a language? If we have objectified our reality, it is (from the perspective of this book) for two principal reasons. First, because there is a gap in our perception which permits us to do so. Second, because the assimilation of language splits our reality into independently conceived subjects and objects, thereby providing us with a means of objectifying what is presumed to be "out there."

The gap in our awareness has to do with the way we apprehend our reality. We know that the reality we perceive is not a reflection of what is "out there," in the way that a mirror reflects our image (Rorty 1979; Jackendoff 1987). Most today would agree that our manner of being must contribute to what we perceive. Yet we do not have access to how this is done. Like the beating of our hearts, this process occurs automatically, outside of our reflective awareness. As a result, we must infer the nature of the process whereby we apprehend our reality. That is, we cannot avoid making some such assumptions if we are to understand the nature of people and of their universe. The choice we make as to what to assume is a critical one, since it will have a bearing upon everything that follows.

Two ways of filling in this gap are not in much repute these days. The first, known as naive realism collapses the duality of the person and his or her world by seeing the person's reality as a reflection of that world. The second way denies the reality of the world and collapses the person-world duality in favor of the person; i.e., everything stems (as in Bishop Berkely) from the mind. Neither of these assumptions has been very fruitful of late in generating ideas. This is not to say that they won't at some future date. Today however, they have been eclipsed by the two main contenders for explaining how we apprehend our reality. Simply put, the first of these (as proposed among others by the developmental psychologist Jean Piaget) states that we apprehend our reality by building a *representation* of that reality. The second contender (as proposed for example, by the pragmatists) maintains that the process of apprehending a reality is in fact one in which we construct our reality. In this text, I have promoted the constructive view over the representation view. I have argued that whereas the constructive view permits us to grasp the limitations of the representation view, the obverse does not hold. Also, I have maintained that the constructive view permits us to understand the nature of transformation, discovery, and change in a way that the representation view may not.

The representation view of how we apprehend our reality is akin to what a number of contemporary authors who concern themselves with language and philosophy refer to as "objectivism" (e.g., Richard Rorty 1979, 1982; Harold Brown 1979; Hilary Putnam 1981; Richard Bernstein 1983). As described by Bernstein: "By 'objectivism,' I mean the basic conviction that there is or must be some permanent, ahistorical matrix or framework to which we can ultimately appeal in determining the nature of rationality, knowledge, truth, reality, goodness, or rightness" (8).

For Putnam (1981), the objectivist approach expresses a deeply felt need to anchor our reality in some immutable truth. Objectivism (which Putnam refers to as "metaphysical realism"), is therefore a response to our deep-seated dependency needs; needs which presumably propel us to seek out a "God's eye view" which will guide and protect us once we have found it. Putnam believes that for this reason, objectivism has characterized our theory of reality since the Greeks and Romans. Referring to the fact that we have only recently caught on to this form of self-deception, Putnam states: "What we have is the demise of a theory that lasted for over two thousand years. That it persisted so long and in so many forms in spite of the internal contradictions and obscurities which were present from the beginning testifies to the naturalness and strength of the desire for a God's Eye View" (74).

In this text, I have proposed that the objectivism we find in our theories is a function, not of a perverse need for the security of an immutable truth, but of the way language functions. It arises when an inquiry is limited to its initial literal phase, in its potential development as metaphor for our reality. By this view, the motive or need for a "God's Eye View" does not of itself explain the means whereby we distort meaning. In order to force our meaning into the procrustean bed of metaphysical realism, we would have had to distort the meaning that is inherent to our functioning; namely, that our meaning is not, and could not be independent of the context in which it arises. That is (short of being abstracted out of its context by language) a meaning will always pertain to a particular time and place. Only with language might we abstract-out ahistorical matrices or algorhythms which might then appear to exist independently of the contexts in which they arise. By this view, then, the objectivism identified by Putnam, Rorty, Brown, Bernstein and others, corresponds to a particular phase of creative discovery (the literal phase), which must first be established before one might reach beyond it. Objectivism may therefore be seen as a mistaken identification of this phase with the entire process.

This is not to deny that something exists "out there," independently of how we function. But that "something," in contributing to the reality we create, should not be referred to as our reality; i.e., it does not become a reality for us until it has been forged within the crucible of our organismic and sociocultural frames of reference as a realization. To say that the reality we forge is a representation, is (by this view) to ignore the part we bring to its realization. Hence the view of reality as something which we create. As described by Putnam (1981): "[Our conceptions] depend upon our biology and our culture; they are by no means 'value-free'. But they *are* our conceptions and they are conceptions of something real. They define a kind of objectivity, *objectivity for us,* even if it is not the metaphysical objectivity of the God's Eye view" (55).

In this last quote, Putnam is addressing a principal barrier to this shift in our understanding; i.e., the fear that if we abandon our belief in an independent reality, we must also give up our belief in objective standards of rationality and knowledge. That is, if we give up objectivism, we will fall prey to a relativism in which there are no standards; a relativism in which opposing theories are deemed incommensurable, or beyond productive comparisons, and in which therefore, anything goes. But what if (as per Rorty 1982), a different approach is adopted as to the nature of truth? That is, what if the question, What is the true nature of our reality? only makes sense to ask within a theory of creative expression? This book has attempted to spell out the implications of making just such an assumption.

In this book, I subscribe to a functional view of how we conceive our reality—that our thinking is characterized by the way in which we function as organisms. This assumption is not new; its more recent expression is to be found in an appreciation of man which emerged in Europe with Husserl's phenomenology, and in the United States with the pragmatism of Peirce, Mead, James, and Dewey. Not so long after the emergence of these two philosophical schools, philosophy itself took a "linguistic turn" (Rorty 1967), which is still being digested. Over the past forty years or so, much of the philosophical discourse in the English-speaking world has focused upon the degree to which the questions we ask in philosophy are really questions about language. This has led to an in-depth questioning of the assumptions we make as to the nature of meaning, reality and truth. The conundrum we have been led to is this: if we are to arrive at a common understanding of the nature of meaning and truth, we need a frame of reference that is grounded in facts that all may agree to. But what we call facts depends upon the theory one uses to define them. There is therefore little reason to believe that we will ever arrive at a common paradigm for our behavioral sciences and our philosophies, since the facts that must be accounted for are a function of the frame of reference you use to invent them.

From the perspective of this book, this conundrum arises when one fails to distinguish between two distinctly different forms of meaning: the verbal and the nonverbal. Our language mode is presented here as parasitic to our nonverbal mode, in the same way that the Morse code is parasitic to language. While the terms of our theories require a frame of reference in order to have meaning, all theories must in the end accord with the nonverbal meanings that are built into our biological adaptation. The conundrum is resolved, not because we might today envisage a single, and unequivocal answer. Rather, it is resolved because we may now see how we had framed the problem in the wrong way.

If there is an answer, it lies (by this view) not in the facts and their explanation, but in the integrity of the quest. It is the pursuit of knowledge, not its possession that must serve our institutions. Objectivity here inheres, not in the discovery of a transcendental (independent) reality in itself, but in the ongoing deliteralization and renewal of our concepts. Our concepts might therefore be compared to a set of spectacles which must be wiped clean every so often in order to work; and which must be appreciated as a means to an end, not the end in itself. What might that end be? For this essay, it is to be found in the integrity of the quest.

Feyerabend (1965), has noted that it takes time to build a good theory. Only gradually do we come to define the underlying implications and assumptions that go with a particular view; i.e., the metaphysical premises which must be made explicit if a theory is to be challenged and to grow. "A science that is free from all *metaphysics*" (notes Feyerabend, and he includes philosophical systems in this category as well), "is on the way to becoming a *dogmatic* metaphysical system (ibid., 150). For these reasons, it would seem important to conclude this book with an overview of the metaphysics which support its premises. I have elected to draw on the metaphysical foundations of pragmatism for several reasons. The pragmatic school has the good fortune of joining Peirce's revolutionary grasp of how we realize meaning as a semiotic system, with Mead's critical emphasis upon (and demonstration of) the social origins of shared meaning. In addition, Peirce and Mead (who were the seminal thinkers of pragmatism), had the depth and breadth of knowledge to pursue the meanings of their terms to their ultimate implications. By paraphrasing their position and casting it in a more contemporary language, I will attempt to show how their cosmology supports a shift in our understanding that bears more than a casual resemblance to phenomenology and existentialism; namely, that far from adhering to some immutable ahistorical standard, the "reality that is there" (as Mead would say) is in a continuous state of becoming. And that only in making such an assumption might we account for the creative transformations that sustain our adaptation to our world.

PEIRCE'S SYNECHISM

A first premise of pragmatic metaphysics is that man exists as a part of an ecological system which is inherently meaningful. Within this system, meaning arises out of the reciprocal involvement of all elements of the system. The important shift that is apparent in this cosmological view, is that the cosmos is not taken literally as a collection of planets in space, but metaphorically as a holistic meaning system. For Peirce, this premise was described as *synechism,* "the doctrine that all that exists is continuous" (Vol. 1, P. 172), and served as a basis for his development of semiology. Several consequences follow from this holistic view of man and nature. First, we do not naturally come by the notion that man is a subject in an objective world. As an intrinsic part of nature's ecology, there is no reason (short of the objectification of language) for man or woman to be conceived of as independent of the meaning system he or she partakes of. Second, the reciprocal interpenetration of the parts of this system constitutes it meaning; i.e., a meaning that has evolved over millions of years, as an adaptive and evolving biological system. Meaning in other words arises out of the adaptive contexts it is a feature of, and could not therefore be reduced to some independent, abstract matrix. Third, in a universe where all things are continuous, the universe itself must be undergoing a continuous growth from nonexistence to existence. As described by Peirce, "The very first and most fundamental element that we have to assume is a Freedom or Change, or Spontaneity, by virtue of which the general vague nothing-in-particular-ness that preceeded the chaos took a thousand definite qualities" (Vol. 6. P. 200). This freedom however is meaningless unless it refers to a choice of actions. Every freedom or potentiality must sooner or later be realized; and in being realized it annuls itself by becoming determined. That is, choices establish patterns, and patterns link with other patterns. In this manner, a "habit taking tendency" arises, and gives birth to time, when (as per Peirce), "events . . . have been bound together into something like a continuous flow" (Vol. 1. P. 412). An essential ingredient of this biological meaning system is therefore the ongoing polarity between continuity and change.

PEIRCE'S "THIRDNESS" AND MEAD'S "FUNCTIONAL IDENTITY"

For both Peirce and Mead (and in keeping with the last point), the emphasis (in attempting to understand our reality) shifts from, "What is the nature of reality?" to, "How do our realities come into being?" What matters in this nondeterministic view is the *process* whereby our realities emerge, since it is this emergence (and not some immutable reality), that is the subject of our inquiry. Second, the habit forming tendency, which today would be better described as the constraints that are placed upon the possibilities of meaning, are meaningful by virtue of what Mead referred to as the functional identity of a response (*cf.* Miller 1973), and Peirce referred to as *Thirdness* (*cf.* Turley 1977). For Peirce, there are meanings in nature which connect a potential realization or law with an actual realization. Each realization is but one instance of its law, yet the law exists only in the form of the instances it permits. Peirce's thirdness would appear to conform to the objectivist belief in some ahistorical framework for determining truth. If thirdness corresponds to a law, and laws exist independently of the circumstances they organize, then Peirce must be an objectivist. The law in question however, is not one which could exist outside of the context it organizes, insofar as it establishes a functional (as opposed to an abstract) identity. This critical point is perhaps more clearly seen in Mead's notion of the functional identity of a response. For Mead, two hammers are similar, not because they have an identical shape or are made of the same material, but because both are used to hammer nails. The identity is in the functional use, not in some abstract category. By this view, existentially different objects (having separate identities) can be similar if they function the same way. If (to borrow Miller's example [1973, 13]) I say "Close the door" to you, the meaning is the same whether it is closed by me or by you; and the existentially different acts of closing it are functionally identical.

An objection might be raised at this point, insofar as when one says "function *alike*", one is presupposing the very thing one would explain. That is, one is presuming the alikeness that is purportedly functional. As described by Miller (1973), "Mead, with Peirce, would no doubt answer that we must take habit, thirdness, law, as a basic category whose meaning is not explained in terms of other more primitive concepts or notions" (15). In this text, Peirce's thirdness and Mead's functional identity are ascribed to our inherent ability to discover analogies; i.e., how things are alike (see Appendix). That is, the ability to discover analogies is built into the system, so that we need not explain how we discover this ability (though one would sorely like to know how it arises!). For the moment however, I would underscore this critical point for two reasons. First, it offers an alternative to the "representational" position insofar as this ability must emerge creatively out of the contexts in which it arises, and could not be a function of simply duplicating what is "out there." Second, it is basic to the two most significant developments to grow out of pragmatism: Mead's explanation of the social origins of shared meaning; and Peirce's explanation of meaning in terms of his *semiotics*.

THE SEMIOTICS OF PEIRCE AND SAUSSURE

Peirce referred to himself as "a pioneer, or rather a backwoodsman, in the work of clearing and opening up what I call *semiotic*, that is the doctrine of the essential nature and fundamental varieties of possible semiosis" (Vol. 5. P. 488). Within virtually the same time frame (Peirce lived from 1839 to 1914, Saussure from 1857 to 1913), Ferdinand de Saussure was teaching his *Cours de linguistique générale* (1959) in Geneva, to be published by his students only after his death. Like Peirce, Saussure saw language as but one of the many sign systems that contribute to our meaning. Also like Peirce, he christened it *"Sémiologie (du grec semeion, 'signe')";* a science which would teach us the laws which regulate signs (*"Elle nous apprendrait en quoi consistent les signes, quelles lois les régissent"*). Working separately and on different continents, Peirce and Saussure each inaugurated a revolution in our understanding that we have as yet barely caught up with. This still very young science of semiotics is not only the fruit of a lengthy process of dereifying our reality—only now are we in a position to appreciate meaning without having to refer to a literal world; it also conforms to the recent findings in infant observation (described in the Appendix) that have revolutionized our view of infant development.

Our commonsense view has been that our signs refer us to things in the real world, which are called the referent. Yet a referent is not by this view an actual state of the world that validates the sign. As pointed out by Peirce, in order to know something about the referent as sign, one must indicate it through another sign, and so on. The referent can only be grasped through a series of signs. The sign may not therefore owe its meaning to the referent it refers to, since that referent is itself defined by the sign!

At this stage of our understanding, the manner in which signs perform this feat is not altogether clear. The very notion of a sign (as presented by these two pioneers of semiology) leaves something to be desired. Saussure saw the sign as a twofold entity—a signifier or sign-vehicle, and a signified or content—an insight which according to Eco (1976) "has anticipated and promoted all correlational definitions of sign function" (14). But, (Eco goes on to say), "Saussure did not define the signified any too clearly, leaving it half way between a mental image, a concept, and a psychological reality" (ibid., 14,15). For Saussure, the relationship between the signifier and the signified is established on the basis of a system of rules *(la langue)*. Signs by his view are necessarily artificial, as they belong to conventional systems of meaning. The perceptual side of the equation is left quite vague.

For Peirce, a sign is "something which stands to somebody for something in some respects or capacity" (Vol. 2. P. 228). For this meaning function to occur however, there must always be cooperation of three subjects: "A sign, its object and its interpretant" (Vol. 5, P. 484). That is, a sign can stand for something only because it is mediated by an interpretant, which is another sign. What a sign produces in the mind is called the *interpreter*. The interpre*tant* (Peirce insisted) is not the interpre*ter*.

Rather, the interpretant is another sign which refers to the same object. In order to establish what the interpretant of a sign is, it is necessary to name it by means of another sign. This establishes a process of unlimited semiosis which according to Eco, is "the only guarantee for the foundation of a semiotic system capable of checking itself entirely by its own means (1976, 68). One might add that unlimited semiosis presents us with the problem of envisaging a meaning system that makes no clear reference to an outside world. The reference is there in that something gets interpreted, but it is hard to get at what the "something" is.

There is a further problem with the notion of a sign. Peirce and Saussure belonged to a generation which took the knowledge of Greek for granted among cultivated men. It was not therefore, a coincidence that (unbeknownst to each other), they adopted the same name for their fledgling science, deriving the word semiology (or for Saussure, *sémiologie*), from the Greek *semeion*. This gift from Greece stands today as a kind of Trojan horse, insofar as it perpetuates the ancient duality of the sign as a representation. From the perspective of this essay, the notion that signs represent our reality not only detracts us from the process of signification; it reifies the sign as being separate from the reality it is said to represent. A final problem with the notion of the sign is that Saussure and Peirce differ in what they perceive to be its range of applicability. For Saussure, signs are always established on the basis of some conventional agreement. For Peirce, we also have natural signs, i.e. signs which are inherent to the way in which we realize meaning.

One response to these difficulties is to deconstruct the sign as representation, in order to imagine signification as a process. To do so, one might ask how the notion of a sign relates to the revolution in infant observation described in the Appendix. That is, if infant observers are now able to say something about how infants think, how might these observations assist us in understanding the role of the sign in the realization of meaning? As described above, the main implication to be drawn from the discoveries of infant observers is that infants have a built-in capacity to tune into the invariant properties of events. The problem of course is that one is hard put to imagine how meanings arise, if there is no realm of pure, fixed, univocal meanings for us to reflect or internalize. Herein lies the importance of the notion proposed separately by Peirce and Saussure, that our signs carry meaning by referring to each other. That is, signs do not refer us to the objects they stand for, as a label might refer us to the content of a jar. A sign owes its meaning to the network of signs it is a part of. Our perceptual system, as a system of signs, might best be described as being in the service, not of representing an extrinsic reality, but of discovering analogies. The analogy in question would not be one which points to a common meaning shared by different subjects, since this is tantamount to assuming that these analogies correspond to some state in the real world. Rather, the analogies in question have to do with the kinds of relations we discover. That is, what is common to the things compared is not a presumed reality "out there," but the likeness itself.

PEIRCE'S TYCHISM AND MEAD'S SOCIAL ORIGIN OF THE ACT

Finally, the notion that we create a reality is fundamental to both Peirce and Mead. If everything happens in accordance with a fixed rational plan, or according to fixed ends, there could be no novelty or creativity. Mead was mindful of the implications of the theory of relativity in physics, particularly with regard to how it precludes the possibility of an absolute, immutable perspective. He also understood that, unless you assume that we creatively synthesize our reality as an emergent, you can't account for how situational aspects such as motives and values become a part of that reality. For Peirce, indeterminacy or "chance" is as real an ingredient in nature as lawful change. According to Peirce's doctrine of Tychism, the universe must include some of the spontaneity which characterized the evolutionary point of departure. By chance, Peirce means lawlessness; i.e., departures from law which in the physical universe are infinitesimal and consequently known only in an indirect way (Vol. 7. P. 514). Mead cast these ideas in terms of the social act, adopting Hegel's notion of the historical process of meaning as a dialectic. But unlike Hegel, Mead conceived of the individual as a principal source of creativity, and saw this creative process as one in which personal experience comes into conflict with accepted theories and laws. Herein lies Mead's fundamental concern with the relationship of the individual to the group; i.e., for the individualism and the open society which are essential to man's creative adjustment.

Both Peirce and Mead were somewhat vague (as was Hegel), as to the medium whereby this evolutionary development or dialectic occurs. Peirce indicates that in people it arises through the deployment of our signs; whereas Mead addresses this question with his metaphor of the *I* and the *me*. By this view, the *I* is existential and attuned to the "world that is there," whereas the *me* represents the social self-conscious self structured by language. Hence the view that we each bear within us an ongoing dialectic whereby the societal constraints we must adopt to be a part of society are gradually broadened and personalized in our confrontations with our more existential self.

THE PROBLEM OF OBJECTIVE TRUTH

If today our sense of objectivity may no longer be ascribed to some independent standard, what is it to depend on? What is the nature of the *objectivity for us* alluded to by Putnam? Peirce's attempt to resolve this question was not entirely successful. Peirce characterized truth as that "which is independent of what you or I or any group or generation of man may opine upon the subject" (Vol. 2. P. 153); but this amounts to saying that what we mean by truth is determined by "the opinion which is fated to be ulitmately agreed to by all who investigate" (Vol. 5. P. 407). That is, truth is social in nature, and demands an endless investigation as well as an unlimited community of investigators. Peirce defines it as "that concordance of an abstract statement with the ideal limit towards which endless investigation would tend to bring scientific belief, which concordance the abstract statement may possess by virtue of the confessions of its inaccuracy and one-sidedness, and this confession is an essential ingredient of truth" (Vol. 5. P. 565). Thus, even if one is to assume that investigation will continue and reach ultimate agreement, no law could be pronounced unqualifiedly true. Since truth and reality demand an infinite investigation for their recognition, there are no grounds for proclaiming even the probable truth of a particular law.

Peirce's principal of *fallibilism* offers an alternative approach to objectivity, which is the one adopted by this book; i.e., to view objectivity not in relation to some independent standard, but as inhering in one's ability to question one's beliefs. The objectivity of one's beliefs is attributed, not to a belief's congruence with an abstract standard, but to its ability to be challenged and to grow. The obverse of this process—the objectification or reification of our beliefs—is seen here as a principal source of dogma. An objective belief system is therefore one which allows us to deepen and to broaden what we know. What is added to Peirce's fallibilism is the idea that if our beliefs must be continuously questioned, it is because of the nature of the language we use in stating them. Language *literalizes* our meaning. As used here however, *literal* refers to a distortion in the attribution of meaning that occurs when we assimilate a language. As was described in chapter 3, in the initial stages of being assimilated to words, meanings are taken by the child to be a property of the words that express them. At this early stage of language acquisition, the child is not yet able to reflect upon meaning, or to understand language as being about the possibilities of meaning. For this reason, the literalness of the child's verbal grasp of the world must (in his or her development) be continuously broadened to recapture the breadth and textural richness of nonverbal meaning that is sacrificed to the incursion of language; and to establish the reflective potential of language as a source of discovery.

The same might be said of our theories. In their earlier stages, the terms of a theory tend to be quite literal, as in the theory of numbers in ancient Greece which was thought to refer to real numbers; or the separation of the sacred and the profane, which was thought of in terms of real spaces. By this view, the theoretical cast we bring to our understanding must be continuously broken so as to counter the literalizing and objectifying tendencies of language, and to grow and expand in meaning.

The French author François Rabelais (1494–1553) has offered the following theory of poetry appreciation: *"Il faut briser l'os et sucer la substantifique"* (one must break the bone, and suck out the marrow). In a similar vein, language is viewed here as a kind of cast which objectifies our reality, and which must be continuously broken so as to broaden and enrich the content of meaning. Each new discovery is in turn objectified as it emerges in our discourse, so as to be challenged anew. By this view, the assimilation of language might be compared to what happens when a wild animal is captured and trained to perform in a circus. In the wild, the animal's inherent and considerable skills are finely tuned to the ecological requirements of its milieu. In the circus, the potential breadth and depth of these skills are severly and cruelly constrained and curtailed so as to adapt the captured animal to the performance requirements of the circus. The analogy breaks down at this point, as the animal lacks language and cannot adapt its training to the purposes of intentional communication. Circus animals are not only deprived of the opportunity to become responsible members of the circus community; they are (as are children) vulnerable to being cruelly taken advantage of. Contrary to these victimized animals however, humans may use language to join ranks with the responsible members of a social group. The full humanity of our being, however, will not arise short of challenging the reified beliefs of our childhood and of society.

Hence the relevance of this text to the interpretive work of psychotherapy. If language is the vehicle whereby we distort meaning, then it is from an understanding of how this occurs that these distortions will be corrected. The interpretive process of psychotherapy is therefore presented as a perfect example of how failures or distortions in the realization of meaning are brought to light and corrected. That is, the work of the psychotherapist is grounded in a process of creative discovery that pertains to all of our cultural pursuits.

I would not wish to convey the impression that it is solely to the *structure* of language that one must look if one is to understand the nature of objectivity. That is, while objectivity (as understood here) results from our ability to continuously challenge and thereby broaden the meaning of our terms, it is not a goal of our inquiry in the sense of leading to a final result. Rather, objectivity is more appropriately seen as a quality of the process of inquiry. In chapter 6 this quality was described as being *purposeful, responsible* and *uniquely individual,* and as essential to the symbolic realization of meaning. A loss of this objective stance on the other hand, is seen as a principal condition for the distortion of meaning; i.e., for claiming truths on the basis of what we think they should mean or what we wish them to mean.

Thus, by this view, the reification of our reality with language is not merely something to be overcome with understanding and growth. One might not underestimate the politics of reification as it is used to fortify a dogmatic stance, or is placed in the service of arrogance and pretentious mediocrity. The reification of our beliefs pervades every aspect of our lives, from the reified brutalities that may arise in our interpersonal relationships, to the callous indifference of the haves to the have-nots. Examples of this failure of objectivity are rarely obvious in our scientific reports, as they originate *not* in the form of an inquiry, but in the unstated assumptions and motives which underlie that inquiry. Needless to say, assumptions of this sort are most destructive to the enterprise of knowledge *not* because they assume a certain view of reality (which might always be challenged), but because they are grounded in a self-serving arrogance. Might one make such a claim without sounding arrogant oneself? And should an essay on language adopt such a moralistic tone?

The point seems unavoidable, as the reifications I refer to, while made possible by language, are not caused by language, but by the people who use them. I do not here refer to the mediocrity of falsified data, or the presentation of fiction as fact, though these may be in the service of the stance I am describing. Rather, it is the position that because one holds a belief, that belief must be unassailably true; or that because one believes, all who do not share in one's belief are infidels and fools. In short, any position which fails to respect the free and responsible realization of meaning as a basic value; and which fails to appreciate and to support the conditions which promote the emergence of meaning.

The goal of understanding (in the absence of this respect and appreciation) is readily subverted to one of selfish need, as when the objectified position which should be but a phase in the dialectical expansion of knowledge is seized upon by a particular group as an eternal truth; or when a belief is dogmatized so as to empower the position of those who are the "keepers of the truth"; or when the inquiry is in the service of motives such as the need to enhance one's status and power. Then the free play of differences which must be permitted in any creative exploration cannot be maintained. A slant or bias has crept into one's inquiry, and objectivity has given way to objectification.

Appendix
ON THE POSSIBILITY OF FREE CHOICE, AND THE INTEGRITY OF KNOWLEDGE

The theory of meaning presented in this book requires that one address the following question: How does a meaning system that is biologically determined allow for free choice and the integrity of knowledge? If (as in this text) human beings are said to be essentially *creators of meaning*, it should be possible to explain how a biologically determined meaning system could allow for the purposeful, responsible, and uniquely individual elaboration of meaning, described in chapter 6. In order to address this question, I will start with a discussion of the revolution in infant observation described by Stern (1985), so as to spell out the paradigm shift on our appreciation of meaning that is implicit in these findings, and that pertains to how infants create a reality.

To appreciate the recent revolution in infant observation, one must be willing to challenge the empiricist assumption that lies at the heart of our earlier beliefs about the nature of meaning. The main question to be asked in child development was, To what degree is the brain programmed to function in the world? The answer was, As little as possible! Why had this assumption persisted for so long? Perhaps in a democratic, forward-looking society, it has not been seemly to attribute who we are to our genes. Rather, we pride ourselves to the extent that we are self-made. Hence the assumption that children (as has been claimed until recently) learn to make sense of their world from their experience. Only gradually do they form beliefs about the nature of physical reality based upon what they surmise from their experience. This basic assumption entails the following beliefs in our most respected theories of child development:

1. Children at first lack the capacity to understand their environment or to reason about it coherently. The infant, as per William James, starts life in a state of "buzzing confusion," or, as per Jean Piaget in a state of total "egocentrism," or in the words of the psychoanalyst Margaret Mahler, in a state of "autism."
2. The child's ability to represent his or her reality must be acquired gradually, as the child learns to coordinate the various sense modalities. "No pain, no gain" might be the motto for this work-oriented ethic; our infants must work to attain the fundamental building blocks of a mind.

Today the pendulum has swung to the opposite position. Could it be mere coincidence that this occurred at a time when cognitive scientists began comparing the mind to a computer? Given the inordinate success of computer technology, and its ability to simulate what the mind does, it would be surprising had we not come up with a metaphor of the mind as computer. By today's view, the role of experience has virtually disappeared, and the mind is viewed as springing forth like Athena out of the head of Zeus, fully equipped to construct and represent a reality from the start. Yet so important a change of view (as described in Putnam 1987) has been centuries in the making, and must be related to deeply rooted transformations of our understanding of who we are. We may also appreciate this change as growing out of innovations which have appeared in increasing number in the field of childhood observation. I will therefore briefly review some of these innovations, as they constitute the main evidence for the "biological" view of meaning proposed here.

A first example is the discovery (Wolff 1966) that infants do not start life in a state of "buzzing confusion" or "autism." From the very start, infants reveal moments of alert inactivity in which they are clearly responsive to what goes on. A shift away from the empiricist paradigm had to have been made by Wolff to permit this observation, for it countered everything we had assumed about infants. The same may be said for the discovery that voluntary activities such as looking, sucking, and head-turning could be used to determine what infants are capable of recognizing. Infants, it was discovered, can be made to answer questions on their own, if we only ask the right question. Here again, the very notion that infants act with "intention" went against the grain of our empiricist and behavioristic assumptions, and could not have taken root had there not been a significant shift in the way we understand the infant's mind.

The final innovation to be considered is the all-important discovery that infants habituate fairly quickly to familiar situations, and therefore permit us to appreciate the recognition of events in terms of what they fail to attend to. Here again, a paradigm shift is evident in the view of the infant as actively realizing (and then habituating to) meaning, rather than passively registering it. As is often the case with paradigm shifts, one case will establish itself as prototypical of the shift taking place. This appears to be true of a study that completely and definitively turned the empiricist assumption about infants on its head. To prepare us for this paradigm case, Andrew Meltzoff and Keith Moor (1977) demonstrated how infants between twelve and twenty-one days of age can imitate both facial and manual gestures, in a way that cannot be explained in terms of either conditioning or innate releasing mechanisms. Meltzoff and Richard Borton (1979) then showed how infants ranging in age from twenty-six to thirty-three days old, can recognize an oddly shaped nipple across modalities in a way that indicates that he or she can represent the abstract, invariant features of events. To demonstrate this mind-boggling feat, these experimenters had to assume that infants could do what most infant observers assumed they couldn't do. In their demonstration, Meltzoff and Borton showed conclusively that infants don't need repeated experiences to make sense of an event; and that they can represent and subsequently recognize the invariant features of events by the third week, across modalities. In this clear refutation of the tenets of empiricism, one must conclude that these skills are innate, and occur as automatically as the beating of our hearts. As a biological function, meaning is an inherent feature of who we are as organisms. This challenge to our presumptions must rank with the discoveries of Copernicus, Darwin, and Freud as the latest assault upon our narcissistic presumptions. We are not, it now seems clear, responsible for what we find preverbally meaningful, any more than for any biological function of our body. Once we have absorbed this discovery, the finding makes sense, for were this not so, we would lack a basis for agreement in our communications.

But how, one might now ask, do these findings affect the assumptions we make about the nature of our reality? One way of understanding how infants accomplish what Meltzoff and Borton show the infant can do, is to assume that infants have a coding system for representing their reality that is built into the nervous system. The question is, how does this coding system work? It could work like a TV camera, and generate a facsimile of what is "out there." Or the infant's coding system could embody a system of assumptions about the nature of reality that enable the infant to construct a reality. The first possibility (dubbed a "weak" hypothesis) sees the code as reflecting some extrinsic, independent standard. The second possibility (dubbed a "strong" hypothesis) sees the code as *being* reality. By this second view, we do not represent a reality so much as bring one into being. The evidence we have today supports this strong hypothesis. An infant who represents reality from the start could not merely duplicate what's "out there," since these representations would have to be meaningful from the start in order to *be* representations; i.e., they would have to encode a reality that has meaning, not in itself but from the perspective of the infant.

There are, however, problems associated with a strong hypothesis. For example, how does one escape the solipsism of assuming that we construct our reality? If the basic assumptions we make about reality are "wired in," how is such a reality to be challenged? How could wired in assumptions ever change? Furthermore, if our awareness is of a reality we construct, how do we tell the difference between what we bring to this construction, and that which exists independently of what we bring? And if our representations don't reflect an external reality, what do they represent?

For those who subscribe to a computation model of consciousness, one consequence (if not a resolution) of hewing to a strong hypothesis is to divorce phenomenal awareness from meaning. For the empiricist, awareness plays a critical role in establishing meaning, since our awareness enables us to reflect an external reality. For the computationist, the construction of meaning occurs unconsciously. We do not need awareness to discover meaning, since meaning emerges outside of our awareness. Awareness therefore pertains to the *form* information takes, not to the meaning it has. Following Jackendoff's (1987) description in *Consciousness and the Computational Mind,* the information that impinges upon our sense receptors is organized in terms of a peripheral, an intermediate, and a central organization. The intermediate level, which is stored in short-term recall, corresponds to the representational form meaning takes. The centrally organized level, which is stored in long-term recall, corresponds to the meaning per se.

There is a good deal of evidence today to the effect that perceptual processes are not identical to phenomenal experience (Marcel and Patterson 1978; Marcel 1979; Marcel and Wilkins 1982). An example cited by

Marcel (1988) is the phenomenon of cortical blindness showing "blindsight," where the person is phenominally blind in one visual half field, even though the visual functions are intact. The person suffering from this condition sees, but doesn't *know* that he sees. As in the Meltzoff and Borton study, meaning appears to be made up of a phenomenal representation (which we can use to represent a meaning because it can be felt, seen, or heard), and an amodal meaning (which we construct unconsciously, and somehow attach to this representation). The question then becomes, do these findings justify the computation model's divorce of the modal representation of meaning from its amodal content? For the computationist, the shapes and dimensions we compute unconsciously and then project as our extrinsic reality have meaning in that we can orient ourselves in this projected space. But neither the process nor the content of thought are revealed to us in our phenomenal representations.

A question raised by this assumption is that if we don't really know *why* what we are aware of has meaning, how do we know when our computations have gone wrong? In an automobile, the fuel-battery-oil gauges tell you when something needs attending. What accomplishes this for the mind, if our awareness has nothing to do with what things mean? Jackendoff's answer to this question is to appeal to an area that is normally ignored by computationists. He claims that it is our affects that serve this function. There is a felt aspect of meaning which tells us if an event is good or bad, interesting or indifferent, right or wrong, attractive or repulsive, intrinsic or extrinsic, and so on. But there is still a problem with this solution, in that it holds that the mind operates like an autocratic parent. The mind tells us what to do (in response to these evaluations) but not why! And the problem with not knowing why, is that if you do something a certain way and suddenly it doesn't work, you have no means of altering what you do, short of blind trial and error. How, given such a view, would we ever correct our mistakes?

Jackendoff's position on phenomenal awareness counters the assumption many would make that awareness plays an important role in learning. For Jackendoff, our awareness cannot affect the meaning we compute unconsciously without operating like a mind's eye or a "little person in the brain." This fiction was an unavoidable implication of the empiricist assumption; i.e., if your awareness reflects a reality, then someone has to be "in there" perceiving this reflection. Therefore, to avoid the notion of a mind's eye, you have to divorce awareness from meaning. As described by Jackendoff, "The stream of consciousness is essentially nothing but our evidence that thought is taking place; both the process of thought and its content are inaccessible to awareness" (320). Our knowledge will always be implicit, based upon the representations we have access to, but not upon the computations which inform them.

Clearly, the problem Jackendoff creates is as ornery as the one he wants to avoid. If our awareness does not alter what we know, how do we learn? If the meanings associated with our representations do not change as a function of our conscious needs and desires, how do we survive? Without a means of explaining how awareness guides our thought, how can we be viewed as purposeful beings with a free choice over what we do? If the preverbal child does not already have a capacity for purpose, how could he or she adopt a procedure such as language, which is an instrument of purpose? How, from a computation point of view, could there ever emerge an individual sense of self, if our affects cannot change on the basis of our awareness? If the computationists are correct, then conducting a psychotherapy is (at best) a well-intentioned hoax.

A different kind of difficulty is faced by theories of meaning which bypass these questions and attempt to establish the individual's sense of self as emerging out of an affective sharing with a caretaker. For example, psychoanalysts generally assume that the infantile self emerges out of an empathic mirroring or sharing of affective experiences with an adult caretaker. As pointed out by Stern (1985) however, it is not at all clear how one can share an experience in the sense of getting inside another person's subjective experience and then letting them know you have arrived there, without using words. For an affective state to be shared, not only must a parent read the infant's state and respond in a way that corresponds to that state, but the infant must in turn relate to the parental response as having to do with its own experience. In other words, the infant must be capable of inferring that the adult's communication is directed at his or her own subjective state, at a time when the infant is unaware of *having* a subjective state. Stern's solution to this dilemma is to appeal to the "affective attunement" that occurs when a parent matches a child's response. When these matchings are cross modal (as when a gesture is used to reflect a sigh, or a grunt is used to reflect a fall), they treat the child's subjective state as a referent, and the overt behavior as one of several possible manifestations of that referent. In this way, the infant presumably comes to refer to his or her own feeling state. Thanks to the parental attunement, the child's focus shifts from the behavior itself, to what is behind the behavior, i.e., to the quality of feeling being shared. In this manner, a sense of self emerges in the child, as a state the child may him or herself refer to.

The problem with this explanation is that in order for the child to respond to the parental matching in this way, he or she must be capable of interpreting the parental gesture as an intentional communication. That is, the child must appreciate the fact that the parent is using a gesture in order to have the child infer a meaning the gesture is a sign of. In other words, Stern is assuming the very quality he would account for, insofar as the child must already possess what he or she supposedly learned from being attuned to in this manner. If the infant is to conceive of the caretaker as intending a communication, he or she must be capable of thinking metalinguistically of the adult's communication as a gesture that is about something; and of reflecting upon the intent of this communication as bearing upon its own experience. Neither of these requirements are possible to meet without language.

What we need, then, is a way of accounting for discovery and change that does not rely entirely upon an independent reality to explain how this occurs, as well as a way of explaining how we come to share meaning that does not rely upon qualities that could only occur with language. Finally, we have to be able to explain how, in a biologically determined meaning system, you nonetheless can have a range of free choices where the meaning of what you do is not wholly determined by the system that enables you to have meaning.

Long before Jackendoff hit upon the idea of using our affects as our principal conveyor of nonverbal meaning, the philosopher psychologist Eugene Gendlin (1962) elaborated a theory of felt meanings as a source of what we find meaningful. In his theory, Gendlin points out how the significance of much of what we know is something we *feel*. Gendlin uses this idea to present what (to my knowledge) remains our only explanation of how meanings change. A change in meaning is not a function of finding new words. Rather, it comes from focusing upon the felt meaning our words refer to. In a psychotherapy, for example, one often sees how a panic or a compulsion may fade as an individual is supported in the act of reflecting upon the felt significance underlying these forms of behavior. Something about focusing upon the feeling that underlies our words enables the patient to get a better grip on what the words he or she is using mean, and to integrate better that meaning within the fabric of what he or she consciously knows.

How might Gendlin's notion of a felt meaning be viewed today? Chances are, his seminal notion would today be placed within a context. In a special issue of *American Psychologist* on children and their development, Greeno (1989) describes how recent research on general thinking abilities has generated a "new" perspective. Many researchers today see thinking and learning as existing within contexts of beliefs. As an example, he cites the work of Dweck and her associates (Dweck 1983) who found that while some children believe their intelligence is fixed, other childern view their intelligence as a result of their activities, and as something they can change. The first group, viewing intelligence as a fixed quantity, consider tests as occasions in which their weaknesses will be exposed. The second group sees tests as opportunitites to become smarter. The point being that just as the revolution in infant observation permits one to appreciate how the organism must emerge equipped with built-in assumptions in order to construct a reality, so too do children adopt beliefs as meaning contexts in order to make sense of their world. What this has to do with Gendlin's notion of felt meaning will be explained in a moment.

The notion of context is in fact not very new, as it is related to the idea of "adaptation level" proposed by earlier theorizers (Bruner 1957; Allport 1955; Helson 1947), as well as to the more recent emphasis upon "frames" in cognitive psychology and artifical intelligence (Minsky 1975; Schank and Abelson 1977; Clark and Carlson 1981), and in sociology (Goffman 1974). Perhaps the most graphic current use of the role of contexts is to be found in the work of Bernard Baars (1988) who describes a context as "a representation that shapes a conscious experience without itself being conscious" (278). Here is Baars's description of how our contexts pertain to our conscious experiences:

> The assumption is that the nervous system can be treated as a collection of specialized unconscious processes, including perceptual analyzers, output systems, action schemata, syntax systems, planning and control systems, etc. In general, these specialists are highly efficient in their own domains, but not outside of them. The system is fundamentally decentralized or "distributed." Interaction, coordination, and control of the unconscious specialists requires a central information exchange, a "global workspace;" once there, the message is broadcast to the system as a whole. (273)

Baars likens this situation to a roomful of human experts who work together to solve a problem that no single expert can solve alone. Consciousness is like a blackboard that everyone can see, but upon which only one expert can write at any single time. The homunculus notion that Jackendoff would shun appears to have been reintroduced with a vengeance! Except that Baars explains consciousness in a way similar to William James's "ideomotor theory" of voluntary control of action. For James, it is the momentary consciousness of a goal which serves to put unconscious effector systems into action. In other words, Baars's "global workspace" is one in which competing systems may vie for the organism's limited capacity for conscious control. Given this metaphor of the mind, change may be seen as a "resetting" of conscious contents as a result of surprise or challenge. A sudden, unfamilar representation, for example, could cause us to alter the expectation we have of a particular event, and to interpret it differently. One would then have a source of discovery and change that does not depend upon a little person in the head, or upon a reified reality.

But what of Jackendoff's insistence that awareness could not have an effect upon what we know? We could (as does Anthony Marcel [1988], in keeping with Helmholtz) turn this assumption on its head and assume that our phenomenal awareness is itself conceptually mediated. Marcel cites evidence to the effect that conceptual categories shape our phenomenal experience in the perception of speech and visual space, and in the experience of pharmacological effects. The influence of cultural assumptions upon visual illusions and on pain perception is also well known (Marcel 1988). Marcel concludes "that what we consciously experience and the way we experience it (systemic awareness and its phenomenology) are subject to the existence of conceptual categories and to tacit beliefs we hold about the world and about our perception, such categories and beliefs being themselves nonconscious" (1988, 173).

Granted, the beliefs and categories Marcel is alluding to are probably structured by language, else they could not serve as *cultural* assumptions. Language is necessary to transmit assumptions that are not built into the organism's structure. Yet these effects nonetheless demonstrate how our affects are influenced by the meaning context we bring to interaction. That is, the affects which represent what we know (our felt meanings) are sensitive to the meaning contexts which (as per Baar) shape our conscious experience. This last point would have to be true of the contexts that are wired-in or our feelings could not represent these contexts. It also appears to be true of the contexts we acquire as the result of adopting a language, as pointed out by Marcel. For this to be possible, however, our affects would have to be an integral part of what we know, and not just a signal of the inaccessible process and content of "thought taking place" as described by Jackendoff.

What we need is an approach to this issue which will enable us to ask what it is we know, when we say we are aware of something. To start, let us say that our affects and their contexts exist in some sort of reciprocal relationship. We still have no means of imagining how such a relationship would work. Baars's graphic description of our unconscious contexts offers a view of what its structure would be like, but not of its process. For a sense of how affects relate to their context, we might compare the realm of what we feel (our sensations as well as our felt meanings) to a language system. The purpose of this system, however, would not (in contrast to a language of words) be to communicate information. Rather, it would be to embody information in a form we can be aware of, so as to represent our moment-to-moment relationship to our environment.

Following the computationists, we can further assume that a part of what contributes to our "felt" knowing is not itself knowable. We could compare this aspect of representation to a formatting system like the ones writers use on a word processor. You can format a text by deciding the form it should have—the number of words per line, the number of lines per page and so on—and then not have to think about this aspect of your task since it occurs automatically. The unconscious mind as context is presumably similar in that it computes the form of our experience automatically, without our conscious intervention. How the mind formats our experience is not something we can have an explicit awareness of. We know this only implicitly, as a result of the forms themselves. The question then becomes, If our awareness doesn't provide us with this kind of knowledge, what does it provide?

As a feedback system, awareness would have to convey two kinds of information. First (and this is the truly mysterious part) it would have to embody our experience as qualities we feel. Our computer analogies of the mind have nothing to say about this kind of transformation. But then, neither—to my knowledge—does any one else! Second, it would have to (following Jackendoff) inform us of the area in which a particular representation is being processed. We need a felt representation of what is intrinsic to the organism, as opposed to what is extrinsic. This would depend upon our knowing that a representation is peripherally as opposed to centrally organized. A peripheral organization (e.g., the perception of edges and textures) is "closer" to the imput that impinges on our sense receptors. A central organization (e.g., the ability to perceive a constant object in spite of peripheral changes) integrates what we perceive with information stored in long-term memory. In this manner, we may tell the difference between what we expect of a situation, and what exists independently of our expectation.

An example will attempt to illustrate how this would work. Imagine that you are walking down the street, and suddenly you perceive someone in the distance who has the same lilting gait as Leroy, your nemesis! As your growing fear begins to grip your throat, you frantically scan this figure for signs of recognition, until you realize with enormous relief that this is merely someone who has the misfortune of walking like Leroy. In this experience, your knowledge does not pertain to how you recognize Leroy; rather, it has to do with knowing the difference between Leroy, and his look-alike. What we learn (by this view) is not how to construct our representations (since this is built into the organism), but how to use our representations more efficiently. That is, with each new encounter, we refine and deepen our grasp of what we know, by comparing that knowledge with previous experiences; i.e., by differentiating the elements of our representation system in relation to each other.

What I have attempted to illustrate is the idea that the system of representations made up of our feelings operates like a filing system in reverse. That is, it does not (as does language) classify existing information into generalized categories. Rather, it embodies our information in a form we may then use to better adapt to our world. As with language, the way in which meaning is constructed is only implicitly known. We don't know why we see a table as flat, but we do know that the table is flatter than the sofa. The embodiment of meaning as sensations and feelings provides us with a representation system that does not reflect a reality so much as bring one into being. A reality that is imbued from the start with our states of need and desire, as the "value component" of what we feel. A reality, in other words, that is meaningful in every sense of that word from the start of our existence in the world. Hence the claim that our phenomenal awareness participates in the ability we have to deepen our grasp of what we know by expanding its field of relevance. A meaning system based on differences grows from being challenged.

A final point before returning to Gendlin's seminal notion has to do with an observation R. B. Zazonc (1988) makes in questioning how a person remembers a particular event:

> I don't just remember Mr. X or Ms. Y, but I remember meeting them on a specific occasion in a specific place, and above all, I remember how I reacted to them on that occasion, and how I shook hands with them, whether I had to look up because they were taller or bend down because they were sitting, and what my impression was. Thus, a part of the self is very much involved in the trace. It might be only the part that observed the object or event, perhaps only the part that processes the information, or perhaps only the part that reacted. But any combination of these elements may be retrieved. (358)

In other words, a state of consciousness would always include some self-trace or schema that is juxtaposed with the particular representations called forth at any given moment. The notion of a schema harks back to Bartlett (1932), Asch (1946), and Piaget (1970), and has recently made a comeback in the work of authors such as Bandura (1982), Marcel (1988), and Horowitz (1987). As described in Horowitz (1988b): "Schemas summarize past experience into holistic, composite forms, thus allowing incoming information to be measured against the existing composite for 'goodness of fit'. In forming a conscious experience of thought, information from the internal composite may be used to fill out forms missing from the external stimulus information . . ." (13, 14).

Getting back to Gendlin's idea of a felt meaning, one way of understanding why focusing upon what we feel can have the effect he describes is to view the act of reflection (which he views as promoting this focusing) as an act in which a self-schema is summoned in order to simultaneously consider and juxtapose different meanings. Zajonc's (1988) point regarding the "channel capacity" of consciousness, that one should not underestimate the human channel capacity to maintain a multiplicity of simultaneously ongoing mental processes would be relevant as well. Reflection need not then be seen as the act of a homunculus in the brain, but as a kind of binary opposition of meanings, whereby a particular felt meaning is brought to awareness by virtue of being contrasted with some other felt meaning (as described in chapter 7). The contrast in turn would help to deepen our appreciation of what each means in relation to the other. This kind of binary opposition has not only been claimed by some (e.g., Jacobson and Halle 1956) as a principal operation of the mind; it is also implicated as a principal basis for the discovery of new meaning in poetry. The point being that if the juxtaposition of felt meanings is indeed a source of discovery and growth, then we also have (as I will now attempt to indicate) a basis for explaining free choice.

One of the premises adopted in this text is that the preverbal meanings we produce are biologically determined. This kind of determinism, however, could not account for how meanings are juxtaposed, since this would depend upon factors not under the organism's control. The organism has a limited control over the information that impinges upon its sense receptors. Granted, you might say, but this information is determined in another way, since it impinges upon these receptors from an external world. Between these two kinds of determination, however, the juxtaposition of experiences allows for a kind of discovery that conveys a degree of freedom to the individual. That is, experience (as the empiricists would have it) does teach us one critical lesson. This lesson pertains, not to "what's out there," but to how our experienced feelings function in relation to each other. That is, our environment must account for the information that impinges upon our receptors, and our brain must account for how that information is interpreted. But neither can determine what meanings are juxtaposed in the course of going about our lives.

This last point should not come as a surprise. If (from the perspective of a constructionist view) our access to "what's out there" is mediated by our representations of "what's out there," then the main events in the realization of meaning must occur between representations. This (as I understand it) is the basic idea of the semiology elaborated separately by Peirce and Saussure, as well as of the "meaning holism" subscribed to by philosophers such as Putnam and Quine. Representations owe their sense (as defined earlier, p. 57–58), not to what they represent, but to their relationship to the other representations that are a part of the meaning system they participate in. One might then further assume that juxtaposing two representations (within the context of a purposeful self) would enable one to clarify what each means in relation to the other, as this would free up the content that is otherwise kept implicit.

In other words, there are grounds (both empirical and theoretical) for assuming that our feelings are the main conveyors of meaning; and that we may deepen our grasp of what these meanings are and alter what we know by juxtaposing them against each other. It is then but a short step to assume that this process of juxtaposition is what we refer to as an act of reflection; i.e., that Gendlin's focusing brings to light features of meaning that emerge in contrast to other features, as well as to a purposeful state of mind. Granted, the evidence to justify this view of reflection is still speculative and indirect. Yet it presents the only solution to the homunculus problem that allows us to appreciate how we come to make choices in our lives. Given this view of reflection, we may assume that once we (as children) have learned how reflection works, we are free to use it to promote new meaning. By this view, what is free about our choice is the freedom to deepen our understanding of what we know. Acts of preverbal reflection are most likely limited and dependent upon structures which we don't readily control. The example of reciprocal smiling that follows, for example, must be structured by the parent. Yet this notion of reflection as the juxtaposition of meanings can be used to explain how we share meaning and how we generate a purposeful sense of self *prior* to the assimilation of language, as in the following illustration:

In the reciprocal smiling that occurs by the twenty-sixth week (Kaye and Fogel 1980), the infant spontaneously smiles at the mother, who smiles back at the infant, thereby inducing a further smile in the infant. It seems not farfetched to assume that this permits the infant to oppose a self-initiated experience (spontaneous smiling) against a passively induced experience (maternally induced smiling), in a way that qualitatively distinguishes each in relation to the other. It could then become possible for the infant (having grasped the sense of active smiling) to promote this sequence of experiences by smiling at the mother. The mother's ability to reciprocate the infant's gesture has become a setting for the infant's exploration of one of his or her first purposeful interpersonal involvements. Notice that this shows how the infant could relate the parental response to its own long before he or she might define that response as belonging to the parent, or before the infant could refer to its own experience as belonging to a self. In other words, the sharing of affective responses that (for the psychoanalyst) is the basis for *having* a self, may be seen to occur in the infant's ability to share a reaction induced by the adult, by juxtaposing it with a self-initiated reaction. This act of shared meaning does not implicate intentional communication, as does Stern's notion of affective attunement. Spontaneous and induced smiling, as role and reciprocal to that role, occur as a function of the way in which the mind constructs meaning within a structure provided by the parent. The point being that this structure (along with what we may assume about the infant's mind) promotes a pattern of interpersonal involvement that allows for purposeful interaction prior to having a language with which to define the self.

With words, the act of reflection becomes something one may pursue systematically (as in a psychoanalysis) or with the help of poetic expressions. For example, the expression "love's sweet sorrow" enables one to juxtapose a state of sadness with a state of happiness, and to define the feeling of each in relation to the other by qualifying pain in relation to pleasure, or melancholy with joy, and so on. In this manner I may come to appreciate how my feelings are subject to a deepening understanding; an understanding which in turn alters the underlying assumptions of my verbal contexts, by making them more explicit.

One last point. Among the many questions raised by this theory of meaning is the following: Why should the juxtaposition of felt meanings or conscious schemas result in new meaning? The fact that they may become more differentiated in relation to each other doesn't explain how a representation acquires meaning from an unknowable computation system. One view of this process (following Ortega y Gasset, see p. 153 of this text) is that the juxtaposition of meanings—be it in recognition of or between disparate meanings—generates a gap. That is, if the degree of difference between two meanings skirts the limits of the expectable or comprehensible, the underlying meaning system which embodies a conscious meaning is forced to yield a new synthesis. Skirting the ineffable in our meaning system forces it to kick in with a reformatting that enables us to reconcile disparate meanings. A more detailed description of this process is offered in chapters 6 and 7 of this book.

BIBLIOGRAPHY

Adorno, T. W. (1966). *Negative dialetics*. Translated by E. B. Ashton. New York: Seabury.

Adorno, T. W., and M. Horkheimer. (1982). *Dialectic of enlightenment*. New York: Continuum.

Allport, F. (1955). *Theories of perception and the concept of structure*. New York: Wiley.

Apter, M. (1982). Metaphor as synergy. In *Metaphor: Problems and perspectives*. Edited by S. Miall. Atlantic Highlands, N.J.: Humanities Press.

Arieti, S. (1955). *Interpretation of schizophrenia*. New York: Brunner.

——— (1967). *The intrapsychic self: Feeling, cognition, and creativity in health and mental illness*. New York: Basic Books.

——— (1973). The interpersonal and the intrapsychic in severe psychopathology. In *Interpersonal explorations in psychoanalysis*. Edited by E. G. Witenberg. New York: Basic Books.

Asch, S. (1946). Forming impressions of personality. *Journal of Abnormal and Social Psychology* 41: 258–90.

Austin, J. L. (1961). *Philosophical papers*. Oxford: Oxford University Press.

Ayer, A. (1946). *Language, truth, and logic*. Rev. ed. London: V. Gollancz.

Baars, B. J. (1988). Momentary forgetting as a "resetting" of a conscious global workspace due to competition between incompatable contexts. In *Psychodynamics and cognition*. Edited by M. Horowitz. Chicago: University of Chicago Press.

Bandura, A. (1982). The self and mechanisms of agency. In *Psychological perspectives on the self.* Vol. 1. Edited by J. Sals. Hillsdale, N.J.: Erlbaum.
Bar-Hillel, Y. (1954). Indexical expressions. *Mind* 63: 359–79.
Barnett, J. (1966). On cognitive disorders in the obsessional. *Contemporary psychoanalysis* 2: 122–34.
——— (1973). Sexuality in the obsessional neurosis. In *Interpersonal explorations in psychoanalysis*. Edited by E. G. Witenberg. New York: Basic Books.
Barron, F. (1968). *Creativity and personal freedom*. Princeton: Van Nostrand.
Bartlett, R. C. (1932). *Remembering: A study in experimental and social psychology*. Cambridge: Cambridge University Press.
Basch, M. (1983). Empathic understanding: A review of the concept and some theoretical considerations. *Journal of the American Psychoanalytic Association* 31: 101–26.
Bateson, G., and D. D. Jackson. (1964). Some varieties of pathogenic organization. In *Disorders of communication,* edited by David Rioch, vol. 42, 220–83. N.p.: Association for Research in Nervous and Mental Disease.
Becker, E. (1975). *Escape from evil*. New York: Free Press.
Bernstein, R. (1983). *Beyond objectivism and relativism*. Philadelphia: University of Pennsylvania Press.
Bernstein, R., ed. (1985). *Habermas and modernity*. Cambridge: MIT Press.
Bion, W. R. (1957). Differentiation of the psychotic from the nonpsychotic personalities. In *Second thoughts: Selected papers on psychoanalysis*. New York: Jason Aronson.
Bower, T. G. R. (1978). The infant's discovery of objects and mother. In *Origins of the infant's social responsiveness*. Edited by E. Thoman. Hillsdale, N.J.: Erlbaum.
Brenner, D. (1982). *The mind in conflict*. New York: International Universities Press.
Brentano, F. (1973) [1874]. *Psychology from an empirical standpoint*. Edited O. Kraus and L. McAlister. London: Routledge and Kegan Paul.
Breuer, J., and S. Freud. (1895). *Studies on hysteria*. In The standard edition of the complete psychological works of Sigmund Freud. Vol. 2. London: Hogarth Press.

Brown, H. (1979). *Perception, theory, and commitment.* Chicago: University of Chicago Press.
Bruner, J. S. (1957). On perceptual readiness. *Psychological Review* 64: 123–52.
——— (1977). Early social interaction and language acquisition. In *Studies in mother-infant interaction.* Edited by H. R. Schaffer. London: Academic Press.
Burke, K. (1957). *The philosophy of literary form: Studies in symbolic action.* Rev. ed. New York: Vintage Books.
Burnham, D. L. (1970). Varieties of reality reconstruction in schizophrenia. In *The schizophrenic reaction.* Edited by R. Cancro. New York: Brunner.
Carnap, R. (1936). Testability and meaning. *Philosophy of Science* 3: 419–71.
Chein, I. (1962). The image of man. *Journal of Social Issues* 18: 1–35.
Chukovsky, K. (1963). *From two to five.* Translated by Miriam Morton. Berkeley: University of California Press.
Clark, H. H., and T. B. Carlson. (1981). Context for comprehension. In *Attention and Performance.* Edited by J. Long and A. Baddeley. Vol. 9. Hillsdale, N.J.: Erlbaum.
Cohen, L. B., and P. Salapatek. (1975). *Infant perception: From sensation to cognition.* Vol. 2, *Perception of space, speech, and sound.* New York: Academic Press.
Cohen, L. B., and M. Straus. (1979). Concept acquisition in the human infant. *Child Development* 50: 419–24.
Colby, K. M., and R. J. Stoller. (1988). *Cognitive science and psychoanalysis.* Hillsdale, N.J.: Analytic Press.
Culler, J. (1975). *Structuralist poetics: Structuralism, linguistics, and the study of literature.* Ithaca, N.Y.: Cornell University Press.
——— (1982). *On deconstruction: Theory and criticism after structuralism.* Ithaca, N.Y.: Cornell University Press.
Dare, C. (1983). Entry for "psychoanalysis" in *The encyclopedic dictionary of psychology.* Edited by R. Harré and R. Lamb. Cambridge: MIT Press.
Derrida, J. (1978). *Writing and difference.* Chicago: University of Chicago Press.
——— (1981) *Positions.* Chicago: University of Chicago Press.
Doramus, E. Von. (1944). The specific laws of logic in schizophrenia. In

Language and thought in schizophrenia. Edited by J. S. Kasin. Berkeley: University of California Press.

Dretske, F. I. (1981). *Knowledge and the flow of information*. Cambridge: MIT Press.

——— (1988). *Explaining behavior: Reasons in a world of causes*. Cambridge: MIT Press.

Dummet, M. (1974). On the significance of Quine's indeterminacy thesis. *Synthesis* 27: 351–97.

Dweck, C. S. (1983). Children's theories of intelligence. In *Learning and motivation in the classroom*. Edited by S. G. Paris, G. M. Olson, and H. W. Stevenson. Hillsdale, N.J.: Erlbaum.

Eco, U. (1976). *A theory of semiotics*. Bloomington: Indiana University Press.

Edelson, M. (1977). Psychoanalysis as science. *Journal of Nervous and Mental Disease*. 165, no. 1: 1–28.

——— (1984). *Hypothesis and evidence in psychoanalysis*. Chicago: University of Chicago Press.

——— (1988). *Psychoanalysis: A theory in crises*. Chicago: University of Chicago Press.

Erdelyi, M. (1985). *Psychoanalysis: Freud's cognitive psychology*. New York: W. H. Freeman.

Fairbairn, W. R. D. (1952). *An object relations theory of the personality*. New York: Basic Books.

Feather, N. T. (1975). *Values in education and society*. New York: Free Press.

Fenichel, O. (1941). *Problems of psychoanalysis technique*. New York: Psychoanalytic Quarterly Press.

Feyerabend, P. (1965). Problems of empiricism. In *Beyond the edge of certainty*. Edited by R. C. Colodney. New York: Prentice Hall.

——— (1975). *Against method: Outline of an anarchistic theory of knowledge*. Atlantic Highlands, N.J.: Humanities Press.

Flavell, J. H. (1963). *The developmental psychology of Jean Piaget*. Princeton: Van Nostrand.

Fodor, J. A. (1987). *Psychosemantics: The problem of meaning in the philosophy of mind*. Cambridge: MIT Press.

Foucault, M. (1973). *The order of things: An archaeology of the human sciences*. New York: Pantheon.

Freud, S. (1895). Project for a scientific psychology. Standard Edition 1: 283–387, London: Hogarth Press.

——— (1925). An autobiographical study. *Standard Edition* 20: 7–74. London: Hogarth Press.

——— (1951). *Psychopathology of every day life.* Translated by A. A. Brill. New York: Mentor Books.

Friedrich, P. (1979). *Language, context, and the imagination: Essays by Paul Friedrich.* Edited by A. S. Dil. Stanford: Stanford University Press.

Fromm, E. (1947). *Man for himself.* Greenwich, Conn.: Fawcett.

——— (1951). *The forgotten language: An introduction to the understanding of dreams, fairytales, and myths.* New York: Holt, Rinehart and Winston.

Gadamer, H. G. (1975). *Truth and method.* New York: Seabury Press.

Gendlin, E. T. (1962). *Experiencing and the creation of meaning.* Glencoe, Ill.: Free Press of Glencoe.

——— (1964). A theory of personality change. In *Personality change.* Edited by P. Worchel and D. Byrne. New York: John Wiley.

——— (1974). The role of knowledge in practice. In *The counselor's handbook.* Edited by G. F. Farwell, N. R. Gamsky, and P. Mathieu-Coughlan. New York: Intext Educational Publishers.

Getzels, J. W., and P. W. Jackson. (1962). *Creativity and intelligence: Explorations with gifted students.* New York: John Wiley.

Gill, M. M. (1976). Metapsychology is not psychology. *Psychological Issues* 36: 71–105.

Ginsberg, H., and S. Opper. (1979). *Piaget's theory of intellectual development.* 2d ed. New York: Prentice Hall.

Goffman, E. (1974). *Frame analysis.* New York: Harper.

Gopnik, A. (1984). The acquisition of "gone" and the development of the object concept. *Journal of Child Language* 11: 273–92.

Gopnik, A., and A. Meltzoff. (1984). Semantic and cognitive development in 15- to 21-month-old children. *Journal of Child Language* 11: 495–13.

——— (1985). Words, plans, things, and locations: Interactions between semantic and cognitive development in the one-word stage. In *The evelopment of word meaning.* Edited by S. Kuczaj and M. Barrett. New York: Springer-Verlag.

——— (1987). The development of categorization in the second year, and its relation to other cognitive and linguistic developments. *Child Development* 58: 1523–31.

Gramont, P. de. (1986a). Meaning, reality and the practice of psychotherapy. *Contemporary Psychoanalysis* 22: 278–305.
——— (1986b). The self and symbolic realization. *Contemporary Psychoanalysis* 22: 603–28.
——— (1987). Language and the self. *Contemporary Psychoanalysis* 23: 77–121.
Green, G. M. (1989). *Pragmatics and natural language understanding.* Hillsdale, N.J.: Erlbaum.
Greenberg, J. (1987). Of mystery and motive: A review of "the ambiguity of change" *Contemporary Psychoanalysis* 23: 689–703.
Greeno, J. G. (1989). A perspective on thinking. *American Psychologist* 44, no. 2: 134.
Greespan, S. I. (1988). The development of the ego: Insight from clinical work with infants and young children. *Journal of the American Psychoanalytic Association* 36 (Suppl.): 3–56.
Grice, H. P. (1957). Meaning. *Philosophical Review* 67.
——— (1975). Logic and conversation. In *Syntax and semantics 3: Speech acts.* Edited by Cole and Morgan. New York: Academic Press.
——— (1978). Further notes on logic and conversation. In *Syntax and semantics 9: Pragmatics.* Edited by Cole. New York: Academic Press.
Grunbaum, A. (1984). *The foundations of psychoanalysis.* Berkeley: University of California Press.
Habermas, J. (1971). *Knowledge and human interests.* Translated by J. J. Shapiro. Boston: Beacon Press.
——— (1984). *The theory of communicative action.* Vol. 1. Translated by T. McCarthy. Boston: Beacon Press.
——— (1985). Questions and counterquestions. In *Habermas and modernity.* Edited by R. J. Bernstein. Cambridge: MIT Press.
——— (1987). *The philosophical discourse of modernity.* Translated by F. Lawrence. Cambridge: MIT Press.
Hampden-Turner, C. (1981). *Maps of the mind.* New York: Collier Books.
Harré, R., and R. Lamb. (1983). *The encyclopedic dictionary of psychology.* Cambridge: MIT Press.
Helson, H. (1947). Adaptation level as a frame of reference for prediction of psychological data. *American Journal of Psychology* 60: 1–29.
Hobbes, T. (1958) [1654]. *Leviathan, or the matter, form and power of a commonwealth, ecclesiastical and civil.* Edited by H. W. Schneider. New York: Liberal Arts Press.
Holt, R. R. (1976). Drive or wish? A reconsideration of the psychoana-

lytic theory of motivation. In *Psychology versus metapsychology: Psychoanalytic essays in memory of George S. Klein*. Edited by M. M. Gill and P. S. Holzman. *Psychological Issues* 36: 158–97. New York: International Universities Press.

Holtzman, P. S. (1976). Theoretical models and the treatment of schizophrenia. In *Psychology versus metapsychology: Psychoanalytic essays in memory of George S. Klein*. Edited by M. M. Gill and P. S. Holzman. *Psychological Issues* 36: 134–57. New York: International Universities Press.

Horkheimer, M. (1968). *Kritishe theorie*. Vols 1 and 2. Frankfurt: Fischer Verlag.

Horowitz, M. J. (1987). *States of mind: Configurational analysis of individual psychology*. 2d. ed. New York: Plenum Press.

——— (1988a). *Introduction to psychodynamics*. New York: Basic Books.

——— (1988b). Psychodynamic phenomenon and their explanation. In *Psychodynamics and cognition*. Edited by M. J. Horowitz. Chicago: University of Chicago Press.

Hudson, L. (1966). *Contrary imaginations: A psychological study of the English schoolboy*. New York: Schocken.

Hunt, M. (1982). *The universe within*. New York: Simon and Schuster.

Husserl, E. (1960). *Cartesian meditations*. Translated by D. Cairns. The Hague: Martinus Nijhoff.

——— (1969) [1913]. *Ideas toward a pure phenomenology and phenomenological philosophy*. Translated by W. R. Boy. New York: Humanities Press.

Jackendoff, R. (1987). *Consciousness and the computational mind*. Cambridge: MIT Press.

Jacobson R., and M. Halle. (1956). *Fundamentals of language*. The Hague: Mouton.

James, W. (1950) [1890]. *The Principles of psychology*. 2 vols. New York: Dover.

Johnson, C. N. (1982). The acquisition of mental verbs and the concept of mind. In *Language development*. Vol. 1, *Syntax and semantics*. Edited by S. Kuczaj. Hillsdale, N. J.: Erlbaum.

Joseph, R. (1982). The neuropsychology of development: Hemispheric laterality, limbic language, and the origin of thought. *Journal of Clinical Psychology* 38: 4–33.

Jung, C. G. (1967). Symbols of transformation. *Collected works*, Vol. 5. 2d ed. Princeton: Princeton University Press.

Kagan, J., R. B. Kearley, and P. R. Zelazo. (1978). *Infancy: Its place in human development.* Cambridge: Harvard University Press.

Kaye, K. (1982). *The mental and social life of babies: How parents create persons.* Chicago: University of Chicago Press.

Kaye, K., and A. Fogel. (1980). The temporal structure of face-to-face communication between mother and infant. *Developmental Psychology* 16: 454–64.

Kessen, W., M. M. Haith, and P. Salapek. (1970). Human infancy: A bibliography and guide. In *Carmichael's manual of child psychology.* Edited by P. Mussen. New York: Wiley.

Kernberg, O. (1975). *Borderline conditions and pathological narcissism.* New York: Jason Aronson.

Klein, G. S. (1976a). Freud's two theories of sexuality. In *Psychology versus metapsychology: Psychoanalytic essays in memory of George S. Klein.* Edited by M. M. Gill and P. S. Holzman. *Psychological Issues* 36: 14–70. New York: International Universities Press.

——— (1976b). *Psychoanalytic theory: An exploration of essentials.* New York: International Universities Press.

Klein, M. (1964). *Contributions to psychoanalysis, 1921–1945.* New York: McGraw-Hill.

Kohlberg, L. (1978). Revisions in the theory and practice of moral development. In *New Directions for child development: Moral development,* no. 2. Edited by W. Damon. San Francisco: Jossey-Bass.

Kohut, H. (1971). *The analysis of the self.* New York: International Universities Press.

Kuhn, T. S. (1959). *The Copernican revolution: Planetary astronomy in the development of western thought.* New York: Vintage Books.

——— (1970). *The structure of scientific revolutions.* Rev. ed. Chicago: University of Chicago Press.

Lakoff, G., and M. Johnson. (1980). *Metaphors we live by.* Chicago: University of Chicago Press.

Lamb, M. E., and L. R. Sherrod, eds. (1981). *Infant social cognition.* Hillsdale, N.J.: Erlbaum.

Langer, S. (1942). *Philosophy in a new key.* Cambridge: Harvard University Press.

——— (1967). *Mind: An essay on human feeling.* Baltimore: Johns Hopkins University Press.

Langs, R. (1973). *The technique of psychoanalytic psychotherapy.* New York: Jason Aronson.

——— (1976). *The bipersonal field.* New York: Jason Aronson.
Langs, R., and H. Searles. (1980). *Intrapsychic and interpersonal dimensions of treatment: A clinical dialogue.* New York: Jason Aronson.
Lashley, K. (1923). The behaviouristic interpretation of consciousness. *Psychological Review* 30.
Lax, R. F., S. Bach, and J. A. Berland. (1986). *Self and object constancy: Clinical and theoretical perspectives.* New York: Guilford Press.
Levenson, E. (1972). *The fallacy of understanding.* New York: Basic Books.
——— (1983). *The ambiguity of change.* New York: Basic Books.
Levinson, S. C. (1983). *Pragmatics.* Cambridge: Cambridge University Press.
Lipsitt, L. P., ed. (1983). *Advances in infant research.* Hillsdale, N.J.: Erlbaum.
Locke, J. (1959) [1690]. *An essay concerning human understanding.* New York: Dover.
Loewald, H. (1971). On motivation and instinct theory. *Psychoanalytic Study of the Child* 26: 91–128.
Lowenstein, R. M. (1951). The problem of interpretation. *Psychoanalytic Quarterly* 20: 1–14.
Lyons, W. (1986). *The disappearance of introspection.* Cambridge: MIT Press.
Lyotard, J. F. (1984). *The postmodern condition: A report on knowledge.* Translated by G. Bennington and B. Massumi. Minneapolis: University of Minnesota Press.
Mace, C. A. (1948). Some implications of analytic behaviorism. *Proceedings of Aristotelian Society* 9: 7.
Mahler, M. (1968). *On human symbiosis and the vicissitudes of individuation.* Vol. 1, *Infantile psychosis.* New York: International Universities Press.
Mahler, M., F. Pine, and A. Bergman. (1975). *The psychological birth of the human infant: Symbiosis and individuation.* New York: Basic Books.
Marcel, A. J. (1979). Phonological awareness and phonological representation—investigation of a specific spelling problem. In *Cognitive processes in spelling.* Edited by U. Frith. London: Academic Press.
——— (1987). Conscious and unconscious perception: Experiments on visual masking and word recognition. *Cognitive Psychology* 15: 197–237.
——— (1988). Electrophysiology and meaning in cognitive science and dynamic psychology—comments on "unconscious conflict: A convergent psychodynamic and electrophysiological approach." In *Psy-*

chodynamics and cognition. Edited by M. Horowitz. Chicago: University of Chicago Press.

Marcel, A. J., and E. K. Patterson. (1978). Word recognition and production: Reciprocity in clinical and normal studies. In *Attention and Performance, vol. 7.* Edited by J. Requin. Hillsdale, N.J.: Erlbaum.

Marcel, A. J., and A. J. Wilkins. (1982). Is cortical blindness a problem of visual function or visual consciousness? Paper presented at the Fifth International Neuropsychology Society European Conference, Deauville, France, June.

Marcuse, H. (1968). On hedonism, in *Negations: Essays in critical theory.* Boston: Beacon.

Marx, K. (1932). *Economic and philosophcal manuscripts.* Berlin: Marx and Engels Verlag.

——— (1954). *Early Writings.* New York: McGraw-Hill.

Mead, G. H. (1909). Social psychology as counterpart to physiological psychology. *Psychological Bulletin* 6: 401–408.

——— (1934). *Mind, self and society.* Chicago: University of Chicago Press.

Meltzoff, A. N., and W. Borton. (1979). Intermodal matching by human neonates. *Nature* 282: 403–4.

Meltzoff, A. N., and M. K. Moore. (1977). Imitation of facial and manual gestures by human neonates. *Science* 198: 75–78.

Merleau-Ponty, M. (1962). *Phenomenology of Perception.* Translated by C. Smith. London: Routledge and Kegan Paul.

——— (1964). The child's relations with others. In *The primacy of perception and other essays on phenomenological psychology, the philosophy of art, history, and politics.* Translated by W. Cobb. Edited by J. M. Edie. Northwestern University studies in phenomenology and existential philosophy. Evanston: Northwestern University Press.

——— (1973). *Consciousness and the acquisition of language.* Translated by H. Silverman. Evanston: Northwestern University Press.

Miller, D. L. (1973). *George Herbert Mead: Self, language, and the world.* Chicago: University of Chicago Press.

Miller, L. (1986). Some comments on cerebral hemispheric models of consciousness. *Psychoanalytic Review* 73: 129–44.

Millet, J. A. P. (1962). The changing faces of psychoanalytic training. In *Modern concepts of psychoanalysis.* Edited by L. Salzman and J. Masserman. New York: Citadel Press.

Minsky, M. (1975). A framework for representing knowledge. In *The psychology of computer vision.* Edited by M. Winston. Cambridge: MIT Press.

Money, J. (1986). *Lovemaps. Clinical concepts of sexual/erotic health and pathology, paraphilia, and gender transposition in childhood, adolescence, and maturity.* New York: Irvington.

Mundle, C. W. K. (1979). *A critique of linguistic philosophy, with second thoughts—an epilogue after ten years.* London: Glover & Blair.

Murray, H. A. (1962). The personality and career of satan. *Journal of Social Issues* 18: 36–54.

Nagel, E. (1961). *The structure of science.* London: Routledge and Kegan Paul.

Nisbett, R. E., and T. de C. Wilson. (1977). Telling more than we can know: Verbal reports on mental processes. *Psychological Review* 84.

Nunberg, G. (1978). *The pragmatics of reference.* Bloomington: Indiana University Linguistics Club.

Ortega y Gasset, J. (1956). *The dehumanization of art and other writings on art and culture.* New York: Doubleday.

——— (1975). An essay in esthetics by way of a preface. In *Phenomenology and art.* Translated and edited by P. W. Silver. New York: Norton.

Papineau, D. (1979). *Theory and meaning.* Oxford: Clarendon Press.

Pattison, E. M. (1984). Psychoanalysis and the concept of evil. In *Evil, self, and culture.* Edited by M. C. Nelson and M. Eigen. New York: Human Sciences Press.

Peirce, C. S. (1931–58). *Collected papers of Charles Sanders Peirce.* Vols. 1–6 edited by C. Hartshorne and P. Weiss. Vols. 7–8 edited by A. W. Burks. Cambridge: Harvard University Press.

——— (1940). Logic as semiotic: The theory of signs. In *Philosophical writings of Peirce.* Edited by J. Buchler. New York: Routledge and Kegan Paul.

Perry, H. S. (1982). *Psychiatrist of America: The life of Harry Stack Sullivan.* Cambridge: Harvard University Press.

Peters, R. S. (1958). *The concept of motivation.* London: Routledge and Kegan Paul.

Piaget, J. (1926). *The language and thought of the child.* New York: Harcourt Brace.

——— (1929). *The child's conception of the world.* New York: Harcourt Brace.

——— (1949). Le problème neurologique de l'interiorization des actions en opérations reversibles. *Archives Psychologiques* 32: 241–58.

——— (1951). *Play, dreams, and imitation in childhood.* New York: Norton.

——— (1970). *Structuralism.* Translated by C. Maschler. New York: Basic Books.

Popper, K. (1972). *The growth of scientific knowledge.* 4th ed. London: Routledge and Kegan Paul.

Pulver, S. E. (1988). Psychic structure, function, process and content: Toward a definition. *Journal of the American Psychoanalytic Association* 36 (Suppl.): 165–90.

Putnam, H. (1981). *Reason, truth, and history.* Cambridge: Cambridge University Press.

——— (1987). *The many faces of realism.* La Salle, Ill.: Open Court.

——— (1988). *Representation and reality.* Cambridge: MIT Press.

Quine, W. V. (1960). *Word and object.* Cambridge: MIT Press.

——— (1969). Ontological relativity. In Quine, *Ontological relativity and other essays.* New York: Columbia University Press.

Rapaport, D. (1951). Toward a theory of thinking. In *Organization and pathology of thought: Selected sources.* Translated with commentary by D. Rapaport. New York: Columbia University Press.

Rice, L. N., and L. S. Greenberg, eds. (1984). *Patterns of change.* New York: The Guilford Press.

Rieff, P. (1959). *Freud: The mind of the moralist.* New York: Viking.

——— (1966). *The triumph of the therapeutic. Uses of faith after Freud.* New York: Viking.

Rogers, C. R. (1950). A current formulation of client-centered therapy. *Social Science Review* 24: 4

Rokeach, M. (1968). *Beliefs, attitudes, and values.* San Francisco: Jossey-Bass.

Rorty, R. (1967). *The linguistic turn: Recent essays in philosophical method.* Edited with an introduction by R. Rorty. Chicago: University of Chicago Press.

——— (1979). *Philosophy and the mirror of nature.* Princeton: Princeton University Press.

——— (1982). *Consequences of pragmatism.* Minneapolis: University of Minnesota Press.

——— (1985). Habermas and Lyotard on postmodernity. In *Habermas and modernity.* Edited by R. Bernstein. Cambridge: MIT Press.

Ross, G. S. (1980). Categorization in 1- to 2-year-olds. *Developmental Psychology* 16: 391–96.
Ryle, G. (1949). *The concept of mind.* London: Hutchinson.
Sanford, N., and C. Comstock. (1971). *Sanctions for evil.* San Francisco: Jossey-Bass.
Sartre, J. P. (1956). *Being and nothingness.* Translated by Hazel Barnes. New York: Philosophical Library.
Saussure, F. de. (1959). *Course in general linguistics.* New York: Philosophical Library.
Schafer, R. (1976a). Emotion in the language of action. In *Psychology versus metaphyschology: Psychoanalytic essays in memory of George S. Klein.* Edited by M. M. Gill and P. S. Holzman. *Psychological Issues* 36: 105–33. New York: International Universities Press.
——— (1976b). *A new language for psychoanalysis.* New Haven: Yale University Press.
——— (1978). *Language and insight: The Sigmund Freud Memorial Lectures 1975–1976. University College London.* New Haven: Yale University Press.
——— (1983). *The analytic attitude.* New York: Basic Books.
——— (1988). Discussion of panel presentations on psychic structure. *Journal of the American Psychoanalytic Association* 36 (Suppl.): 295–312.
Schank, R. R., and R. P. Abelson. (1977). *Scripts, plans, goals, and understanding.* New York: Halsted.
Schutz, A. (1962). *Collected papers I: The problem of social reality.* Edited by M. Natanson. The Hague: Martinus Nijhoff.
——— (1967). *The phenomenology of the social world.* Translated by G. Walsh and F. Lehnert. Evanston, Ill.: Northwestern University Press.
Shapiro, T. (1979). *Clinical psycholinguistics.* New York and London: Plenum.
——— (1988). Language structure and psychoanalysis. *Journal of the American Psychoanalytic Association* 36 (Suppl.): 339–58.
Sherman, T. (1985). Categorization skills in infants. *Child Development* 56: 1561–73.
Stern, D. (1985). *The interpersonal world of the infant: A view from psychoanalysis and developmental psychology.* New York: Basic Books. Copyright © 1985 by Basic Books, Inc. Quotations in this volume reprinted by permission of Basic Books, Inc., Publishers.
Strauss, M. S. (1979). Abstraction of prototypical information by adults

and ten-month-old infants. *Journal of Experimental Psychology: Human Learning and Memory* 5: 618–32.

Strawson, P. F. (1960). On referring. *Mind* 59.

Sugarman, S. (1982). Developmental changes in early representational intelligence: Evidence from spatial classification strategies and related verbal expressions. *Cognitive Psychology* 14: 410–49.

Sullivan, H. S. (1953). *The interpersonal theory of psychiatry.* New York: Norton.

Thomason. B. C. (1982). *Making sense of reification.* Atlantic Highlands, N.J.: Humanities Press.

Trevarthan, C. (1979). Communication and cooperation in early infancy: A description of primary intersubjectivity. In *Before speech: The beginning of interpersonal communication.* Edited by M. M. Bullowa. New York: Cambridge University Press.

Turley, P. E. (1977). *Peirce's cosmology.* New York: Philosophical Library.

Vendler, H. (1984). *The New Yorker,* March 19.

Wallace, E. (1981). Freud and religion: A history and appraisal. In *Psychoanalytic study of society.* Vol 10. New York: International Universities Press.

Watzlawick, P. J., B. Bavelas, and D. D. Jackson (1967). *Pragmatics of human communication.* New York: Norton.

Webster's new universal unabridged dictionary. 2d ed. (1979). New York: Simon and Schuster.

Wellmer, A. (1985). Reason, utopia and the dialectic of enlightenment. In *Habermas and Modernity.* Edited by R. J. Bernstein. Cambridge: MIT Press.

Whitebook, J. (1985). Reason and happiness: Some psychoanalytic themes in critical theory. In *Habermas and modernity.* Edited by R. J. Bernstein. Cambridge: MIT Press.

Whitehead, A. N. (1938). *Modes of thought.* New York: Macmillan. Reprint: Free Press, 1968.

Winnicott, D. W. (1958). *Through pediatrics to psychoanalysis.* London: Hogarth Press.

——— (1965). *The maturational process and the facilitating environment.* New York: International Universities Press.

——— (1971). *Playing and reality.* Middlesex, England: Penguin.

Wittgenstein, L. (1953). *Philosophical investigations.* New York: Macmillan.

Wolff, P. H. (1960). The developmental psychologies of Jean Piaget and psychoanalysis. *Psychological Issues* 2, no. 5.

——— (1966). The causes and controls and organization of behavior in the neonate. *Psychological Issues* 5, no. 17.

Wundt, W. (1912) [1911]. *An introduction to psychology.* Translated by R. Pintner. London: George Allen.

Younger, B. (1985). The segregation of items into categories by 10-month-old infants. *Child Development* 56: 1574–85.

Zazonc, R. B. (1988). Prolegomena for the study of access to mental events: Notes on Singer's chapter. In *Psychodynamics and cognition.* Edited by M. Horowitz. Chicago: University of Chicago Press.

Zucker, H. (1967). *Problems of psychotherapy.* New York: Free Press.

——— (1989) Premises of interpersonal theory. *Psychoanalytic Psychology* 6 (4): 401–19.

INDEX

Abelson, R. P., 264
Adorno, T. W., 219
Allport, F., 264
Amodal perception, 46, 259–60
Apter, M., 154
Arieti, S., 11, 89, 165, 206–8
Aristotle, 50
Asch, S., 268
Augustine, Saint, 109
Ayer, A., 12, 108, 113–14

Baars, B. J., 264–65
Bandura, A., 268
Bar-Hilel, Y., 77
Barnett, J., 165, 206–8
Barron, F., 13, 156, 157
Bartlett, R. C., 268
Basch, M., 135
Bateson, G., 12, 137–38
Bavelas, J. B., 10, 64
Becker, E., 135
Bernstein, R., 244
Binary opposition, 155; and oxymoron, 155–56, 271; and creativity, 155–57; and psychoanalytic interpretation, 173–76
Binswanger, L., 135
Bion, W. R., 231
Boss, M., 135
Bower, T. G. R., 130

Brenner, C. B., 37
Brentano, F., 110
Brown, H., 244
Bruner, J. S., 90, 92, 264
Burke, K., 218, 223, 225, 241
Burnham, D. L., 142

Capturing, 13, 137–45, 200; affective, 13, 142–44; ideological, 13, 140–42; in all distortion, 143–45; literal self as, 191; in clinical case, 170–71
Carlsen, T. B., 264
Carnap, R., 57
Chein, I., 135
Chukovsky, K., 89–90
Clark, H. H., 264
Cohen, L. B., 85
Colby, K. M., 166, 167, 172
Computation metaphor of the mind, 51–59, 260–62
Comte, A., 111
Conscience, 198–202; and narcissistic core, 199–200; and language, 200–201; and evil, 201–2; and cultural metaphor, 201
Cooley, C. H., 192
Culler, J., 99, 100, 125

Dare, C., 189
Deconstruction in Derrida, 99, 102; in

Deconstruction in Derrida (*Continued*)
  Ortega y Gasset, 151–52; in H. P.
  Grice, 79; of Saussure's sign, 101–2; of
  Piaget, 84
Derrida, J., 7, 12, 22, 99–102, 151
Descartes, R., 15
Dewey, J., 245
Dooley, L., 232
Doramus, E. Von, 11, 89
Dreams, 169; Jim's dream, 169–71
Dretske, F. I., 11, 64, 73, 82–83, 130, 193
Dummet, M., 104
Dweck, C. S., 264

Eco, U., 2, 62–63, 250–51
Edelson, M., 8, 38–39, 166
Erdelyi, M., 166–67

Fairbairn, W. R. D., 14, 49, 165, 187
Fallibilism (Peirce's notion of), 253
Feather, N. T., 201
Fenichel, O., 158–59
Feyerabend, P., 104, 246
Flavell, J. H., 26, 27
Fodor, J. A., 10, 43, 50–53, 54–56
Foucault, M., 40
Frankfurt School, 14, 219–22
Frankl, V., 135
Friedrich, P., 89
Freud, S., 7, 16, 42, 49–50, 132, 136, 143, 198, 220–21, 237; mainstream Freudian theory, 36–41; early emphasis on meaning, 8, 161; neglect of language, 132–37; drive theory, biological model (see Rapaport), 50; circularity of theory, 42
Fromm, E., 138–39, 169, 233–35

Gendlin, E. T., 11, 67, 147, 149, 152, 154, 160, 263–64, 268, 270; and felt meaning, 67, 264
Getzels, J. W., 13, 156, 157
Gill, M. M., 37, 49
Ginsburg, H., 118
Goffman, E., 264
Gopnik, A., 85; and A. Meltzoff, 11, 73, 85–87; and categorization, 85–87
Green, G. M., 75–77

Greenberg, J., 236–42
Greenberg, L. S., 174
Greeno, J. G., 264
Greenspan, S. I., 40–41
Grice, H. P., 11, 45, 73–78, 93; intentional nature of communication, 74–75; principle of cooperation, 77–79
Grunbaum, A., 166

Habermas, J., 14, 209, 211–16, 217, 218; and life world, 211–12; and validity claims, 212–14
Hadley, E., 232
Halle, M., 13, 155, 268
Hartmann, H., 30, 48
Heidegger, M., 96, 211
Helmhotz, H. von, 265
Helson, H., 264
Hobbes, T., 109
Holt, R. R., 37
Holtzman, P. S., 37
Horkheimer, M., 219
Horney, K., 235
Horowitz, M. J., 9, 29, 268
Hudson, L., 13, 156, 157
Humboldt, W. von, 111
Hunt, M., 51
Husserl, E., 112, 245

Integrity, 225–41

Jackendoff, R., 11, 67, 243, 260–62
Jackson, D. D., 10, 12, 64, 137–38
Jackson, P. W., 13, 156, 157
Jacobson, R., 13, 155, 268
James, W., 110, 148, 245, 258, 265
Johnson, C. N., 118
Johnson, M., 106
Joseph, R., 205
Jung, C. G., 169

Kaye, K., 74, 201; and A. Fogel, 270
Keller, H., 93
Kernberg, O., 165
Klein, G., 37, 46, 161, 165; active reversal, 161
Klein, M., 49, 231
Kohlberg, L., 217
Kohler, W., 136

INDEX

Kohut, H., 14, 49, 160, 165, 188
Kubric, S., 178
Kuhn, T. S., 36, 45, 104, 105, 214

Lakoff, G., 106
Langer, S., 2, 74
Langs, R., 14, 165, 226–31
Language, 45, 60–80; as independent measure of the mind, 45; and intention, 72; and filing-system metaphor, 2, 65–70; and distortion, 87–95, 127–45; and creativity, 145–57; and metaphorical dimension, 6, 197; and conscience, 198–202; and reflection, 120–26; and logical positivism, 69; and the objectification or literalization or reification of meaning, 5, 36, 83, 91–95; as purposeful, responsible, and uniquely individual act, 139, 157, 158; and depression, 206–7; and obsessional neurosis, 207–8; and neutrality of the sign, 73–75; and psychoanalytic interpretation, 157–65; and culture, 189–93; and primary process, 32–33; and motives, 193–98
Lashley, K., 112
Levenson, E., 162, 236–41
Levinson, S. C., 78
Locke, J., 109
López Picó, 150
Lowenstein, R. M., 159–60
Lukacs, G., 220
Lyons, W., 12, 117–20
Lyotard, J. F., 209

Mace, C. A., 112–13
Mahler, M., 14, 49, 186, 258; and F. Pine and A. Bergman, 186
Marcel, A. J., 260, 261, 265, 268; and E. K. Patterson, 260; and Wilkins, 260
Marcuse, H., 219, 221
Marx, K., 138–39, 220
May, R., 135
Mead, G. H., 2, 11, 12, 27, 47–48, 64, 71, 74, 98, 111, 120, 127–28, 147–57, 238, 245; language and mind, 71; language and reflection, 27, 111–12; functional identity, 248–49; social origin of the act, 252–53; transcendental union of I and me, 152–53

291

Meaning holism, 54–55, 104–5, 180, 269
Meltzoff, A. N., 11, 73, 84, 85–87, 259; and Borton, 22, 89, 259; and M. K. Moore, 259
Meninger, K., 234
Merleau-Ponty, M., 13, 147, 149, 151, 152, 154; and silent structure of language, 151; and dislocation of language, 151; definition of love, 152, 153; metaphorical meaning and the self, 177–83
Mill, J. S., 111
Miller, D. L., 248–49
Miller, L., 205
Millet, J. A., 233
Milosz, C., 153
Minsky, M., 264
Money, J., 165
Motives, 193–98; as objectification in psychoanalysis, 194–95; and beliefs, 195
Mullahy, P., 236
Mundle, C. W. K., 113–17
Murray, H. A., 135

Nagel, E., 103
Narcissistic core, 13, 183–88, 199; relationship to evil, 199–200; as definition of the self, 184–86; and capturing, 185; in mainstream psychoanalysis, 186–88
Nicholas of Cusa, 181
Nisbett, R. E., 118
Nunberg, G., 77

Objectivity, 95–107; in J. Derrida, 99–102; in A. Schutz, 95–99; in scientific inquiry, 102–7; and objectification, 107, 255–56
Opper, S., 118
Ortega y Gasset, J., 13, 138–39, 147–57, 271; and reflection, 139; and metaphor as decreation, 152, 153

Papineau, D., 103–6
Pattison, E. M., 187, 198, 201
Peirce, C. S., 2, 74, 247–54; semiotics, 249–52; synechism, 247–48; thirdness, 248–49; tychism, 252; objective truth, 253–54
Perry, H. S., 232, 235
Piaget, J., 2, 7, 11, 16, 17–28, 51, 74, 84

Piaget, J. (*Continued*)
   85, 91–92, 131, 186, 217, 258, 268; egocentrism, 7, 17–19; view of language, 21–23, 84; magical thinking, 24–25; object constancy, 22, 27, 85; reversibility, 26–27; reflection, 20; representation, 22; genetic epistemology, 28
Preverbal distortion, 202–5
Psychoanalysis (mainstream) current state in U.S., 36–41; neglect of language, 134–37; attribution of language function to preverbal meaning, 33–36, 48–50; change in view of interpretation, 158–62
Pulver, S. E., 39–40
Putnam, H., 10, 42, 45, 50, 53–56, 70, 104, 243, 244, 245, 253, 258
Putnam-Fodor debate, 48–59

Quine, W. V., 10, 42, 45, 54, 56–58, 62, 66, 68, 104; relativistic thesis, 56–58

Rabelais, F., 254
Rapaport, D., 8, 28–36, 48, 106, 134, 148; and creativity, 35–36; and countercathexis, 32; and drive derivatives, 32, 33; and language, 33, 34; and primary process, 34, 35
Reflection, 108–26; in history of philosophy, 108–17; in A. Ayer, 113–14; in G. Ryle, 114–17; in W. Lyons, 117–20; role of in psychotherapy, 173–76; as creative act, 153–57
Rice, L. N., 174
Rieff, P., 135
Rogers, C. R., 160
Rokeach, M., 201
Rory, R., 136, 209, 236, 243, 244, 245
Ross, G. S., 85
Rousseau, J. J., 181
Ryle, G., 12, 108, 114–17

Sartre, J. P., 96, 143
Saussure, F. de, 2, 101–2, 249–52
Schafer, R., 36–37, 49
Schank, R. R., 264
Schutz, A., 12, 95–98, 100
Self as metaphor, 177–83, 197; as reification, 123; reflective self, 123, 179; as system of belief, 196; literal self of childhood, 191–93; as soul, 180; and creativity, 197; and conscience, 198–202; and narcissistic core, 183–89; and capturing, 137–45; as literal template, 192
Shapiro, T., 41, 159
Sherman, T., 85
Sociocultural factors in development, 189–93
Stern, D., 2, 5, 10, 11, 46–47, 61–62, 71–72, 86, 88, 188, 202–3, 257, 262–63, 270
Stoller, R. J., 166
Straus, M., 85
Strauss, M. S., 88
Strawson, P. F., 63, 69
Sugarman, S., 85
Sullivan, H. S., 133–34, 192, 232–36

Thomas Aquinas, Saint, 109
Thomason, B. C., 95, 97–98
Tichner, E. B., 112
Turley, P. E., 248

Veblen, T., 192
Vendler, H., 13, 153

Wallace, E., 198
Watzlawick, P., 10, 64
Weber, M., 209–11, 219
Wellmer, A., 210
Whitebook, J., 222–24
Whitehead, A. N., 60, 180, 198; doctrine of mutual immanence, 180–81
White Institute, 232–35
Wilson, T. de C., 118
Winnicott, D. W., 13, 28, 134, 154, 163, 187, 191, 199, 202; transitional object and symbolization, 154
Wittgenstein, L., 75
Wolff, P. H., 222, 258
Wundt, W., 110
Würzberg School, 112

Younger, B., 85

Zazonc, R. B., 268
Zucker, H., 38, 164, 226; role of premises in theory, 38; need for evidence in interpretation, 164, 226

www.ingramcontent.com/pod-product-compliance
Lightning Source LLC
Chambersburg PA
CBHW071955290426
44109CB00018B/2033